THE BACKBONE OF ENGLAND

THE BACKBONE

LANDSCAPE AND LIFE ON THE PENNINE WATERSHED

ANDREW BIBBY

PHOTOGRAPHS BY JOHN MORRISON

F

FRANCES LINCOLN LIMITED
PUBLISHERS

OF ENGLAND

Frances Lincoln Limited
4 Torriano Mews
Torriano Avenue
London NW5 2RZ
www.franceslincoln.com

CONTENTS

PREFACE

There are innumerable watersheds the length and breadth of Britain. Every hill, every little bit of higher ground acts as a divide for water, separating the drops and trickles which flow down one side from those neighbouring drops and trickles which make their way down the other. Before long, however, these rivulets and streams are likely to join up and continue on their way together.

There is however one watershed in England, *the* watershed, where this doesn't happen. This is the line of high ground (and sometimes, more surprisingly, much lower ground) which separates water which is making its way westwards to the Irish Sea and the Atlantic from that heading in exactly the opposite direction to end up in the North Sea. A few yards, perhaps a few feet or – in theory – even a few inches, can be all that it takes. When it comes to the map of England and its river systems, this is the divide that really matters.

It can be an interesting exercise to plot the line of this watershed as it meanders through southern England and the Midlands, round the edge of the Thames basin through Wiltshire and Gloucestershire, along the line of the Cotswolds to the hills of Northamptonshire almost to Market Harborough, then through Coventry and round the west side of Birmingham, squeezing between the Severn and the Trent headwaters close to the Potteries and then north-east to the hilly ground between Macclesfield and Buxton. But I'd decided to set my sights on the route that the watershed takes north of here, once it reaches the Pennines proper and begins to make its way up through the north of England. I was interested in the line it takes where England has a backbone of hills to divide the two sides of the country.

Not that the watershed is entirely single-minded in its choice of direction even when it arrives at the Pennines. The general direction may be northwards, but there are all sorts of deviations and diversions needed to get round the headwaters of the streams and rivers which run off the hills: here a tack to the west, there a big sweep around to the east. Furthermore the watershed doesn't like to be obvious. It shuns some of the best known hills in the Pennines – Pendle, Ingleborough, Whernside, Great Whernside and Great Shunner Fell, to give a few examples – and instead seeks out some lesser-known summits like Boulsworth Hill near Haworth and Great Knoutberry in the northern Yorkshire Dales.

How do you know where the line of the watershed goes? In my case, I simply pulled out the maps and worked it out mile by mile, though I also found that there are maps of England's river systems on the Environment Agency's website which helped me in my task. Just once or twice my pencil faltered: south of the Yorkshire Dales near the Leeds and Liverpool canal and again in limestone country where streams have the knack of disappearing underground without notice to reappear sometimes miles away. Initially I got the line slightly wrong much further north, too, near Cold Fell, where I had unilaterally tried to reroute a tributary of the Tyne to flow instead to the Solway Firth. The local RSPB reserve manager put me right.

But in general it didn't take long: soon I had a set of seven Ordnance Survey 1:25,000 maps from the Dark Peak to Hadrian's Wall, each marked with a long thin pencil line. And then the task was simply to get out to follow this line on the ground.

I'm not suggesting that you will necessarily be planning to retrace my steps – this is not intended as a walking guide – but it is perhaps worth making the point that it's only a handful of years since it's been possible to follow the Pennine watershed in this way. Before the legislative changes which introduced the concept of open access land came into force in 2004 and 2005, most of the line of the watershed was private moorland where access by the general public was not permitted. Admittedly, there is still a short section of the Pennine watershed in Lancashire where it enters farmland and where it's still necessary to make brief diversions from the route to seek out rights of way, but with this small proviso the whole line of the watershed is now access land and available for all to enjoy. Someone will almost certainly come forward to correct me, but I'd like to claim that I was the first person to take advantage of this new right in this way.

So if this isn't primarily a walking guide, what has been my intention in writing the book? It's partly a travel book, partly a traditional celebration of a fine stretch of countryside, helped of course by John Morrison's beautiful landscape photographs. But I've tried to do something beyond this: my real objective has been a little more ambitious, and that is to provide a way of interpreting the northern English landscape.

My journey along the Pennine watershed for this book is not just a physical one, it is also a journey of discovery which I try to share. I attempt to offer a range of keys which can open up a sense of understanding of why the land looks as it does. This involves exploring what has happened in the past and, particularly, what is going on up in these hills now to create the countryside we look at and enjoy today.

For some people, the upland Pennine moorland from Kinder Scout to Hadrian's Wall may seem one continuous expanse of emptiness and wilderness. It's not. The landscape is ever changing, and – as the book seeks to demonstrate – a wide variety of people live and work up here on the high ground. There are clues to their activities wherever you look: a recently erected wire fence, a curious metal pin sticking out of the peat, a pile of white grit, a footpath through the heather. Small features like these, taken together, help to build up the full picture.

To meet the task I set myself involves a number of forays into what might normally seem the territory of more specialist books. You may not necessarily be expecting to read, let's say, about moorland hydrology, or about the European Landscape Convention, or about carbon sequestration, about moorland grips and Larsen traps. But I promise this is not a book for specialists only. Whatever the subject, I try to tackle it gently. And I will have failed if I don't convey to you my own fascination with what I discovered. I hope you, too, will enjoy the journey through this special area of England.

Day gives way to night around a North Pennine farmhouse.

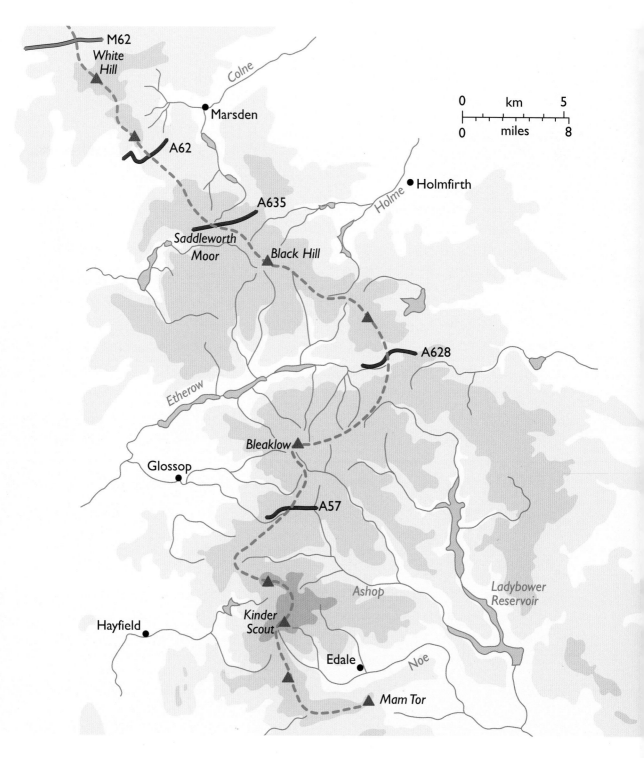

I. KINDER SCOUT

Mam Tor – Brown Knoll – Kinder Low – Crowden Head – Mill Hill – Snake Pass (A57)

I started at Mam Tor.

Or, more precisely, I took a train from Manchester Piccadilly early one Saturday morning in July. The train wove its way down through the Stockport suburbs, crossed over the rivers Etherow and Goyt (both west-flowing out towards the Mersey estuary, I noted with more than usual attention), and then turned and headed for the hills.

I wasn't the only person heading for those hills. The Hope Valley line between Manchester and Sheffield is one of the few railway journeys in England you can make where there is a whiff of the outdoors as soon as you enter the carriage. The only other line which has the same sort of feel for me is the train out from Leeds past Skipton on the Settle–Carlisle line, where cheery walkers and accompanying rucksacks congregate patiently, waiting for the Yorkshire Dales national park to come alongside the window.

Mam Tor, the 'shivering mountain', marks the point where the White Peak of gleaming limestone scars gives way to the Dark Peak, a more rugged landscape of peat haggs and Millstone Grit.

There may be, of course, people who take trains like these for ordinary, workaday, reasons. But on a Saturday in summer, heading from Manchester to the beautiful wild lands of the Dark Peak, they were in a minority. Next to me in my compartment were three young people, getting out the sun cream from their rucksacks almost as soon as the train pulled out of Piccadilly. Standing over by the sliding door was a cyclist sporting a bright lycra top. (There was no sign of his bike, but nobody advertises Credit Agricole on their body if they haven't got a bike secreted somewhere close.) There were more rucksacks parked on the floor at the far end of the carriage. And there was a palpable buzz of anticipation, which fitted my own mood perfectly.

We, most of us, disgorged from the train at Edale. Edale station serves a village with a population of about 300, so some people might think that it's fortunate still to have a station served by regular hourly trains each way. I expect the locals appreciate their good fortune, but for anyone wanting to get out to the heart of the Peak District countryside Edale station is a wonderful facility to have. You can come here for a stroll up Grindsbrook to visit, say, the rocky outcrop known as Ringing Roger. Or you can stride up Edale's main street to take your first few steps on the 270-plus mile journey on the Pennine Way, since Britain's most famous long-distance footpath conveniently starts just up the road beyond the village church.

But though I had a journey ahead of me north to Northumberland, perversely I initially turned due south. I left the station and headed up the old bridleway track out of the Vale of Edale, accompanied for a time by a redstart which darted out of the hedgerow beside me, showing off its orange rump and chest. I was making for the prehistoric hill fort at Mam Tor. Here was where I'd decided my journey along the watershed would start.

Mam Tor's earth banks and ditches are impressive, and so too is the view south towards Castleton and the head of the Hope valley and north to the heartland of the Dark Peak behind Edale. The hill fort itself dates back at least to the Iron Age, though the site was almost certainly occupied before this, back into the Bronze Age, the era which is usually taken to have begun around 2000 BC.

The earthworks at the summit of Mam Tor have survived the centuries, but lower down the hillside to the east it's a different matter. Mam Tor bears an alternative name of Shivering Mountain in recognition of the propensity of the loose shale to slide away downhill after heavy rain. The main A625 from Stockport to Sheffield used to come this way before the road was carried off in a landslide in the 1970s. Now both ends of the road end abruptly, the trunk road has been purged from road maps, and to get through by car at all involves diverting on to a minor road through nearby Winnats Pass.

I set off from Mam Tor west along the ridge which marks the effective boundary between the two halves of the Peak District. It's a geological divide. To the south is limestone country, the light colour of the stone giving this area the name of the White Peak. This is where to go to visit the famous Derbyshire caves, the 'bottomless' pit of Speedwell Cavern, Blue John cavern, and the Devil's Arse or, more politely, Peak Cavern. Here too is a gentler, predominantly agricultural landscape, with the limestone being used to create the network of field boundaries. To the north is something very different: the much rougher, more muscular lands of the Dark Peak, reflecting the Millstone Grit rock which predominates.

I noticed the change immediately, as I turned northwards beyond Lord's Seat to cross the moorland at the head of the river Noe, the river which flows through the Edale valley. From here on, the ground gets squelchier. This was my first encounter with the terrain known as blanket bog, a reference to the deep blanket-like covering of peat which clothes the ground

The Edale valley, fields neatly defined by walls and hedges, has the Kinder escarpment as a backdrop.

and which can be six, twelve, even eighteen feet deep in places. There is a lot of blanket bog to enjoy along the Pennine watershed.

A prominent air shaft marks the route of the railway underneath, passing through Cowburn tunnel. I'd been under there, a short time earlier. But now in the fresh air I was striding ahead, a pair of curlews accompanying me, past Brown Knoll, down to the bridleway where the Pennine Way comes in from Edale, and then up again to the rocks at Kinder Low.

From Kinder Low, most sensible people keep heading northwards, along the edge of the Kinder escarpment until the waterfall known as Kinder Downfall is reached. This is the way the Pennine Way takes you, and this is the place and the view celebrated in the Manchester Rambler song, written by Salford-born Ewan MacColl and perhaps the best-known anthem of the outdoor movement:

> I've stood at the edge of the Downfall
> And seen all the valleys outspread
> And sooner than part from the mountains
> I think I would rather be dead.

But for anyone following a watershed, the rule is simple: *never cross running water.* Arriving at a waterfall is a sure sign that something is wrong. Instead, keeping to the Pennine watershed here means making a detour into the heart of the barren peat lands of the Kinder plateau, heading towards the inconspicuous lump of peat known as Crowden Head where a small pile of stones fights a losing battle for attention.

If you're bashing about at the back of Kinder, it helps to have the right vocabulary. The peat channels which crisscross this land, and there are plenty of them, are groughs. The residual mounds of peat teetering on the brink of falling into the groughs are known as haggs or, perhaps, hags.

This is a distinctive landscape. Louis Jennings, a nineteenth-century gentleman from Lewes in Sussex who came rambling this way, talked of the 'savage beauty' he found here: 'There is a mass of stern and lonely hills, many of them with rounded tops, and beyond them again is a wild and trackless waste of moss and heath and bog, intersected by deep runnels of water, soft and spongy to the tread, and dotted over here and there with treacherous moss. So strange, so wild, so desolate a region it would be hard to find elsewhere in England.'

Nevertheless, Jennings admitted he found the landscape curiously compelling: 'There was, indeed, a somewhat forbidding aspect over this dark, weird, apparently impenetrable fastness. Yet it also had a strange fascination with it, and it was only when the twilight began to close in, casting blacker shadows than before over this domain . . . that I reluctantly began to retrace my steps.'

Jennings's view of Kinder, forbidding and fascinating, is one that many have held since. Indeed, despite the haggs and groughs, despite the apparent desolation of the landscape here, Kinder Scout is for many hill-walkers today a favourite location. But more than this, Kinder has an iconic status in the story of the outdoor movement in Britain, as the result of an event which took place here in April 1932.

For much of the nineteenth century right through to the 1950s, Kinder Scout was forbidden land – or, at least, forbidden to the vast majority of the population. The moorland here was reserved for grouse shooting, with gamekeepers employed to keep the heather in good condition, to eradicate vermin and also to stop the general public from venturing up this way. Jennings himself had been warned off exploring the moorland plateau: 'The first discovery which my inquiries brought to light was that Kinderscout is regarded as strictly private property,' he wrote. 'It is not unusual for the game-keepers to turn strangers back even when they are upon paths which are supposed to be fairly open to all.'

These restrictions were not unique to Kinder, but there was a particular frustration for the people who lived in Manchester and the industrial cities and towns near by who wanted to get out to the countryside and who could see the Kinder escarpment and the Downfall on the horizon, tantalisingly out of reach.

Here's how one young man put it at the time:

> We ramblers after a hard week's work, and life in smoky towns and cities, go out rambling on weekends for relaxation, for a breath of fresh air, and for a little sunshine. And we find when we go out that the finest rambling country is closed to us. That because certain individuals wish to shoot for about ten days per annum, we are forced to walk on muddy crowded paths, and denied the pleasure of enjoying to the utmost the countryside.

The demand was, he said, for 'access to all peaks and uncultivated moorland'. It was, he added, nothing unreasonable.

The speaker's name was Benny Rothman and the speech itself was made to a jury in a court room in Derby in the summer of 1932, where he was conducting his own defence on charges of riotous assembly, assault, and incitement to riot. Shortly after delivering the speech (the text comes from his hand-written notes prepared shortly beforehand), he was to find himself beginning a four-month prison sentence. Four other young people were found guilty of similar charges and also sent to prison.

The alleged riotous assembly which this case at the Derby Assizes was concerned with took place on 24th April 1932, and the venue was the hillside flank of Kinder Scout. The event was what has now become known as the Kinder mass trespass.

Benny Rothman was the main organiser. At the time, he was no more than twenty years old, a young man who'd grown up in the north Manchester inner-city area of Cheetham. Like many in this part of Manchester at the time, his parents were part of the city's large Jewish immigrant community. ('Both my father and mother originated from villages, and had an affinity with growing things, trees, plants etc., although neither of them knew much about the countryside,' Benny recalled later in life.)

The early 1930s were not a good time to be young and working class in Manchester. The country was passing through the worst part of the inter-war great depression. The National Government decided the way out was by cutting back drastically on public expenditure (a route which the economist John Maynard Keynes was later to suggest was about the worst possible thing they could have done). Unemployment pay was reduced, and the much-hated means test introduced. The unemployed fought back, sometimes literally. In October 1931, for example, the National Unemployed Workers Movement organised a major demonstration across the Irwell river in Salford which ended with several demonstrators injured after very heavy-handed police tactics. It was a time of acute political tension, in other words.

Benny Rothman was fortunate in that he did have a job. Although he had won a scholarship and could have continued his secondary education, the death of his father when he was twelve meant that the family badly needed whatever income he could bring in. His first work experience was as an errand boy in the motor trade. He was also discovering the countryside beyond the confines of north Manchester. Like many others from working class areas of the city he joined the Clarion Cycling Club. 'I was a seasoned camper and cyclist at the ripe old age of sixteen, or so I thought when I paid my first visit to the Lake District. I was a townie on a heavy 'sit up and beg' bike, home made tent and Woolworths map,' he later recalled.

He was becoming politically active. He was one of the many at the time whose journey towards socialism came in part from reading Robert Tressell's classic novel *The Ragged Trousered Philanthropist*. When he was about sixteen he began to be drawn in to the activities of the Young Communist League, and to sell the *Daily Worker* to his workmates. He was arrested when he was eighteen for chalking an advert for the newspaper on the pavements of central Manchester.

Politics and outdoor interests naturally came together. In his late teens, he helped establish a Lancashire branch of the British Workers Sports Federation and quickly became its secretary. Benny was inspired at the time by a successful protest in Tottenham, north London, where the BWSF had persuaded the London County Council to provide football pitches and changing facilities for local working class amateur football teams.

It was an incident which took place at the BWSF's 1932 Easter camp which provided the spark for the Kinder event a few weeks later. The camp was being held at Rowarth, a few miles due west of Kinder Scout, and the programme included an organised ramble from Glossop on to Bleaklow. Or at least that was the plan. Benny himself tells what actually happened:

> The small band was stopped at Yellow Slacks by a group of gamekeepers. They were abused, threatened and turned back. To add to the humiliation of the Manchester ramblers, a number of those present were from the London BWSF on a visit to the

One of the many gritstone outcrops around the edges of Kinder Scout.

Peak District, and they were astounded by the incident. There were not enough ramblers to force their way through, so, crestfallen, they had to return to camp.

This was written fifty years later, but the sense of humiliation which Benny clearly felt that day – and in front of his southern comrades too – clearly comes through in the writing. Back at camp, retaliation was planned. What was needed, the young people decided, was a body of ramblers so numerous that the keepers would have to give way. What was needed, they decided, was a demonstration on the hills. Someone came up with a name: the mass trespass.

Benny threw himself into the preparations. Flyers were typed: 'If you've not been rambling before, start now, you don't know what you've missed. Roll up on Sunday morning. . . . Come with us for the best day out you have ever had.' Pavements were chalked with the details. Benny also went to the local press, who quickly sniffed out a good story and stirred things up with some provocative headlines. 'Direct action by ramblers,' read one. 'Peak Trespass Protests: Mob law on the moors,' read another.

It meant that when the chosen day, Sunday 24th April arrived, both the landowners and the police were well prepared. Extra gamekeepers had been drafted in to help patrol the edge of the Kinder plateau, while the police had both uniformed and plain-clothes officers in Hayfield, the village below Kinder where this novel type of demonstration was to commence.

The story of that day has been recounted several times, and the broad outlines of what happened are fairly clear. Benny Rothman later wrote his own account, published to coincide with the fiftieth anniversary in 1982. The original plan, to begin with a rally in Hayfield, was altered at the last minute to outwit the police, and instead several hundred young people gathered in an old quarry a short distance from Hayfield in the direction of the open moors. Benny Rothman clambered up to address the crowd. It was, he said, an inspiring picture:

'There were hundreds of young men and women, lads and girls, in their picturesque rambling gear: shorts of every length and colour, flannels and breeches, even overalls, vivid colours and drab khaki (khaki shorts and shirts were fashionable at the time), multi-coloured sweaters and pullovers, army packs and rucksacks of every size and shape.'

By the time he had got down from his rock, the front of the demonstration was already well down the lane leading to the moors and Benny had to content himself with joining the body of the march. The atmosphere, like so often on demonstrations, was good-humoured, and there was plenty of singing: the Red Flag, according to one press report, but Tipperary too according to Benny. And there was another song produced for the occasion, a parody of Harry Lauder's famous *The Road to the Isles*, its words recalled fifty years on by one of those who'd sung it:

> For by Kinder, and by Bleaklow, and all through the Goyt we'll go
> We'll ramble over mountain, moor and fen
> And we'll fight against the trespass laws for every rambler's rights
> And trespass over Kinder Scout again . . .

The idea planned by Benny Rothman and one of his friends was to head northwards close to Kinder reservoir, taking the established right of way up what is now known as William Clough (it was then more frequently called Williams Clough), before breaking off to scramble up the steep hillside towards the Kinder plateau. Another of the trespassers, Sol Gadian, later described the way things worked out:

> When we reached William Clough a whistle sounded and we all stopped, then turned right facing up Kinder, as a second whistle sounded. It was then that I saw against the skyline a line of keepers, some of them wielding sticks. A third blast of the whistle and we started scrambling up the steep incline. The keepers offered little or no resistance and we just walked past them . . . . I was busy helping a girl up the steep slope. Having got past the keepers we lined up and marched about 400 yards on to the moors where we met a group of ramblers from Sheffield.

The plateau of Kinder had been reached, albeit some distance north-west of the Downfall. It was good enough for Benny Rothman. As he put it later, 'We were on the holy of holies, the forbidden territory of Kinder.'

The 1932 trespass on Kinder Scout was by no means the first attempt to raise the issue of access to the hills. Year after year in the late 1920s and throughout the 1930s the more organised (and more respectable) ramblers' movement was organising rallies in the Peak District, held at Winnats Pass just to the south of Mam Tor, which were also calling for a legal right of access to open countryside. These rallies typically attracted several thousand, more than the three or four hundred who had climbed up William Clough that day. Indeed by 1932 there had already been almost fifty years of campaigning in an attempt to persuade Parliament to pass an 'Access to Mountains Act'. The first such bill (at that stage to be restricted to the Scottish hills) had been introduced at Westminster in 1884, and thereafter regular attempts had been made by MPs to bring forward the same legislation: in 1888, 1892, 1898, 1900, 1908 and 1909, each time without success. After the war, there were similar attempts, by now calling for access to mountains and moors throughout Britain. In 1931, for example, the Labour MP Ellen Wilkinson had tried with her own Access to Mountains Bill. It met the same fate as the others.

Benny Rothman was young and impatient and at the time of the mass trespass critical of the tactics being used by the ramblers' organisations. 'The policy of the Ramblers' Federation, the Footpaths Preservation Society and these similar bodies is futile, and is actually preventing ramblers from obtaining Access to Mountains,' he told the Derby jury. 'The numerous annual demonstrations which they hold in the different parts of the country are meetings just to ask ramblers to support this policy of leaving it to a few MPs and officials to ask for Access to Mountains. Nothing is obtained that way . . .'

The ramblers' federations responded in kind. The Manchester Ramblers' Federation, for example, dissociated themselves publicly from the trespass: 'We wish to record our protest against such a method, which we consider can only ultimately prejudice the objects which the orderly rambler has at heart,' wrote the Federation's secretary to the *Manchester Evening Chronicle* in the run-up to the event.

Later, Benny Rothman accepted that he had made a tactical mistake in antagonising the official Ramblers' Federation bodies, though in the context of politics of the early 1930s his stance was perhaps to be expected. However, the bad blood between the trespassers and the organised rambling movement festered for many years and lingered on into the 1980s. It was only when Benny Rothman, by then in his eighties, began to be a regular speaker at Ramblers' Association rallies – still campaigning for the old demand of access to open country – that old ill-feeling was overcome.

Ironically, it was the intervention of the legal system and particularly the imprisonment of the five trespassers, a punishment which was widely felt to be unduly punitive and vindictive, which gave the Kinder event the importance which, by itself, it probably wouldn't have achieved. As the trespassers left William Clough for the top of the hillside, a number of scuffles with keepers broke out. Reports of what happened vary (not least among the police witnesses themselves), but in essence one keeper, a man named Edward Beever, fell or was pushed to the ground and twisted his ankle. The incident gave the police the excuse they were looking for to bring charges.

Looking back in 1982, Benny Rothman was convinced that the trespass, the trial and imprisonment had been effective in raising the profile of the campaign for access. Public awareness grew, people started to think and started to comment, he said. And the continuing resonance which the story of the mass trespass still has today suggests he was right. The fiftieth anniversary celebrations in 1982 were followed by similar events for the sixtieth anniversary in 1992 and again in April 2007 when the seventy-fifth birthday was celebrated. A commemorative plaque is now in place in the quarry near Hayfield where Benny Rothman addressed the demonstrators.

What else has happened since 1932? The long-awaited Access to Mountains Act finally made it on to the statute book in 1939, only for ramblers to discover that they had been conned: in many respects, it benefited only the landowners. The war changed attitudes. A 1945 government report argued for the first time for the benefits of conferring 'public rights of access over *all* uncultivated land (suitably defined)'. The subsequent legislation, the National Parks and Access to the Countryside Act 1949 repealed the unsatisfactory 1939 Act and introduced arrangements for access agreements, though England and Wales had to wait until the 2000 Countryside and Rights of Way Act for implementation of the 'not unreasonable' demand Benny

Rothman had put at his trail in Derby: access to peaks and uncultivated moorland. (Scotland had to wait for legislation from the Scottish Parliament in 2003.)

As for Benny Rothman himself, he remained committed to his political beliefs throughout his life. He took part in demonstrations in Manchester against Mosley and the fascist Blackshirts in the 1930s and for much of his working life was an active trade unionist in the engineering union. Later he became involved in the early environmental movement, campaigning for example to preserve green spaces in the Greater Manchester area and against motorway developments. He also kept an interest in Kinder Scout. In 1982 when the National Trust acquired three thousand acres of Kinder he set up the Kinder Scout Advisory Committee – basically as a ginger group, keeping a wary eye on the NT to ensure they did not backslide on access matters.

In the last years of his life, as interest in access as an issue grew again, he welcomed to his home a growing stream of journalists and TV crews keen to interview him and to hear again the story of the 1932 trespass. And in 1994, he and his wife Lily received a formal invitation from Derbyshire County Council to mark the 62nd anniversary of his trial by attending a reception – held in the Judges' Lodgings in Derby. He died in January 2002.

Walkers can enjoy the views from Kinder Scout today, because of Benny Rothman and the mass trespass of 1932. This plaque, near Hayfield, commemorates the event.

2. BLEAKLOW

Snake Pass (A57) – Bleaklow Head – Bleaklow Stones – Lady Cross – A628

I was given responsibility for the bright yellow trundle wheel. It was my task to set the distance counter on the wheel to zero before we began, push it for exactly fifty metres and then stop. It would be fair to say that I was the junior partner in the task we had ahead.

My rendezvous with Peter McGrory had been on the A57 between Sheffield and Glossop, on the watershed at the head of the Snake Pass. Peter had agreed to take me out with him so that he could initiate me into the work he was currently undertaking. I couldn't help noticing that he had the rather fancier kit – a hand-held computer together with a GPS device which he strapped carefully to his wrist.

For the previous two years or so, I already knew, Peter had been quartering the footpaths of Kinder, Bleaklow and the rest of the Dark Peak as part of a small team engaged in a detailed footpath survey. Although originally from Manchester he'd spent much of his working life, primarily spent in the water industry, down south in Milton Keynes. He had decided to move back north, however, when he'd come to retire. He'd found a place in the Peak District, had signed up to become a national park ranger and had passed the five training modules necessary for his ranger's badge. And that's how he had come to see the memo that had gone round, asking for volunteer surveyors: hill-walking for a purpose.

The plan was for Peter and I to make our way north from the Snake Pass towards Bleaklow along footpath 3.22.022.p, better known to most of us as the Pennine Way. Peter and his colleagues work from detailed maps of the area which show each and every path and track on the ground, including those which are across open access land and which aren't formal rights of way. The maps themselves have been drawn up, with painstaking care, from aerial photographs, with each path given its own distinguishing number.

Peter booted up his Hewlett-Packard PDA, opened the database program, and began the routine he went through each time he started a day's surveying. The first task, he told me, was to enter the GPS coordinates of the starting point, type in a brief description ('junction of Pennine Way and Snake road'), and add of course the path identification number. Only then, at last, were we ready to set off walking.

Being a footpath surveyor, I quickly realised, requires meticulousness and dedication to detail. It requires good powers of observation. It also requires an acceptance of the fact that you won't be getting anywhere very quickly. Fifty metres is simply no distance at all. We had barely left the busy traffic behind on the Snake road before the counter on my trundle wheel showed that it was time for the first stop.

The database that records the data which Peter and his fellow volunteers put in has been designed specifically for the project, and there's a lengthy set of questions to be completed at

Well-defined and dry underfoot, the Pennine Way climbs from the Snake Pass to the broad plateau of Bleaklow.

each survey point. Peter took me through them, one by one. What was the vegetation type beside the path? Was it grassland? Heather moor? Grass and rushes? Was it peat bog? Scrub? Perhaps it was woodland? This was an easy one. Peter and I looked on either side of the Pennine Way and agreed unanimously: the box for heather moor was duly ticked on the little PDA screen in Peter's hand.

Conditions under foot? We agreed 'dry'. Path material? At this point of the Pennine Way the answer was clearly 'man made'. Width of bare ground? Say a metre and a half. Width of worn vegetation? Most people were sticking faithfully to the path, so the appropriate response here was about two metres. Gradient of the path? Level.

And so it went on. The survey required quite detailed reporting of four particular aspects of the path's condition, in turn covering the degree of ground saturation, the evidence of water scarification (or in other words, whether running water was washing away the path's surface), the condition of any drainage channels, and finally the state of the soil structure — whether dips and hollows were developing across the path line, for example.

In each case, Peter and I had to choose between one of five levels, ranging from zero to four. Take the question on water saturation for example. If there was no evidence at all of any standing water (and there wasn't, at this point on path 3.22.022.p), the correct response was clearly zero. A level one path was one which showed: 'transient standing water and/or mud unto depth of 2.5 cm, small isolated areas of transient soft ground in poor condition'. For level two there would be 'semi-permanent standing water and/or mud to 5 cm depth'. Level three had 'soft ground that only dries up in very dry conditions' with mud or water up to 10 cm deep. Peter told me he had learned to assess which level was correct by seeing how far up the side of his boot the water or mud came. I didn't ask, but presumably you knew you'd reached level four when you ended up with a wet woolly walking sock.

The questions all completed and the data entered in the PDA, Peter gave the command. The trundle wheel went back on the path and we were momentarily under way again. Almost immediately, however, the wheel clicked round to 100 metres. Once again, there were the questions on the PDA which needed to be answered. Peter began the routine all over again: Vegetation type? . . .

Of course, you get faster with practice. Even so, Peter told me that it took him an hour or more to go a kilometre. 'I generally do about five kilometres a day,' he said. 'That's roughly six hours' working. Six hours is quite a long time to be doing physical work on the moor. And he also revealed that there had been soul-destroying days when a glitch in the computer had meant all the data had disappeared. All the surveyors had encountered that sort of problem, he said.

Those were the very bad times. All being well, however, Peter would safely transfer the data he had entered as soon as he was back home, sending it by email to the survey coordinator based in an office at the Moorland Centre in Edale. Here what will hopefully eventually become a comprehensive database of all the paths and tracks of the Dark Peak is gradually being built up.

The idea is to categorise all the paths into one of five categories: those which are in a relatively good condition (Green 1 and Green 2), those which have some problems (Amber 1 and Amber 2) and those in a really poor condition (Red, about 7 per cent of the mileage initially surveyed). This sort of simple classification helps ensure that the limited money available for footpath repair gets channelled to the right places – though, interestingly, it's not necessarily the Red paths which get all the attention. Sometimes it makes more sense to focus on Amber paths, I was told, to take remedial work in time before they get any worse.

The footpath work being undertaken by Peter and the other volunteers is one of a number of detailed research surveys which have been undertaken on the moors around Kinder and Bleaklow over the past few years. If you'd been out on these hills in the spring of 2004, for example, you might have come across the team undertaking a detailed study of the location of breeding birds. A total area of over 500 square kilometres – basically the whole upland moorland of the Dark Peak area – was divided into a set of single kilometre squares, and the surveyors' task was to visit each of these squares (or at least all those where the landowners gave permission for access) twice during the nesting season. From this work has come a valuable dataset of bird species and numbers on these moors: around 8,500 pairs of meadow pipits, about 450 pairs of curlew, 400 pairs of golden plover, thirty-one pairs of merlin and just two pairs of goshawks, to give a few examples.

There's an on-going value in datasets like this, in that they can be used in the future as benchmarks for monitoring change. In the case of the bird survey, in fact, the 2004 study could be directly compared with a pioneering earlier study of breeding birds in the same area which had been done in 1990. As a result we know that there has been a steep decline in some species (the twite, sometimes known as the Pennine finch, has clearly had a particularly tough few years), while others such as the peregrine falcon, merlin and short-eared owl have increased their range and numbers. Hill-walkers and farmers who look out early in spring for the arrival of the first curlew, the beautiful wader with the long slender beak whose call is so evocative of these moors, will be pleased to know that they too have significantly increased their numbers in recent years.

So it isn't only Peter McGrory and his colleagues who have been out quartering the moors. The past few years have seen a stream of researchers making their way to Bleaklow, Kinder and Black Hill, many of them researchers from neighbouring universities such as

Manchester, Sheffield and Leeds, looking at particular aspects of the peatland ecological system. As I was later to discover, the evidence of their work is there to be spotted, if you know where to look.

The flurry of attention has much to do with the fact that a significant chunk of lottery money has recently been invested in these hills. Moors for the Future, based in Edale, managed to raise almost £5 million – including over £3 million from the Heritage Lottery Fund – for a project to support and restore the Peak District's peat moorlands. The project, which when it got under way early in 2003 could claim to be Britain's biggest conservation project, focused on three interlinked areas of activity. It worked to help the general public better understand and enjoy the moorlands, it sponsored research and study of the moors (both the footpath survey and the nesting bird survey were undertaken at its behest) and it also engaged in practical conservation work up on the hills. Edale's new Moorland Centre – the most concrete evidence of all this activity – provides both a visitor centre experience for weekend walkers and tourists and, behind the scenes, a major research centre on moorland ecology and habitats.

The moors are certainly in need of a little care and loving. 'The landscape is wrecked. You don't need to be a soil scientist to know that something big is going wrong here,' I was told by one of the Moors for the Future team. And they were right. I'd already picked my way through the barren peat land on the Kinder plateau but the landscape ahead of me at Bleaklow was, if anything, more barren and more bare.

It was time to give up my custodianship of the trundle wheel. If I was dutifully to follow the watershed route, I needed to leave the Pennine Way near Hern Clough to head off westwards towards the trig point on the Higher Shelf Stones outcrop. The path to the rocks passes through the middle of the wreck of a massive USAF photo reconnaissance plane which failed to clear the top of Bleaklow just before eleven o'clock one morning in November 1948. The plane, nicknamed for some reason *Overexposed*, had been a veteran of the atomic bomb test at Bikini Atoll in 1946 before being stationed in Britain during the period of the Berlin airlift. What was to be its last flight should have been a short hop over the Pennines from Lincolnshire to Burtonwood near Warrington. The crew of thirteen aboard were all killed in the crash.

Rather surprisingly, the authorities left much of the plane's wreckage on the hilltop where it crashed, making it today something of a macabre sight. There's a commemorative stone, and a collection of home-made crosses put here by past visitors. Some people will tell you that it feels particularly spooky here, although to be truthful the whole of Bleaklow can be a pretty spooky place when the cloud is down and you're not quite sure where you're going

At the Higher Shelf Stones I mentally counted off the fifth trig point of my journey. The watershed here turns north, heading towards the Wain Stones. It was Alfred Wainwright, when he walked the Pennine Way who pointed out that the Wain Stones look like a couple puckering their lips together in a kiss and so indeed they do, provided you get the angle right. The Pennine Way is met again just beyond the Wain Stones at Bleaklow Head, after which it disappears south-westwards off the plateau towards the reservoir at Torside. Anyone following the watershed has to takes a different, and much more challenging, route straight into the wild bare peat landscape. A line of stakes marks the route east towards Bleaklow Stones, but even in good weather it needs care to find the route. The path threads its way through the deeply eroded groughs, in between the haggs of residual peat which still remain in place.

The Wain Stones, a short stroll from the trig point on Bleaklow, are a happy geological accident.

The groughs and gullies are the territory of the Peak District mountain hare, a fine sight at any time of the year but a particularly special treat in winter, when the hare is wearing its white winter coat. This provides the animal with excellent camouflage against snow, though frankly it's considerably less effective when seen against the dark banks of peat. Since these days there are likely to be as many winter days without snow as with it, it could be that evolution is taking a little longer than it might to help the hares adjust. In fact, the Peak District hares were introduced here in the nineteenth century to add to the shooting potential of the moors, having been brought down from Scotland where a white coat for winter must have been an excellent idea.

Bleaklow is a landscape which walkers either love passionately or find intimidatingly hostile. Whatever your own views, one thing is clear, however, and that is that this landscape is in no sense 'natural'. There would have been a time when Bleaklow was a vast blanket bog, the peat squelchy under foot, the water absorbed like a sponge by the light green sphagnum moss. There would have been moorland grasses and sedges such as the white fluffy cotton grass. There would have been patches of heather, low flowering shrubs such as crowberry and bilberry, lichens, and perhaps also the insect-eating sundew plant. But not any more. Bleaklow, like Kinder and Black Hill, has become what is known to ecologists as a degraded blanket bog. The water table in the peat has dropped and the top layer of peat has cracked and dried out, so that in dry conditions the plateau resembles an empty black desert. The top layers of peat blow away in the wind or are carried off the hillside when the heavy autumn rains appear and sweep down the gullies.

What's to blame for this state of affairs? Could the cause, perhaps, be the pressure that has come from large numbers of people walking this way? As we've seen, this part of the Peak District has been a precious place for generations for walkers from the cities and towns on both sides of the Pennines, and it's true that walkers' boots on bare peat leave their mark, something that became all too apparent in the early years of the Pennine Way on several of the sections across the Dark Peak moorlands. Just the other side of the Snake Pass, for example, the route I followed north-eastwards from Ashop Head towards Moss Castle was a very early disaster zone, as walkers spread further and further off-path into the peat in an attempt to keep their feet dry. By the time remedial work was taken in 1994, the path was reportedly in places an astonishing seventy metres wide.

There have been other 'trample sites' elsewhere in the Peak District, including the ridge route east from Mam Tor past Hollins Cross. Here, as on the Pennine Way, stone flagging has been needed. But generally speaking, pressure from visitors is only a very small contributory factor to the problems of the peat lands hereabouts. Eroded path lines may be an unfortunate consequence of the countryside being loved too much, but they don't explain the miles and miles of bare peat to be found well away from the usual routes of walkers.

Nevertheless, Bleaklow's current state is indeed primarily the result of human activity. There are, in fact, two main causes. The first, and probably the most significant, has been industrial pollution, over 150 years of it. Emissions resulting from industrial activity were carried by the prevailing south-westerly wind from neighbouring towns and cities and deposited on to the high ground of the Dark Peak. It means that Bleaklow is now one of the most contaminated areas in the world in terms of pollution from heavy metals, particularly lead. One study recently found lead levels on Bleaklow thirty times as high as those in a comparable peatland environment near Trondheim, Norway. Overall, the pollution is double the level at which the government decrees that industrial land is contaminated. In other words, if Bleaklow was in a city area you'd have to remove all the top soil before you could even contemplate doing anything with it.

As regular fellwalkers will know, too, the water which accumulates on the peaty high ground of areas like Bleaklow has nothing of the quality which you find in most freshwater lakes and pools. It's highly acidic, down to a pH of about 2.9–3.1 in parts of Bleaklow. If you borrowed some litmus paper from the school chemistry lab to take with you on to the hills, the peat bogs would turn it as red as it could go. 'This is the stuff you'd put on your fish and chips – in fact, we're getting down to battery acid,' one moorland researcher told me.

The second reason has been overgrazing by livestock, particularly sheep who find the succulent new shoots of vegetation a special treat to be nibbled down to ground level as quickly as possible. Until recent times, the main thrust of agricultural policy was towards boosting production and farmers were rewarded for increasing their stock levels. What this meant on some moors was that stock levels were kept at far above sustainable levels, and as a consequence the moorland vegetation suffered.

Not every plant is equally attractive to a hungry sheep. Sheep have only lower incisors and eat by biting and shearing off the most palatable vegetation they can find (by contrast, cattle tend to wrap their tongues around plants and pull). Top of sheep's favoured list will be some kinds of fine leaved grass, bilberry and young heather shoots. Other types of grass, such as purple moor grass (molinia) and mat-grass tend to be much less popular. One consequence of this is that overgrazed moors which have lost much of the variety of vegetation they once had tend to be left with stretches of rampant tussocky molinia or mat-grass, unloved not only by sheep but also by walkers who have to battle their way through the tussocks.

Very heavily overgrazed moorland can be left with no vegetation at all. This is particularly a problem at supplementary winter feeding sites where the sheep tend to congregate, trampling away whatever is under their feet. Corners of fences can also become badly eroded for the same reason.

How many sheep can you keep satisfactorily on a moor before you start getting damage to the vegetation? It depends on the type of moor you have and which expert you believe, but the short answer is – not many. To bring blanket bog back into favourable conditions may mean no more than one sheep on average for every ten hectares (about twenty-five acres), though some recovery of the moorland is likely to be possible with a summer stocking level of one sheep per two hectares. In winter sheep numbers should be reduced or preferably taken off the moor altogether, according to environmentalists. Natural England recommends that sheep are taken off the land altogether where bare peat is exposed.

This is the approach which has been adopted on Bleaklow, where Moors for the Future and a number of partner organisations collaborated recently to fund the erection of a stock fence round the whole of the Bleaklow plateau, about nine square miles in all. The Great Fence of Bleaklow as the media dubbed it stretches for fourteen miles and is intended only as a temporary addition to the landscape, to last for ten years or so by which time, hopefully, some of the damage caused by overgrazing will have been remedied. The fence is designed to keep sheep, not walkers, out, though unfortunately there was some early damage by someone who took wire cutters to a section of it. Unfortunately, too, continuing peat erosion has meant that some sheep have been able to shimmy under the bottom line of wire to make their way into the forbidden zone beyond.

Away from the footpaths, Bleaklow is, like Kinder, riven by deep gullies.

So industrialisation, overgrazing and – to an extent – public pressure have all played their part in making Bleaklow the way it is today. There's a fourth factor, too, and that is fire. Bleaklow suffered a devastating wild fire at Easter in 2003, which swept across around 1700 acres of the hillside and which was probably started, whether deliberately or accidentally isn't clear, by a visitor to the area. It was the latest in a number of serious fires in the area whose effects are still being felt today. Peat is, of course, a highly combustible material, particularly when dry.

The question to answer, though, is whether we should intervene to repair some of this damage. Does it really matter if this part of the Peak District has stopped being a damp boggy stretch of moorland and has turned into what some describe as a moonscape? Humans should perhaps have known better in the past but that in itself doesn't justify throwing the gears into reverse today, investing money and intervening in the landscape to try to go back to a previous moorland habitat which clearly was not 'natural' either.

Is there anything wrong with leaving Bleaklow – and Kinder Scout and Black Hill – as they are today? Well actually yes, say the Moors for the Future team. One of the things which is going wrong is that peat erosion is causing some serious problems further down the valleys. The maze of tiny streamlets which flow north off Bleaklow plateau, building up into the watercourses which tumble down Torside Clough, Wildboar Clough, Shining Clough, Near Black Clough and the other neighbouring steep-sided valleys end up in the Woodhead and Torside reservoirs, two of the chain of reservoirs built in the nineteenth century to provide water for Manchester. Just across the watershed, the streams on the other side of Bleaklow flow down south and east, ending up in Howden, Derwent and Ladybower reservoirs, ready to supply water to Sheffield and its hinterland. The whole of Bleaklow is water catchment land, and when peat particles are carried down the hill they naturally end up as sediment in United Utilities and Severn-Trent Water's reservoirs, causing the water engineers something of a headache.

The tiny particles of peat in what is about to become our drinking water – known as the degree of turbidity of the water – are not the main problem, however. If there are bits of stuff in the water, it's not too hard to arrange to filter them out. What is rather more of a headache is the actual colour of the water itself. When bare peat is carried away by water, some of the peat dissolves into the water itself, changing the water colouration. It's analogous to what happens when you brew up in the kitchen, pouring hot water over a teabag and watching the water deepen and darken as it takes up the tea.

Water which looks (on a good day) the colour of scotch whisky and (on a bad day) the colour of dark molasses is not really a health problem, but it's clearly something which the average householder in Manchester or Sheffield doesn't expect to be coming out of their kitchen taps. The issue is a cosmetic one, in other words, but it still has to be addressed by the water companies. Unfortunately, for reasons which are not entirely clear, colouration has become more of a problem in the past thirty years. Explanations vary: one theory is that, ironically, it's been an unwelcome side-effect of the very commendable efforts to cut back on air pollution and therefore on the amount of acid rain falling on the hills. Perhaps the acid rain was suppressing the amount of peat escaping into the water. Or perhaps the scientific data appear to show an increase in colouration compared with the past simply because more people are measuring it these days.

Whatever the explanation, the best way of dealing with colouration is at source, and that means by trying to reduce the amount of peat coming off the hills. And this in turn means, step by step, trying to restore the moor to a healthier blanket bog environment. One part of this process is to encourage the revegetation of the bare areas of peat. I'd already arranged for Chris Dean, the Moors for the Future project manager, to tell me more about this, and he'd agreed to meet me a few miles north, across the valley on Black Hill in a few days' time.

Just as important as bringing back the vegetation is to restore the moorland hydrology – the way that water flows into, on, under and out of the land. The task in other words is to rewet the moors. Healthy blanket bogs require sphagnum moss to function effectively, and sphagnum had almost entirely disappeared from the Peak District peatlands (perhaps killed off by high levels of sulphur pollution). The good news now is that it is beginning to reappear.

Some of the work on moorland hydrology which has been taking place is not difficult to spot. I'd already noticed some of the gully blocks put in by the National Trust, for instance, when I had been over the Kinder Scout plateau. Gully-blocking is work which has been started relatively recently, the idea being to physically stop the water scouring through the peat groughs and disappearing down the hillsides by creating artificial barriers and mini-dams across the gullies. If gully-blocking works, there's the opportunity behind the dams for water to be retained and for a damp environment suitable for sphagnum moss to develop.

Measures like this, although they've been tried in lowland wetlands, are a relatively recent idea up on the upland moors. Successful recolonisation by sphagnum requires more than just the odd damp patch of ground, it requires the whole water table of the peat to be raised. So to monitor what seems to work, and what seems less successful, whole teams of academic researchers have been up on these moors in recent years.

If the gully blocks were relatively easy to spot, what I hadn't noticed until they were pointed out to me were the other signs in the moorland landscape that hydrologists were at work. Take, for example, the strange light beige plastic cylindrical objects a couple of feet or so high and eighteen inches across which squat in one or two places hereabouts alongside moorland streams. The padlocked lids turn out to conceal a twelve-volt battery, some computer microelectronics, a water pump and – this is what gives their function away – a set of twenty-four water sample bottles, ready to be filled in turn via a pipe that protrudes into the water of the stream.

Automatic water samplers like these can be pre-programmed so that they slurp up a set amount of water when required, with the operator then coming along later to take the samples away for analysis. This sort of device is invaluable if you're a hydrologist wanting to measure, say, the water colouration of a hillside stream but not fancying camping out beside it for weeks on end.

Because bad water colouration can change rapidly as water levels rise and fall, it's also possible to program the software so that water is sampled very frequently – say, every fifteen minutes – but only when the stream is in spate. To do this means monitoring the depth of water in a stream and for this another piece of electronic technology is used, using changes in pressure to detect changing water levels.

Not all the hydrologists' toolkit is quite so high-tech. Detailed study of peat erosion in five areas just to the south of Bleaklow was undertaken recently simply by inserting eighty stainless steel pins about two feet long into the peat and then returning each month to see how much higher above the ground they had become. It might be simple but it worked and the findings have now formed the basis of an academic journal article.

When you start to look around, in other words, Bleaklow and the peat moors hereabouts turn out to be nothing like as empty as they initially seem. Tucked into streams or poked into the peat is a wide array of instrumentation, assessing the health of the area's hydrology and, hopefully, playing a part in trying to make things better.

A couple of miles or so after Bleaklow Head the path through the peat groughs marked out by the line of stakes does an abrupt turn northwards, conveniently just at the point where the watershed does the same thing. Haggs and groughs are, at last, left behind and the landscape opens out. The vegetation returns, particularly once the stock control fence around Bleaklow is crossed. This is pleasant heather moorland walking.

Ahead, a prominent landmark, is the Holme Moss television transmission tower, visible on the other side of the Longdendale valley. Rather closer are the lorries and cars grinding their way up to the summit of another important trans-Pennine trunk road, the A628 between Manchester and Penistone. I dropped down off the path I had been following just as the rivulets started flowing east, not west, paused briefly at the remains of the old Lady Cross – now reduced just to a stump and stone base – and met the traffic at the very head of the Longdendale valley.

3. BLACK HILL

A628 – Holme Moss – Black Hill

Chris Dean examines the ground closely at his feet, and points with satisfaction to the tiniest heather shoot imaginable, which is just showing through the peat. The heather shoot is his doing – or at least, it's the result of the moorland restoration work undertaken by Moors for the Future of which he is the manager.

Chris has walked out with me from the road at Holme Moss, past the television transmitter mast and through the rough moorland vegetation to the trig point at Black Hill, marooned in a desert of bleak peat. The place has, as Chris points out, something of a reputation with Peak District walkers. 'It's something of an icon, in terms of horrendous walking. There's this feeling that you've not really been on a proper hill walk unless you've been up to your knees in peat on Black Hill,' he says.

Certainly, particularly for early walkers on the Pennine Way, Black Hill became known as an ordeal which had to be endured. Typically, those starting out from Edale would spend their first day struggling across the Kinder plateau and the peat bogs and haggs of Bleaklow and collapse with gratitude after sixteen miles' hard slog at the youth hostel or campsite at Crowden. Day two, you feel they must have said to themselves as they pulled on their boots after breakfast, surely couldn't be as bad as day one. And yet day two, after a cruel pull up from the Longdendale valley, would see them battling their way across the featureless badlands of Black Hill. Almost certainly, it would be raining. Almost certainly, they'd lose their way.

The granddaddy of the fells Alfred Wainwright did his bit to contribute to Black Hill's reputation. No other hill, he said, showed such a desolate and hopeless quagmire to the sky. 'Nature fashioned it, but had no plans for clothing it,' he wrote.

He also had what he described as his 'most frightening experience in a long lifetime of fellwalking' on Black Hill, an episode he vividly recounted in his book on the Pennine Way. Several years had passed when he came to write down the story, but some of the terror of the moment surely remain to be glimpsed through the writing: 'I was crossing a small wet channel of peat that seemed innocuous enough, when suddenly my boots sank out of sight followed by several inches of each leg, more inches being submerged as I tried to extricate myself. Desperate struggles made matters worse. I was firmly anchored in bottomless mud, appearing as a man with both legs amputated below the knees. I was trapped in a vice, helpless to break free.'

Wainwright's salvation on this occasion was a national park ranger who by chance was sitting at the trig point and who was called to the assistance. Wainwright, never perhaps the most lithe of men, came out of the mud, as he put it 'like a cork from a bottle'.

So with Wainwright's malediction on the place it is hardly surprising if Black Hill has an image problem with walkers, even if these days the route of the Pennine Way has been flagged all the way across the plateau. But, according to Chris Dean, that image needs to change. Standing beside the trig point with me close to where Wainwright must have been immolated he points to the still bare banks of peat and makes a prediction: 'I'm very confident: we'll turn Black Hill green in a couple of years,' he says.

Despite Wainwright's assertion, it wasn't nature that left Black Hill unclothed with vegetation, it was human activity. Just as on Bleaklow, a toxic mix of industrialisation, overgrazing, fire and walkers' boots has done its damage. I had seen on Bleaklow some of the efforts being taken to reverse this legacy by improving the hydrology of the area. Now it was time to find out more about the complementary work being done to bring back moorland vegetation.

This is no easy task. One problem is that the sort of plants which can grow up here tend, as a survival mechanism, to be slow growing. Even if seeds germinate on bare peat, they face almost insuperable challenges in building up adequate root systems. In winter, the problem is frost heave, which can open up long cracks in the peat, in the process swallowing up fledgling plants. In summer, the peat becomes desert-dry, the wind picking up the top soil as it blows over the summits. So a heather plant, for example, could struggle through a year or two of growth only for the peat on which it is growing to be unceremoniously whipped away from under its feet. Result – an ex-heather plant.

Chris Dean and his colleagues have been trying various techniques to overcome these problems. The main principle is to try to ensure that plants have the time they need to build up an adequate root-mat underneath them, binding them strongly into the soil and helping protect them from winter and summer hazards. One idea is to kickstart the process by putting down meshes of netting on the peat banks. This work has been undertaken in recent years on both Black Hill and Bleaklow.

The mesh resembles fishing nets, or perhaps the sort of string-bags which some people used to use for shopping. It's usually made of jute, something which causes great satisfaction to the member companies of the Indian Jute Mills Association who in recent years have been delighted to discover a new market opening up for what is a very long-established industry in India. Anti-erosion mats for moorland renovation probably start their life being woven in a jute mill in Calcutta before beginning the long journey to places like Black Hill and Bleaklow.

Once they've arrived, Moors for the Future has the task of transporting the large bales up to the hilltops. Helicopters are the solution, with bales being slung beneath the aircraft and (weather and walkers permitting) at the right moment being dropped on the chosen patch of peat below. After that it's the role of contractors to walk out to the sites, unbundle the jute and spread the mesh over the bare ground, pegging it down with large plastic pegs.

Does it work? It works well, according to a number of academics who have chosen to make the study of geo-textiles their preferred area of research. For example, before jute mesh was widely introduced in the real world it had been subjected to a series of tests by research scientists at Grenoble university who built a series of artificial earth walls of different heights and degrees of slope, spread the stuff out and then subjected it to simulated rainfall, everything from pretend light drizzle to pretend tropical downpours. British academics undertook similar studies, too, trying to work out, for instance, the right thickness and roughness requirements which the jute fibre should be woven to meet. A great many people, it was rapidly becoming clear to me, have had an interest in this moorland restoration business.

Apart from jute, there are other techniques which Moors for the Future has been trying out. The small heather seedling which Chris Dean had pointed out to me was the end result

Grass seed pellets being airlifted by helicopter, past the TV mast of Holme Moss.

of one of these. Heather brash — that is, older heather plants that have been cut back and then chopped up — is spread over the bare peat, creating a kind of carpet through which the heather seeds which are held in the brash can germinate and grow. The idea is not dissimilar to the practice which gardeners use of putting down mulch to help conserve surface moisture.

Originally, Moors for the Future arranged for this work to be done by hand. Chris Dean recounts the long winter days when contractors trudged their way from the Snake Pass road on to Bleaklow early in the morning, their way illuminated by head-torches, to spend the day in among the peat groughs raking out the brash. 'They had five and a half thousand large dumpy bags to empty by hand. At the end of the day, they'd walk to the Snake Pass with their torches on again.' As he recounts it, it doesn't sound like a great deal of fun.

Now the heather brash gets delivered to the hills in the same way as the jute mesh, slung underneath a helicopter and then automatically sprayed out from a hopper. 'We have a new project, too, where we're hydroseeding sphagnum. We get a nursery to grow on sphagnum, harvest it and liquidise it, and we then get that sprayed from a helicopter. We know that works,' Chris says.

I didn't get coated with liquefied sphagnum moss during my time on Black Hill. What did nearly land on my head, however, was a sprinkling of what looked remarkably like hundreds-and-thousands cake decoration. I'd arranged to come here on a day which coincided with one of the helicopter forays across Black Hill, and the brief this time had included the sowing of grass seed. Nine tons of grass seed were deposited as I watched on Black Hill. Another seventy-odd tons of the seed were destined for the top of Bleaklow.

Even the sowing of grass seed turns out to be more complicated than you might think. First of all, Chris Dean (or perhaps one of his staff) gets out the cheque book and purchases agricultural grasses from commercial suppliers. A blend of different varieties is what's wanted, but not all the grasses selected will be those that would naturally grow on the Dark Peak's peatlands. What's needed, in fact, are fast-growing grasses that will root quickly, build up the necessary root-mat system under the surface without being put off by summer dust storms or winter frost heave, and will then after four or five years conveniently die off. This is what's known as a 'nurse' crop. By then, the theory goes, seeds from native grasses will have blown in from neighbouring areas and will have been able to root themselves successfully. After a few seasons, Bleaklow and Black Hill will have been returned to the sort of natural moorland grass cover which they haven't seen for many a long year.

Seeding is done by the helicopter ploughing its way up and down the peat bogs in much the same way as a tractor would make its way, furrow by furrow, up and down a field. In fact, the technology used is the same: both tractors and helicopters these days are equipped with sophisticated GPS kit, to ensure that sowing is done with pinpoint accuracy. But sowing grass, even from as low as fifty feet up above the ground, would still be problematic if nothing were done to prevent the seeds flying away in the wind. So first the seeds have to be coated with a mixture of clay and paper pulp, a process known in the trade as prilling.

The seeds turn out to be prilled in Kings Lynn, and arrive in the Dark Peak as an attrac-tive potpourri of brightly coloured pellets, each colour distinguishing a different variety of grass. These are the hundreds-and-thousands which, if you too are on the hills on a day when sowing is taking place, will fall at your feet, creating a surreal carpet over the black peat. And there's more: sowing is also typically accompanied by the dropping of white fertiliser pellets, containing slow-release nitrogen, potash and phosphate. These pellets resemble tiny hail stones, and also take their place on the hillsides.

This part of the process is designed both to reduce slightly the very high level of acidity of the soil, and also to provide some fertiliser to encourage the grasses to grow. It's not entirely without its critics – some people are worried about the implications for the hydrology – and it's certainly true that the first couple of years after the nurse grass crop has germinated do see the hillside turned a rather curious shade of green. 'Yes, it's unnatural. It looks a little like Tellytubby land,' Chris Dean admits. But this is the start of a long-term process, one which will unfold over a period of many years as, all being well, the moorland vegetation gradually re-establishes on Black Hill.

By coincidence, some of the early pioneering work in moorland revegetation took place close to on Black Hill, as part of restoration work after the construction of a new TV aerial on Holme Moss in the early 1980s. The original mast, reaching 750 feet into the Pennine sky, had been put up here by the BBC at the start of the 1950s to bring its embryonic television service to the north of England. London and the Home Counties were the first to be able to watch TV, the rest of the country having to wait its turn. The Midlands had been brought in with the opening of the Sutton Coldfield mast in December 1949, and by January 1950 it was time for the initial work to get under way at Holme Moss. According to the *Huddersfield Examiner*, which was reporting on the construction work, it wasn't always easy work: the paper talked of workers having to cope with 'driving rain and a blustering wind'.

The mast was finally up and functioning by the autumn of 1951, and the BBC proudly launched TV in the North with a special programme from Manchester, with Gracie Fields and Stanley Matthews as the star turns. It was all complicated technology in those days: the pictures were sent to Holme Moss via coaxial cables from Manchester with the sound being

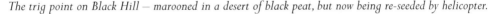

The trig point on Black Hill – marooned in a desert of black peat, but now being re-seeded by helicopter.

sent separately over high-quality GPO telephone lines. Nevertheless, it worked, and thanks to Holme Moss another thirteen million people were able to join the television age.

After thirty years, however, the old mast needed replacing. Among other things, there were concerns about its safety: the TV mast at Emley Moor near Huddersfield (put up a few years later for ITV) had completely collapsed in 1969, brought down by the weight of ice, and icing had also been a problem encountered at Holme Moss. So the decision was taken in the early 1980s to take down the original BBC mast and put up a replacement. Inevitably in the process the peat moorland at the base of the mast was damaged, and in 1984 nine acres were targeted for revegetation. It was one of the first opportunities to try out moorland restoration ideas and techniques which, more than twenty years on, have now been replicated across the whole Dark Peak area.

But it's work which may not necessarily continue in the future. I met Chris Dean as the first stage of his project was approaching its end, and he was engaged in the usual difficult task of finding funding to permit a follow-up phase of Moors for the Future for another few years. Grant-funding policies for the rural economy and the environment change regularly, and in any case the vast majority of the money available is swallowed up by grants to agriculture. What's more, Chris is all too aware that peat moors in the north of England are not as immediately appealing to the general public as more pastoral scenes of the Hay Wain kind. Part of Moors for the Future's work with the general public has been to try to change this, so that people come to appreciate the importance of these stretches of apparently bleak moorland. 'We're trying to get a sea change in the understanding and attitudes of visitors to the area, and of the people who make up the surrounding population,' Chris says. He points to the Moorland Visitor Centre in Edale to illustrate his argument.

The thing is that moorland restoration, of the kind which I saw under way on Black Hill and Bleaklow, takes time. The hundreds-and-thousands at my feet, with luck, will have become by now healthy little grass plants. The heather shoots will have grown into mature plants, safe both from peat erosion and erring sheep. A few more years on the native grasses will, with more luck, have blown in and become rooted. What was once bare wilderness of peat will be returned to real moorland vegetation. But it's a slow process, one which unfolds over a period of ten, twenty or thirty years – not the sort of time frame which most grant-funders or government departments operate within. What happens ultimately up here will depend on public policy towards agriculture, land use and the environment. Black Hill is already no longer the desolate and hopeless quagmire of Wainwright's Pennine Way but there's a long long way to go yet.

The line of the watershed arrives at Black Hill trig point having followed an erratic north-westerly direction from the summit of the A628 at the top of Longdendale. First there are the disused railway tunnels of Woodhead to cross. The railway through Longdendale between Sheffield and Manchester, opened in 1845, was once one of the key railway routes across the Pennines, and considerable investment was made in it after the second world war to upgrade it and electrify it ready for the modern railway age. A new double tunnel was built at Woodhead in 1949 to replace the two original single-line tunnels and in 1955 British Railways Board celebrated the electrification work by bringing out a poster of the line, entitled 'Britain's First All-Electric Main Line'.

However, during the post-Beeching report period of railway rationalisation it was decided to focus on the Hope Valley and Edale line between Manchester and Sheffield and to close the

Stone flags consolidate the route of the Pennine Way, allowing walkers to negotiate Black Hill dry-shod.

Woodhead line. Passenger trains stopped in 1970, and the last train of any kind ran in 1981, with the track being taken up in the mid-1980s. All that is left is the stub to Hadfield, where Manchester-Glossop trains now stop and reverse.

Some people believe that the line should be restored and reopened. However, the track bed has recently been found another use as part of the Trans-Pennine Trail, a 215-mile route from Liverpool to Hull which also forms part of the E8 long-distance path from Ireland to Hungary and (eventually) Istanbul. The Woodhead tunnels have another function, carrying high-voltage electricity power lines through the hills as an alternative to pylons over the top.

North of the route of the tunnels, as the sixth trig point on my journey is reached at Dead Edge End, the watershed links up with what has long been an important administrative boundary, today marking the border between Derbyshire and West Yorkshire. The watershed, and with it the boundary fence which marks it, swings wildly north, then south-west, then north-east, so that the Holme Moss TV mast appears in turn to change its position markedly, first way over to the left, then a moment later off to the right. But eventually the mast lies directly ahead of, and after the crossing of the A6024 Holme road almost directly *above*, the walker.

Black Hill itself provides the first glimpse of the way ahead. Given a good day, there's a view northwards which takes in Pendle hill almost thirty miles away to the north-west and – in the fold of the hills – the wind farm at Cliviger near Burnley which, eventually, the Pennine watershed will encounter. It is time to move on.

4. STANDEDGE

Black Hill – Dean Head Hill – Featherbed Moss – Standedge (A62)

From Black Hill the only way is down. The Pennine Way today heads off to the north, to meet the top of the Wessenden valley at what was previously the site of an inn with the curious name of the Isle of Skye Hotel. The line of the watershed, however, heads north-westwards across the peat, gradually losing height on its way across Dean Head Hill to the Greenfield–Holmfirth road, and more height as it continues across Featherbed Moss and Broadhead Moss.

In the early years of the Pennine Way the watershed was, in fact, the official line chosen for the trail, with the Wessenden alternative created as a bad-weather choice. The Pennine Way acorn sign can still be seen on the occasional finger-post on the old route. It was by all accounts a tough section and Wainwright yet again was an unhappy man ('Featherbed Moss repeats the worst torments of Black Hill and Bleaklow Head in even more virulent form . . . peat sponges . . . a wilderness . . . a filthy slide'). Walkers today have it easier, as the track over Featherbed Moss has been paved over the dampest parts of the moor.

At one of the particularly wet places, a shallow boggy ditch comes in from the west marked today on Ordnance Survey maps as a watercourse. In fact, this ditch is a clue that, despite all the apparent evidence to the contrary, the mill towns of the Pennines are now not far away. The earthworks mark the route of what is called locally the Cotton Famine Road, an early example of a job creation project in one of the darkest periods of the nineteenth century for workers in the cotton industry.

Ironically, the Cotton Famine of the early 1860s followed a boom time in cotton in Lancashire. The decade of the 1850s marked the high-water mark in the industry, a golden period for the mill-owners. The number of mills increased by more than 50 per cent, as did the number of people employed in the cotton mills. Output increased dramatically as Lancashire's inexpensive cotton cloth found a ready market world-wide.

The cotton industry was very dependent, however, on raw cotton imported from the southern states of the US and at the end of 1860 these states announced their secession from the Union to form the Confederacy. Initially, the conflict seemed far off and unlikely to affect Lancashire. Cotton stocks were high, and the crop in both 1859 and 1860 had been good. But in April 1861, as the American Civil War began to get underway, the Union's President Abraham Lincoln announced a new tactic, using the Union's powerful naval supremacy to blockade the Confederate States' coastline including major cotton-exporting ports such as New Orleans and Mobile, Alabama. During the blockade, the quantity of cotton exported fell by 95 per cent.

The price of raw cotton began to rise in England in the summer of 1861, and increased dramatically during the first half of 1862. A pound of raw cotton which had previously sold in

Holme Moss in the fastness of winter, with snow drifting past the TV mast on the horizon.

Liverpool for about seven (old) pence cost over two shillings (24 pence) by mid-1862 and even reached over thirty pence during 1864. At the same time, the price of finished calico cloth rose very slowly, so that what had a short time earlier been a highly profitable industry began to operate at a significant loss. Mills started working at very reduced rates or stopped altogether. Many mill workers faced the prospect of destitution.

There is a powerful reminder of these times in the verse written by the dialect poet Samuel Laycock, whose book *Famine Songs* was a publishing success at the time. Laycock is usually treated as a Lancashire dialect poet, though in fact he was born in 1824 in Marsden in Yorkshire's West Riding and moved as a young man to Stalybridge, then in Cheshire, where he found work as a power-loom weaver in the cotton industry. Like so many others, the Cotton Famine threw him out of his employment.

Laycock's *Famine Songs* were published week by week in local papers, and large numbers were also issued as broadsheet ballads, many being learnt by heart. One which was particularly popular was 'Welcome, Bonny Brid', a gentle verse spoken by a father to his new-born child, welcoming him into the nest of the family even though 'toimes are bad'. Another of his poems addresses the Cotton Famine directly:

One doesn't like everyone t'know heaw they are,
But we'n suffered so lung thro' this 'Merica war,
'At ther's lots o' poor factory folk getten t'fur end,
An' they'll soon be knocked o'er iv th'toimes dunno mend.

Oh, dear! iv yon Yankees could only just see
Heaw they're clemmin' an starvin' poor weavers loike me,
Aw think they'd soon settle the'r bother, an' strive
To send us some cotton to keep us alive.

Some of the more enlightened mill-owners, such as the Fieldens of Todmorden, were prepared to help their workers by keeping them on half-wages during the shut-down periods. In other areas, such as here on Saddleworth Moor, work was artificially created by constructing new roads across the moorland. The Cotton Famine Road, sometimes today known as the 'road to nowhere', can be followed for more than two miles across the Pennine blanket bog.

Beyond Featherbed Moss, as the Pennine Way comes in to rejoin the line of the watershed at Black Moss reservoir, the view opens up and there's a reminder of just how close these moors are to the cities and towns where cotton and wool was spun and woven. The high rises of Oldham come into sight over to the left, while just down to the south-west is Diggle, one of the communities that makes up the collective parish of Saddleworth. On the Yorkshire side, the striking outline of Pule Hill shelters the village of Marsden, barely any distance away.

The main A62 road, which runs between Saddleworth and Huddersfield and which is met at Standedge just beyond Black Moss, is certainly not a road to nowhere. Standedge marks the point where the Pennine range is at its narrowest, with barely half a mile of moorland plateau separating east and west, and for obvious reasons this has been a vital cross-country route for centuries, from the Romans onwards.

Or, perhaps, from before Roman times. Archaeologists have found considerable evidence of the presence of humans in the Saddleworth and Marsden areas during Mesolithic times (the middle stone age, or roughly 7600–3500 BC). Major sites where flints have been found include the summit of Pule Hill itself, which also seems to have been used several millennia later, during the Bronze Age (c.2000–c.650 BC).

The Romans used the Saddleworth–Marsden crossing when they came to build the key trans-Pennine road linking the two important Roman military centres of Chester and York. The road was built some time around AD 79, during the time when Agricola was governor of Britain and was concerned to reinforce the Roman hold on the north of England. The Romans had been having some troubles with the Brigantes, the main tribe in the North at this time. Their queen, Cartimandua, had been for many years a Roman ally, demonstrating her loyalty for example by handing over the leader of the anti-Roman resistance Caratacus after he had fled north after defeat in battle. But then Cartimandua decided to take a new lover. The slighted husband, Venutius, sought revenge, turning against her and against the Romans who protected her. His first revolt was unsuccessful but he tried again in AD 69, at a time when there was Roman instability in Britain, and this time he successfully took the kingdom. The Brigantes, once dependable, became hostile to Rome. The years following 69 saw concerted Roman efforts to stamp down on this unrest.

From Tunnel End, near Marsden, the Standedge Tunnel extends three miles beneath the Pennine watershed.

The Roman road from Chester and Manchester headed in two relatively straight alignments all the way to the edge of the Pennines at Castleshaw just to the west of the A62 Standedge summit. At Castleshaw it's still easy to see much of the *agger*, the artificial mound of stones and soil on which the road was built, in places as much as three feet high and forty to fifty feet across. However, the main focus of attention at Castleshaw is the remains of the fort which the Romans built there at the same time as the road. The fort, which has been excavated several times, was in use until around AD 90 when it was replaced by a smaller 'fortlet', constructed inside its ramparts. Beyond Castleshaw, the Roman road headed over the Pennines before eventually heading off north-eastwards, eventually, to York.

The A62 today at Standedge uses the line chosen by the engineers of a turnpike road opened in 1839. This was the third of three turnpike routes across the hill here, a reminder that improvements in road engineering have a long history. The lines of both the first turnpike, dating back to 1759, and the second constructed in the 1790s, can both be followed on the ground.

However, just as important are the crossings of the hill which were made *underneath* the ground here at Standedge. No less than three railway tunnels were put through between Marsden and Saddleworth, the first built between 1846 and 1849 and the second roughly twenty years later, between 1868 and 1870. The third, a two-track tunnel still used by the Leeds to Manchester trains today, was constructed between 1890 and 1894 and the two earlier single-bore tunnels are now disused.

The fourth of the tunnels under Standedge, the earliest of the lot, is not a railway tunnel at all but was built to take the barges of the Huddersfield Narrow canal through the heart of the Pennines. This was the tunnel I wanted to see for myself. To be fully comprehensive in my account of this part of the watershed, I told myself, I really needed to see what the Pennines looked like from six hundred feet down. No problem, said British Waterways, we'll make a place for you to join one of our boat conveys through the tunnel. Be at Marsden Tunnel End next Wednesday, make sure you're there about 8am. Ask for Fred Carter when you arrive.

Fred and his British Waterways colleagues were already beginning to get ready for the morning's journey through the tunnel, assembling the boats which they would string behind the electric tug like ducklings following a mother duck, as I turned up. Although Standedge canal tunnel is now open once again for navigation after many years of dereliction, you're not allowed to take your own boat through unescorted, a rule which — when you see some of the tight squeezes inside the tunnel which boats have to navigate — makes every kind of sense. Instead, anyone wanting to cruise their boat along the Huddersfield Narrow between the eastern and western sides of the Pennines has to sign up for one of the escorted trips through Standedge, pulled by the tug. In the summer season, there's usually three crossings a week each way.

It's a complicated and time-consuming business. I was expecting to see a flotilla of canal boats assembling at Marsden in front of the tunnel portal but instead there were just five boats waiting patiently. Even a four-boat convoy is quite a challenge, Fred Carter told me. So today's traverse with five boats was going to have to be carefully planned and cautiously executed.

What you don't want to do, I learned, is to put the lightest boat at the back of the flotilla, where it can thrash around like a fish's tail, banging into the sides of the canal tunnel and bringing the whole 'system' of boats to a halt. No, you carefully size up each of the boats, working out the best position in the chain for each, covering them and padding them so that even if they do hit the tunnel side there will – hopefully – be no damage done. Little canal cruisers made of fibreglass need particular care. And even though the level of water in the tunnel was deliberately dropped by about six inches when the tunnel was reopened to give modern canal boats more clearance, there are still some boats on the canal system today where the risk of taking them through Standedge is just too great. These get turned back at the tunnel portals.

Standedge canal tunnel is over three miles long, the longest tunnel on the inland waterway system and also the deepest below ground. In retrospect, building it at all was a pretty foolish idea. But in the years at the start of the 1790s, Britain was going through a time of canal mania not dissimilar to the new technology boom at the start of our own century, and hope, and greed, triumphed over hard business sense. The first meeting to launch the idea of a new trans-Pennine canal, linking up with the existing Huddersfield Broad canal on the Yorkshire side and the Ashton canal on the Lancashire side, was held in Marsden in 1793 with the shareholders enthusiastic for the profits they imagined the Huddersfield Narrow would be able to make them. The plan was for work to start in 1794 and for the new canal to be fully open by 1799. It didn't happen. By 1807, in fact, less than 20 per cent of the tunnel had been completed and, unsurprisingly, the new canal company found itself in crisis.

Nevertheless if things were bad for the shareholders they were rather a lot worse for the navvies who had to undertake the actual work of building a tunnel through the Pennines. Standedge tunnel was dug partly from either end, but deeper inside the hill the technique was to sink shafts several hundred feet from the surface and to dig along from the bottom of these as well. The navvies' task here was to drill holes to take gunpowder, light the fuses and then hang on for dear life to the ropes which hung down the shafts, hoping to be pulled up to safety before the gunpowder exploded. The work had to be undertaken, of course, by candlelight.

There was a time when the work was nearly abandoned altogether. The Huddersfield Narrow's original canal engineer Benjamin Outram had resigned his position, and the surveyor who had been doing most of the actual work of supervising the construction was sacked. Instead, the company's directors turned to the experienced Thomas Telford to help them out. Under Telford's guidance, work on the tunnel began to move much more quickly. It was eventually opened in 1811.

'A lot of the tunnel is virtually like the navvies left it,' Fred Carter told me as, shortly after 9am, the boat convoy began to inch its way forward out of the Marsden daylight. Much of the tunnel is neatly lined with bricks, but there are also sections where the roughly hewn rock has been left unlined. The headlights of the tug pick out the tunnel roof and sides, partly reflected in the dark canal water below.

The trip, I'd been advised, was likely to be conducted at a speed of about one mile an hour. When things go really well, it's possible to get through in not much over two hours, but conversely on bad days when the boats start sticking it can take over four hours before you finally find the daylight again at Diggle. There's no timetable, it just takes as long as it takes. 'Every convoy is different,' Fred Carter said.

The passengers – those of us whose boats were being brought through and those who like me had signed up just for the trip and had been provided with so-called 'hikers' tickets' – were placed in the first boat of the convoy, a glassed-in observation vessel. Each boat behind us had its own British Waterways crew member on board, charged with the task of judging their boat's movement in the water and fending it off if necessary from the tunnel sides. A good transit means likely sticking points are anticipated so the whole boat system slithers through without stopping. Problems occur when boats get stuck and have to be freed; at this point, the slithering act has to be done in reverse.

What do you do as a passenger during the three hours or so inside Standedge tunnel? You peer ahead into the gloom. You notice the numbers on the old legging plates, put up in the days when canal barges had to be propelled by boatmen lying on their backs on the boat roofs and legging it through the tunnel. You look at the brickwork. Periodically, you stand on the little platform at the back of the observation vessel (it's what British Waterways staff like to refer to as the sun deck). If you do, periodically you dive inside for cover as streams of water pour down from the canal tunnel roof.

There are also, from time to time, ghostly companions close at hand. The railway tunnels were built above the level of the canal tunnel, the two dead tunnels a little way off to the left and the active rail tunnel on the right-hand side. When trains pass, you hear the rumble and feel the vibration. You also see their effect as a thin mist settles momentarily on the canal, caused by the change in atmospheric pressure. At only one point in the tunnel, Fred Carter told me, can you actually see the trains flash past, if you happen to be looking upwards at the right moment.

Travelling through Standedge with a hiker's ticket is surely one of the most extraordinary tourist experiences to be had in the north of England. What is so remarkable is that the tunnel, now once again open for traffic, was derelict and ignored for fifty years. The last commercial barge went through Standedge in 1921 and the tunnel was official closed in 1944, though one boat did struggle through in 1948. Thereafter, nature was left to take its course. It wasn't only the tunnel which was closed: the whole of the Huddersfield Narrow was left to decay, and indeed the land on which the canal had been built was used in several

Light and shadow play across South Pennine moorland.

places to construct factories and shops. Bringing the canal back to life, and putting a waterways link back through the Pennines, seemed utterly impossible. And yet, astonishingly, this is what happened, thanks mainly to the voluntary efforts of the Huddersfield Canal Society and the Inland Waterways Association. Their story is as much a tale of triumph against all the odds as was the original successful construction of the canal in the first place.

Roughly half-way through, the trickiest moment of the transit comes as the tunnel reaches a sharp S-bend. Perhaps not surprisingly, given the way it was constructed, it was found when the canal came to be completed that there was a discrepancy of as much as twenty-six feet in the lines being taken from either side. The boat convoy I am on is carefully shepherded around the first right-hand bend, and then back around the left-hand bend which follows almost immediately.

And then there is more tunnel. If, for the first hour or so, I had been actively looking out, watching the progress we were making and counting off the legging plates as they went by, after perhaps two hours a trance-like state came over me. A deep ennui settled, like the mist falling back on the water after the passage of a train. I was grateful I wasn't having to stay alert, driving the electric tug or fending off the boats behind. My brain seemed to close down. Some of the tightest squeezes in the tunnel are just before the western end is reached, but I didn't notice us pass through them. I was ready now for Diggle, and daylight.

And so, finally, we emerged from Standedge. The boats moored and were separated from the convoy. I gave my thanks to Fred Carter and his crew colleagues, and went to catch a bus back to Marsden. The bus took about ten minutes.

5. WHITE HILL

Standedge (A62) – Millstone Edge – White Hill – Windy Hill (A672)

We last left Wainwright complaining about the terrible conditions he was encountering on Featherbed Moss, having already had his hazardous adventure with a man-trap peat bog on Black Hill. Despite his evident dislike of the peaty wastelands of the Dark Peak, however, he wasn't above trying to make his own suggestion as to how the Pennine Way could have been made even tougher.

Given the theme of this book, it's appropriate to recall that he saw this as a route which would trace the actual watershed along the Pennines: 'The *ideal* Pennine Way would follow such a line, keeping always to the highest land ahead and having west-flowing streams consistently on one hand and east-flowing streams on the other; and, because of the complicated topography of the hills, its course would by no means always be on a north–south axis . . .', he wrote in his book *Pennine Way Companion*.

He went on: 'A walk of this nature, keeping strictly to the main watershed, would be extremely arduous, for it is along the *tops* of these moors, especially those with a peat covering, that progress is most difficult . . .' And he added, in one of those inimitable comments which reveal slightly too much of Wainwright's own personal attitudes, 'This would be an undertaking only for the toughest and most resolute of he-men . . .'

From south of Standedge to White Hill and then north again to Blackstone Edge near Littleborough the Pennine Way does, in fact, more or less coincide with the watershed. It's the last time for many miles. The Pennine Way will not be met again until the Yorkshire Dales, on the climb up to Pen-y-ghent, and then only briefly. So this may be the moment to explore something of the background to Britain's first long-distance footpath.

Despite the fact that the worst of the bare peat is now covered with stone slabs, the Pennine Way can still be a challenging undertaking, particularly when the weather is poor and the cloud is down. In the early days – regardless of what Wainwright was implying – it was an even tougher challenge. 'In rain, mist, snow or high winds it can prove arduous and even exhausting for the hardiest walkers, and should certainly not be attempted in such conditions by anyone unable to steer a course by map and compass,' wrote one early guide book, published two years after the official opening in 1965.

But that was how it was supposed to be. Tom Stephenson, the man who more than anyone brought the Pennine Way into being, talked in the early years of his desire for it 'to keep to the heights and rough ground as much as possible'. ('Even so,' he added, 'the keen tramper would still no doubt prefer to take a line of his own off any beaten track . . .')

Stephenson certainly could claim to be a keen tramper himself. He recalled later in life his youth in the years immediately before the first world war, when he was an apprentice printer

The Pennine Bridleway, Tom Stephenson's Pennine Way and the watershed coincide across rocky Standedge.

living in the Ribble valley in Lancashire: 'There were frequent periods of short-time working, perhaps only two or three days a week. This left me with little or no money but ample time for rambling. Passing rich with a few pence in my pocket and with a little food from the family larder, I would set out before sunrise and make a round trip of up to a hundred miles. Nights I spent rolled in a groundsheet in the lee of a drystone wall, or in a barn if one was handy. Sometimes there was a welcome at an out-of-the-way farm and an invitation to a meal. On other occasions a village policeman would question me closely.'

Tom Stephenson was born in 1893 in Chorley, Lancashire and grew up in a working class home. His father was an engraver in a calico print works and his mother worked in one of the area's numerous cotton mills. Tom himself began work at thirteen, following his father into calico printing, but he also worked hard at continuing his education, raiding the Clitheroe public library for books like Darwin's Origin of Species and attending night school in Burnley. In 1915, he won a geology scholarship to the Royal College of Science in London. However, the war was raging and he was a committed conscientious objector. In 1917, his refusal to fight led to a twelve-month sentence of hard labour in Wormwood Scrubs.

After the war he became active politically in the young Labour Party and was a paid member of staff for the party for the whole of the 1920s. But even in his teens he had been contributing articles to newspapers and in 1933 he moved across into journalism full-time, writing on outdoor issues for the *Daily Herald* and editing a small trade union magazine called *Hiker and Camper*. It was in an article which Tom contributed to the *Daily Herald* in June 1935 that the idea of the Pennine Way first received its public airing.

The feature, with its headline 'Wanted – a Long Green Trail', has since been seen as something of a classic in the story of the outdoor movement in Britain. Tom Stephenson's call for 'a Pennine Way from the Peak to the Cheviots' was his response – albeit on a rather more modest, British, scale – to the creation of the 2,000-mile Appalachian Trail and the 2,500-mile John Muir Trail in the United States. And he contrasted the US government support and finance which had gone into these initiatives with the hostile reception so often meted out to ramblers in Britain.

The article began: 'When two American girls wrote asking advice about a tramping holiday in England, I wondered what they would think of our island, particularly of the restrictions placed in the way of those who wished to see some of our most captivating scenery. If, at the end of their tour, these visitors from across the Atlantic are over-loud in their praises of their native "Land of Liberty", who shall blame them?' Tom Stephenson's vision was for a 'meandering way' through the 'lonely entrancing country' of the Pennines. He concluded his article:

> Let us have this through route to health and happiness for this and succeeding gener-
> ations who may thus make acquaintance with some of the finest scenery in the land.
> Whatever the cost, it would be a worthy and enduring testimony bringing health and
> pleasure beyond computation, for none could walk that Pennine Way without being
> improved in mind and body, inspired and invigorated and filled with the desire to
> explore every corner of this lovely island.

The idea of this 'Pennine Way' must have been something Tom Stephenson had been mulling over for some time before the article came to be written, and he had almost certainly discussed possible routes with others in the rambling movement. The call for the Long Green Trail may have been in the form of a newspaper feature, but it was, in reality a detailed proposal with an already well-worked out set of suggestions for where such a Pennine Way would go. What is striking is how many of these suggestions came to be incorporated in the eventual line of the trail: Kinder Scout, Bleaklow, Laddow Rocks, Blackstone Edge, Fountains Fell, Pen-y-ghent, Hardraw, Keld, Tan Hill and Cross Fell are all there in the 1935 article. Even the proposal for the Pennine Way to start at the 'moor-rimmed bowl of Edale' is made for the first time there.

Nevertheless, once the *Daily Herald* piece had appeared there was a need to try to turn the Pennine Way idea into reality, and among other things that involved further discussion about where exactly it could go. One possibility considered early on, for example, was whether to route it over Pendle, Lancashire's dominant whaleback hill, and then perhaps via the eastern edge of the Forest of Bowland towards Ingleborough. ('We did discuss the possibility of including Pendle and the Bowland country but finally decided the traverse across the Burnley district was not worth it. It would moreover have meant missing the Malham district,' Tom Stephenson wrote to a correspondent in 1938.)

Much of the crucial detail of the route seems to have been talked through in discussions which Tom Stephenson had with Edwin Royce, a leading member of the Manchester ramblers' movement, from 1936 to early 1938. The discussions took place through the medium of regular correspondence between the two men, Stephenson writing from his home on Clapham Common in London and Royce from Levenshulme in south Manchester. The letters, which have survived, demonstrate both men's extensive knowledge of the Pennine uplands and the care they took over the details.

To give some flavour of these exchanges, here, for example, is Royce writing to Stephenson in November 1936, talking about options in the Cross Fell area: 'As you know there is the Maiden Way from Skirwith . . . there is also the old mine track over the shoulder of Crossfell to Garrigill . . . ought we to be satisfied with these or ask for a more direct route entirely on the "rough"?'

Here is Stephenson writing a few weeks later: 'One of the difficult paths I think would be across the pastoral land of Craven . . .' He goes on:

> A right-of-way would be necessary from Gt Shunner Fell into Swaledale. From Thwaite to Tan Hill would not present much difficulty. . . . If possible I think the route should proceed from [Bowes Moor] to Middleton-in-Teesdale, thence there is a path up the Yorkshire side of the Tees almost to High Force . . . After visiting Cauldron Snout there is of course the recognised route to High Cup Nick. For the sake of accommodation it would no doubt be necessary to descend from there to Dufton . . .

And Royce again, early in the New Year of 1937, with a list of the missing rights of way links and the comment: 'The worst bit is the passage in Lancashire from Blackstone Edge . . . it provides a surfeit of mill chimneys.'

By early in 1938, Stephenson and Royce felt able to present their thoughts more widely. Together with two other leading ramblers they called a weekend conference at the end of February at a guest house run by the Workers Travel Association in Hope, in the Peak District, to which the various Northern ramblers' federations and outdoor organisations were invited to send delegates. The *Daily Herald* had been prevailed upon by Stephenson to continue its connection with the Pennine Way idea and to stump up the cost of the delegates' accommodation expenses, a total of £7.10s.

The suggested route was presented to the Hope conference marked up on 1-inch Ordnance Survey maps in either red or green ink. Red meant there were problems of access; green meant that no problems were foreseen. Fortunately, most of the route was coloured green: of the total estimated length of the proposed Pennine Way of 251 miles, only 68 miles required new legal rights. Nevertheless, this 'red' section included the grouse moors of Kinder and the Peak District, what Royce referred to 'trespassers will be prosecuted country'. It wasn't necessarily all going to be plain sailing.

Out of the Hope conference came a stirring resolution, agreed unanimously, which echoed in many ways the language of Stephenson's original newspaper article. The Pennine Way, it stated, was desirable for 'the physical and spiritual well-being of the youth of Britain'. The resolution went on: 'The wide, health-giving moorlands and high places of solitude, the features of natural beauty, and the places of historical interest along the Pennine Way give this route a special character and attractiveness which should be available for all time as a national heritage of the youth of the country and of all who feel the call of the hills and lonely places'.

There was, however, some disagreement, most notably on the Sunday morning when the discussion turned to the extent to which the Pennine Way route should be waymarked. Nobody much liked the continental European habit of splashing daubs of paint as waymarkings for paths, but it seems that some people – presumably the 'keen tramper' element who were attracted to places like Kinder and Bleaklow precisely because of their remoteness – were unhappy at the idea of any kind of waymarking up on the high moors. (This very early debate was to resurface in an unfortunate way in 1951, in an internecine dispute among ramblers about whether the Pennine Way should be routed – as Stephenson wished – up Grindsbrook to cross the Kinder Scout plateau, or should be rerouted via Upper Booth and Jacob's Ladder, leaving the back of Kinder for the serious wilderness walker and free from the walking masses. The issue went to a public enquiry and the compromise was for the Upper Booth route to be a bad weather substitute. It has since become the only official route out of Edale.)

But generally the mood as the Hope conference finished was very upbeat. The meeting had agreed to create a Pennine Way Association, which would meet regularly to pursue the idea. What's more, local ramblers' federations had volunteered to take on the task of checking the exact alignment of the route on the ground, looking at the legal status of the paths being proposed and at the state of the ground underfoot.

There was a sense of things moving quickly, reinforced by considerable media interest. Other journalists apart from Stephenson began writing about this Pennine Way idea. The *Manchester Guardian* wrote a piece which appeared shortly after the conference, as did the *Manchester Evening News*, and so too did *The Times*. This latter may not have been entirely helpful. Tom Stephenson received a letter immediately afterwards from a Hampshire clergyman who demanded rather peremptorily: 'Would you be so good as to give me some details of the Pennine Way, which I gather from *The Times* is a footpath extending some 200 miles. I am thinking of taking a walking holiday next week, and should like to know particularly where the path starts, where it stops and what particular halts there are by the way.' Stephenson had to respond, 'In reply to your enquiry, the Pennine Way at the moment is an unachieved ideal . . .'

And despite the high hopes, there were reasons to be cautious. The world political situation at the end of the 1930s was far from encouraging. As early as January 1937, Edwin

Another trig point, marking the highest land on Standedge.

Royce had finished a letter to Stephenson about the route with the comment 'The times are unpropitious. Have you bought a gas mask yet?' His concern was justified. War intervened before the fledgling Pennine Way Association could finish its initial research work.

Ironically, however, it must be acknowledged that it was the war and more particularly the post-war public mood for change which created the conditions which saw the Pennine Way brought to fruition. The Pennine Way was endorsed in 1945 by the Dower committee, which was set up to consider the creation of national parks in England and Wales and which led to the eventual passing of the 1949 National Parks and Access to the Countryside Act. Sections 51–5 of this Act empowered the newly established National Parks Commission to recommend the provision of long-distance routes. The Act also gave powers for local authorities to overrule recalcitrant landowners and to create the new legal rights of way necessary.

Tom Stephenson, by 1948 the first full-time secretary of the Ramblers' Association, was now well placed to push forward the Pennine Way through official channels. There were still some storms ahead (for example, there were battles with water authorities concerned with the risk of possible water pollution from walkers over the route both to the south and to the

north of Black Hill which had to be resolved, and there was also the unhappy business of the Kinder Scout disputed route). Nevertheless, the principle of the Pennine Way was well-established. Hugh Dalton, the minister for local government and planning, formally approved the Pennine Way in July 1951. The route itself was completed and officially opened in 1965. It had taken thirty years for the long green trail to become reality.

The Pennine Way signposts follow the watershed north from the A62 at Standedge to the trig point at Millstone Edge, on through the National Trust's Marsden moorland estate, past the trig point at White Hill, and up to the A672 near Windy Hill. Beyond here is the M62, the latest of centuries of trans-Pennine highways to be put across these hills. An elegant pedestrian bridge takes the footpath over the motorway. A long way below, lorries and cars criss-cross incessantly. Above, walkers usually pause briefly, and then press on.

A remarkable feat of engineering in itself, the trans-Pennine M62 motorway rises to the highest point — the mast on top of Windy Hill.

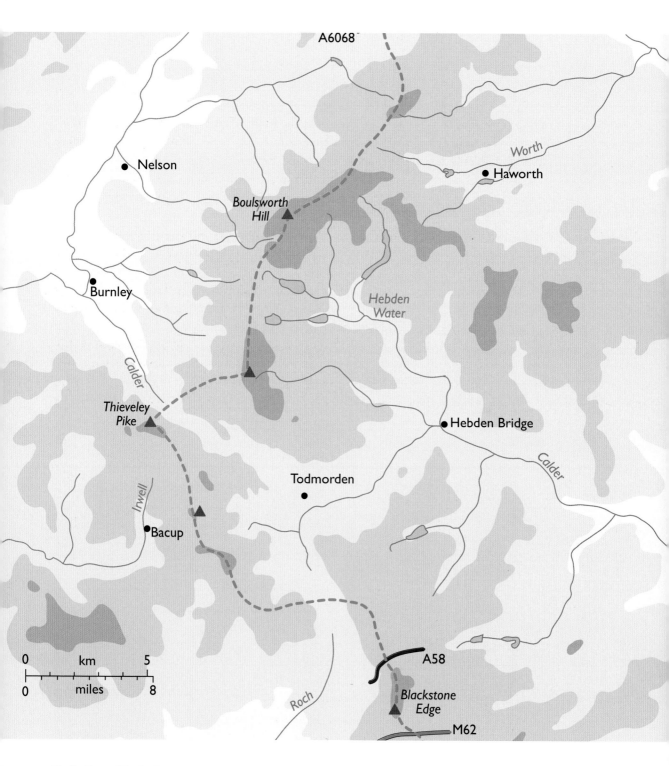

6. BLACKSTONE EDGE

Windy Hill (A672) – Blackstone Edge

It's a fine view from Blackstone Edge. Not since the Kinder Downfall, way back south almost to Mam Tor, has the English watershed delivered quite such an extensive panorama. Here the hills stop suddenly, leaving the Lancashire plain directly below stretching away towards the Irish Sea. Rochdale is close at hand. A little further off, and a little more to the south, the high-rise offices and flats of Manchester are obvious landmarks. And the view extends further, too, always provided the weather is kind.

I was lucky. The weather was clear, showing off the view to the full. In one direction, the sun was glinting off the top section of the TV mast high up on Winter Hill near Bolton, at the end of the high land of the West Pennine moors. To the south, the Pennine range proper could be seen curling round, past Kinder to the moors east of Macclesfield at the head of the Goyt valley. Beyond Manchester, to the south-west, I could even catch a glimpse of the Clwydian Hills and the hill ridges near Wrexham.

Many places in Britain have been commemorated in verse – think of Tintern Abbey (Wordsworth), or Wenlock Edge (Housman), or Adlestrop railway station (Edward Thomas), or Little Gidding (T.S. Eliot). Blackstone Edge can join this list, thanks to a nineteenth-century political leader and poet called Ernest Jones. His verse 'The Blackstone Edge Gathering', written more as a song than a poem and set to a popular tune of the day, was composed in 1846.

Jones begins by looking down from Blackstone Edge over the plain – or at least trying to. Instead of his eye being led to far horizons, however, what greets him is industrial smoke and pollution, the product of the cotton mills which, as we have already seen, had been transforming the landscape and the economy of this part of Lancashire. It was not a pretty sight. In fact, Jones suggests, there is something about it which is against the natural order of things:

> O'er plains and cities far away
> All lorn and lost the morning lay
> When sank the sun at break of day
> In smoke of mill and factory.

On Blackstone Edge itself, however, high above the Lancashire plains, it's a different story:

> But waved the wind on Blackstone Height
> A standard of the broad sunlight
> And sung that morn with trumpet might
> A sounding song of liberty!

Juggernauts judder to a halt on the M62, with Windy Hill on the horizon.

We know exactly which 'morn' Ernest Jones was referring to: it was Sunday 2nd August 1846. The poem itself, as its title suggests, commemorates an event which took place here, up on the Pennine escarpment, during the heyday of the Chartist movement.

Walking past the Blackstone Edge rocks today it's hard to imagine this as the setting for a mass political rally. Nevertheless, that Sunday in August saw about thirty thousand people gathered here, at least according to a report a few days later in the Chartists' own newspaper the *Northern Star*. There would have been banners and pennants ready to be waved by the wind, there would have been speeches (and they would have been long), but there'd have been a party atmosphere too, rather like on most demonstrations today. Chartism was strong on both sides of the Pennines, both in the larger mill towns such as Halifax, Bradford, Rochdale and Oldham and in the smaller towns such as nearby Todmorden, and rallies on moorland tops were a feature of the movement, it presumably being rather easier to discuss radical politics away from the immediate attention of the mill-owners and their supporters. Blackstone Edge was a convenient place to bring together people from both the Lancashire and Yorkshire towns 'all of whom' (this is the *Northern Star* again) 'must have travelled three miles, and many of whom had travelled thirty to renew the covenant with their fellow men.'

The Chartist movement doesn't seem to feature much these days in history, a fact which seems surprising given that Chartism was one of the most important and the most influential popular movement of the past two hundred years, able in its time to mobilise hundreds of thousands of people. Their basic demand, converted into modern demo-speak, can be summed up something like this:

> What do we want?
> Votes for all!
> When do we want it?
> Now!

It was the Chartists who helped define the shape of our modern democracy, arguing the case for a political system where voting is the responsibility and right of all, not just of those with money and wealth. And, much to the concern of the British state which periodically set about arresting and imprisoning the Chartist leaders, it was also the first time that a working class in Britain made its presence firmly felt on the national political landscape.

When Ernest Jones joined the crowds at Blackstone Edge, the Chartist movement had already been in full flow for eight or more years. Chartism took its name from the People's Charter, which carried the demands of the movement and which was first published in May 1838. There were six demands: universal male suffrage (or in other words, votes for all men aged twenty-one and over), a secret ballot, no property requirements to become an MP, payment of MPs, equal constituencies and annual parliaments. 1838 was a year of activity and mass mobilisation throughout Britain. Newcastle, for example, had a mass demonstration in June, Birmingham in August and Manchester in September. Each city and town made their choice of delegates to attend the Chartist National Convention, which met for the first time the following February. In June 1839, the first Chartist petition (three miles long, by the time it arrived in London) was presented to Parliament, and of course firmly rejected (the voting was 235 against to 46 in favour).

Thereafter followed several years of ups and downs. 1839 saw an abortive rising in Newport, Monmouthshire, and early 1840 would see other attempts at armed uprising, in places such as Sheffield, Bradford and Dewsbury. In general, this was a time generally when the State regained the upper hand, and several Chartists found themselves in prison for various alleged public order offences. The next high-water mark for the movement was the year of 1842, when a second petition was taken to Parliament and when, later in the autumn, the mill towns of Lancashire and Yorkshire were convulsed by a wave of industrial protests known to historians as the Plug Riots. (This had nothing to do with bathroom plumbing. An effective way, the protesters found, to stop the mills from working was to remove the plugs from the boilers of the engines which drove the machinery.) Thereafter once again the tide receded. Chartists began to turn their attention from demanding parliamentary reform to creating their own land colonies, a back-to-the-land strategy more than a century before the alternative movement of the 1970s and 1980s tried the same thing.

But Chartism was to have one final year of mass political activity in 1848, a year which was also marked in mainland Europe by a wave of revolutions. By 1846, therefore, there was perhaps a sense that the movement was once again on the move. This certainly is how the *Northern Star* reported the Blackstone Edge rally: 'Sunday last may be considered as the resurrection day of Chartism,' the report began. Ernest Jones himself was clearly moved by the spirit of the event. His verse (and it must be time by now to get back to that) continued:

> And grew the glorious music higher
> When pouring, with his heart on fire
> Old Yorkshire came with Lancashire
> And all its noblest chivalry:
>
> The men who give – not those who take!
> The hands that bless – yet hearts that break –
> Those toilers for their foeman's sake
> Our England's true nobility.

Blackstone Edge, overlooking the Lancashire plain, where Chartists gathered in 1846.

> So brave a host hath never met
> For truth shall be their bayonet
> Whose bloodless thrusts shall scatter yet
> The force of false finality.

This last comment was something of a barb at the man who had become Prime Minister earlier that 1846 summer, Lord John Russell. Russell had a few years earlier pronounced himself completely satisfied with the way the British electoral system functioned, declaring (and I may be paraphrasing his exact words a little) 'Nobody else gets the vote, and that's final'. Thereafter to his political enemies Russell came to be known as Finality Jack.

Jones and his fellow Chartists not surprisingly had a different idea from the Prime Minister. Jones continues 'The Blackstone Edge Gathering' in optimistic mood:

> Though hunger stamped each forehead spare
> And eyes were dim with factory glare
> Loud swelled the nation's battle prayer
> Of – death to class monopoly!

Then every eye grew keen and bright
And every pulse was dancing light
For every heart had felt its might
The might of labour's chivalry.

Jones concludes his poem by returning to Blackstone Edge itself, the 'high hill' from which the message of Chartism is to be carried out to the world:

And up to Heaven the descant ran
With no cold roof twixt God and man
To dash back from its frowning span
A church prayer's listless blasphemy.

How distant cities quaked to hear
When rolled from that high hill the cheer
Of hope to slaves! to tyrants fear!
And God and man for liberty!

'The Blackstone Edge Gathering' was written by Jones immediately after the rally, and published about three weeks later in the *Northern Star*. The event was important for Jones, for as well as being its chronicler he was also one of the main speakers, the first time he had taken the platform publicly in support of the Chartist cause. He had an unusual background: his father was an Army major, his mother came from a large landowning family in Kent and his godfather was the Duke of Cumberland, uncle to Queen Victoria. Jones was born and brought up in Germany and this upbringing gave him a natural ability with other languages. His family returned to England in 1838 when he was nineteen, and thereafter he qualified and practised as a barrister. The initial years of Chartist agitation passed him by. But something happened to change the course of his life, and by the start of 1846 he had thrown in his lot with the Chartist cause. He went on to become one of the national leaders, suffering two years of harsh treatment in prison at the end of the 1840s on what were effectively trumped-up charges. He met Karl Marx a number of times (Marx told Engels that he found Jones a little egotistical) and probably read Marx's writings in the original German. He tried to keep the Chartist flame alive in the 1850s and for a time produced his own newspaper *The People's Paper*. He also continued to write poems and songs.

Chartist orators must have had powerful lungs, particularly at large open-air events like that at Blackstone Edge. His skills as a barrister would have helped, too, to hold the large crowd. The text of the speech he made at the Blackstone Edge rally has survived and it shows him in powerful form. Here's a short extract, just to give a flavour of his language:

> What? Are pounds sterling or living souls to be represented in our House of Parliament? What? Are the interests of a man possessing a million pounds to be cared for a million times more? This – this is what their argument involves. This, then is their philanthropy! Out upon them! They have but legislated for their money bags – we will legislate for our fellow-men. The interests they tried to promote was the interests of their vested capital – the interests we will further shall be those of humanity all over the world.

At the time you might have accused Jones of being impossibly visionary in campaigning for votes for all and a democratic House of Commons. On the other hand, we know now that it was Jones and the Chartists who had the ear of the future, rather than Finality Jack.

Even in those days, it seems there was something of an issue about public access to moors where grouse were shot, for the rally's chairman having called for silence began by telling the crowd, 'The squire had made a request that in their passage across the mountain they would not disturb the rest of his birds.' (The Chartist press reported that this was greeted with 'great laughter'.) But we don't know exactly where on Blackstone Edge the rally took place. The *Northern Star* talked of a 'beautiful amphitheatre' on the summit of what the reporter described as a 'wild mountain', overlooking the plain below.

There's certainly no plaque at Blackstone Edge to commemorate this moment in the history of the north of England. Nevertheless, the Chartists' memory is not entirely forgotten in these parts. As I was beginning the work on this book a small photocopied leaflet came my way: it was to announce a walk up to the stones at Blackstone Edge, organised by a group in Halifax for a summer Sunday lunchtime, to remember that day in 1846 and to commemorate the Chartist legacy in the Halifax area. The echoes of the 'sounding song of liberty' resonate still up here.

7. ON THE SOUTH PENNINE MOORS

Blackstone Edge – White House – Light Hazzles Reservoir – Summit (A6033)

Just as the appearance of the Pennine moorland changes subtly mile after mile, so too do the particular sounds associated with the land.

We tend to read the countryside with our eyes rather than our ears, however. We're also good at blocking out particular sounds. As the M62 crossing is approached near Windy Hill, for example, the motorway traffic's continual low growling is ever present, dying away only as the hills near Blackstone Edge gradually provide a natural shield against the sound. When you're made conscious of the traffic, it's impossible to ignore. And yet it's possible to walk the moors near the motorway and effectively fail to hear it.

Walking north from Blackstone Edge past the White House (the first habitation met so far on the watershed, incidentally: a bonus for the walker that it's a pub), I began to be conscious that I was hearing a sound that I'd never heard before in these parts. It was a deep metallic sound, like the beating of hammers on iron, and it was reverberating around the hillside. No chance of ignoring this particular noise. It also got louder as I progressed southwards, a slightly alarming sensation.

The explanation was over the next hill. High up – eighty feet? a hundred feet? – above me, sitting on the support struts of a large electricity pylon in an apparently precarious manner,

The White House: the first pub encountered by watershed walkers.

were two men, engaged in renovating the pylon's metal work. The men would have been difficult to notice, but the sound their tools were making was being carried widely over the surrounding moors.

There are two chains of high voltage pylons which cross the Pennines close to the White House and Blackstone Edge, and not surprisingly they were a controversial addition to the landscape when they were first put up. A writer in *Yorkshire Life* magazine in 1968, just before a public enquiry into the first set of pylons, expressed her disgust at the prospect. Never since the German bombers flew over in the second world war, she claimed, had the countryside been at greater risk: 'The enemies this time are metal giants. . . . In an age when men can test the surface of the moon and lay cables across the earth's great oceans, is it too much to ask that the cables be put underground?'

Well, yes, it was too much to ask. Originally the proposal was to route the pylons further north, close to Haworth and the moors associated with the Brontës, but the government was persuaded by guardians of the Brontë heritage to think again. Blackstone Edge became the chosen route.

All sorts of additions and excrescences have been made to the upland landscape which, were they to be proposed again now, would almost certainly invite protest. If a government mapping service was to suggest today, for example, erecting a string of pillars made of concrete and painted bright white on the summits of many of the country's most loved mountains, it is hard to believe that they would be welcomed, and yet the old Ordnance Survey trig points are now familiar friends to many walkers. Prominent landmarks like the stone obelisk of Stoodley Pike, erected in 1814 a few miles north of Blackstone Edge on the hillside overlooking the Calder valley and now a visitor feature, might also be controversial were they to be proposed today.

On the other hand, and try as I might, I have not yet managed to fall in love with electricity pylons. I do, however, recognise that the two chains of pylons at Blackstone Edge have to take

Electricity pylons stride across the moors, either side of the trans-Pennine A58.

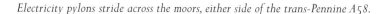

their place in any account of the Pennine watershed. The transit of these hills which the power lines make is as significant for our own economy and our own way of life as was the Huddersfield Narrow canal tunnel for its day, or going back further, the military road across Standedge for the Romans.

And I am grateful that there are people like Sean Prendergast prepared to tackle the hazardous task of maintaining the condition of the pylons. I met Sean and several of his fellow workers on the pylons late one afternoon as they sat in their van at the end of a day's shift. Sean told me he was from Doncaster and had worked as a car mechanic before deciding to head for the high life on the pylons. He'd thought originally that he was applying for a job which would involve working on scaffolding in some way – or at least that's what he implies when telling the story. He hadn't been entirely serious in applying for the job: his CV had been written on the back of a beer mat, he says.

But now, six years on, he'd been at work on pylons all over the country: Birmingham, North Wales, London, Dungeness, Folkestone. Newport in south Wales was the highest he'd worked: 500 feet above the ground, working on the very top wire at the pylon apex. That was unusually high: typically he could be working 160 or 180 feet above ground level.

Was it as frightening as it sounded? Sean admitted that, despite the three weeks' training in working at height which he'd undergone, the first ascent had been very scary. Windy weather in particular could make a pylon seem a precarious place, he told me, but whatever the weather the work was often cold and hard. Tough for partners and families, too: Sean himself has three children, but spends weeks at a time away from home, living in caravans and often working fifty or more hours a week. Work has to be undertaken with the knowledge all the time that there are two significant dangers: the risk of falling, and the risk of getting an electric shock. When working on one side of a pylon, the power is usually left on on the other side. Insulation becomes a crucial part of the safety procedures.

There can also be a lot of weather a hundred feet or more up. 'We're working in all weather, in wind and snow,' Sean told me. 'The only thing that stops us is lightning.' The crew receive a special weather report from the Met Office detailing the likelihood of lightning, and at the first suggestion of thunder head for cover.

And what about the scenery? I was interested to know whether the view Sean was getting from several hundred feet up above the Pennines was significantly better than the view I was getting at ground level – and the message back was that it was, well, all right. (A good view, but not a patch on the Isle of Skye, said one of Sean's mates, who then revealed that he came originally from Skye.)

Despite the evident dangers and the hardness of the work, this is a job which some people do year after year. One of Sean's colleagues had recently retired after about twenty years, I was told. There is a strong camaraderie between the men, the sort of bond which comes from people who share risks and rely on each other and which is associated with traditionally male jobs like working on the oil rigs or, in times past, coal mining.

The chains of pylons at Blackstone Edge can stand as a symbol of the way that the moorlands hereabouts have been used to accommodate the needs of an industrial society. This was, of course, the stretch of countryside which Edwin Royce confided in his letter to Tom Stephenson suffered from a surfeit of mill chimneys, and though almost all the mills which those chimneys served are now silent, the moorland near Littleborough, Todmorden and Hebden Bridge has certainly learned how to earn its keep.

Because of this historical legacy, what tends nowadays to be called the South Pennines missed out when it came to the selection of the country's national parks. Not even designation one step down, either, as an Area of Outstanding Natural Beauty. Nevertheless, and in a much lower profile way as far as the public is concerned, the importance of these moorlands has been given official recognition. Indeed, the high ground traversed by the Pennine watershed over Blackstone Edge and beyond can claim a bewildering set of initials, as – among other things – an SSSI, an SPA and an SAC.

It's perhaps time to explain the background to all this. Though one stretch of moorland may look much like another to the casual visitor, each part of the Pennine uplands has been studied, examined for the importance of its habitat, its ecological systems, its vegetation and biodiversity, and assessed. What may seem to some like wild and unfrequented parts are carefully recorded on databases accessible on PCs in government departments and local authorities (and, in fact, to any internet user). The moors are certainly not terra incognita.

There are two sections of the Pennine watershed that are within national parks, the first being the Peak District, which we left behind at Standedge, and the second the Yorkshire Dales, which will be met in another thirty miles or so. Most people are familiar with the idea of national parks, which was a significant initiative of the first post-war government and which was brought in, in England and Wales, through the National Parks and Access to the Countryside Act in 1949. (The idea of national parks in Scotland has come in only since 2000). The original Act established two aims for the national parks, to conserve and protect the landscape and to promote the public enjoyment of them. Unlike national parks in some other countries, the land itself was not taken into public ownership but remained in the hands of those who owned it previously. Today, about three-quarters of the land within national parks is privately owned, though the National Trust and Forestry Commission also have significant land holdings.

Each national park has its own National Park Authority with significant powers, particularly in relation to planning decisions where it has the duties which would normally be the responsibility of a local authority. In fact, a National Park Authority acts a little like a local council, except that control isn't in the hands of directly elected councillors. The authority's Board is made up of two groups of people: just over half are councillors of the local authorities covered by the national park boundary who take on membership of the Board as part of their overall duties, and the remainder are appointed by the government. This latter group is meant to reflect the various interest groups having a stake in the national park: farming and shooting interests are likely to be represented, and so too are representatives of recreational users such as walkers.

National parks are considered the premier league when it comes to the country's most important and beautiful landscapes. The 1949 Act also established the concept of Areas of Outstanding Natural Beauty (AONBs), which perhaps unfairly could be seen as forming a (rather larger) second division in the beauty stakes. There are thirty-six AONBs in England, ranging in size from the Isles of Scilly (6 square miles) to the Cotswolds (790 square miles). The second largest is the North Pennines AONB, at just under 775 square miles, which abuts on to the northern boundary of the Yorkshire Dales national park and will be met in due time, when we arrive at the northern stretches of the Pennine watershed.

AONBs do not have equivalents of the National Park Authorities and planning controls remain with local authorities. Officially, the emphasis within an AONB is likely to be more on the conservation and preservation of the landscape and less on the provision of public enjoyment, although the best AONB teams do a good job in helping the public appreciate their own area's character and value. Each AONB has a local partnership body where organisations and interest groups are represented.

Some road maps of Britain mark national parks and AONBs by colouring them in green, which rather points out the absence of these designations for the South Pennines area, where the map stays resolutely white. But a vast swathe of the moorland here – over 50,000 acres, or if you prefer, over 200 square kilometres – has been designated as the South Pennine Moors Site of Special Scientific Interest. SSSIs were yet another creation of the 1949 Act, and the concept has been developed since then so that now there are well over six thousand SSSIs in Britain. Responsibility for designating and monitoring SSSIs in England is currently given to Natural England which in 2006 replaced the former agency, English Nature.

What this means in practice is that every few years an ecologist is sent by Natural England to walk the SSSI-designated South Pennine moorland, checking the vegetation and assessing its overall condition. They then go back to their desk and file a report of what they've found. Recent reports have not been very encouraging, to put it mildly. In fact, at the time this book was being written, 99.6 per cent of the South Pennine moors were categorised as being 'unfavourable', which is the official way of saying that they were in pretty bad nick. Again and again, overgrazing was given as the main culprit, though for the moors directly north of Blackstone Edge air pollution was also a contributing factor.

If there is some good news, it is that about 16 per cent of these moors, while 'unfavourable', are at least considered to be 'recovering'. On the other hand, another 4 per cent are actually deemed to be getting worse. Given that the government has set a target for 2010 that 95 per cent of all SSSIs should be either in good condition or, at least, recovering, there's a strong sense that the South Pennine moors may not be quite doing their part.

The problems here are not as instantly dramatic as they were at Bleaklow or Black Hill. However, the moorland is, by and large, still not the sort of healthy blanket bog habitat which ecologists would like to see. Instead of a rich variety of vegetation – plenty of sphagnum moss, and dwarf shrubs like crowberry, cranberry and bilberry – there are large areas of acid grassland, dominated by mat-grass and wavy hair grass. Another moorland grass we've already met, molinia (purple moor grass), is here too, particularly on wetter slopes. Molinia, it may be remembered, is particularly prone to develop into barely penetrable tussocks, generally a sign that the land has been grazed too much.

Nevertheless, these moors are valuable for their bird life, particularly for waders. A significant number of curlews breed up here, coming in to the high ground from Morecambe Bay and other areas where they have overwintered. Lapwings breed too, and both the curlews' distinctive cry and the lapwing's pee-wit call are the sounds of spring. Golden plover, snipe and dunlin are other important nesting species, but the largest population of all on these upland moors is that of the little meadow pipit. For me, there's a real pleasure in coming by chance on a pipit's nest, hollowed out in a grassy dip close to the ground, with a set of speckled eggs which are just the size and colour of chocolate Easter eggs. I happened to come across a pipit's nest one year which had been constructed only a matter of inches away from the boots of walkers on the Pennine Way. I took a hasty glance at the eggs nestling together and moved away, trying not to disturb the mother bird.

The South Pennine moors are also the most important habitat in England for the twite – the Pennine finch – so much so that the RSPB has designated the land between Huddersfield,

Rochdale and Keighley as England's 'twite triangle'. It has to be admitted that the twite, a relatively inconspicuous brown bird smaller than a sparrow, is not the most spectacular moorland bird. Nevertheless, its presence here is important, or indeed – to quote the official SSSI designation for the South Pennines – 'vital for the present world distribution' of the bird. Twite in the Pennines, it turns out, are a southern outpost of the main twite family, who can be found in Scandinavia and Scotland. These Europeans are in turn isolated from the main centre of world twitedom, the mountainous areas of central Asia.

It is because of the importance of this habitat for breeding birds, and particularly because birds of prey such as the peregrine falcon, merlin and short-eared owl are here too, that the South Pennine moors have been given a second designation to complement their SSSI status, as a Special Protection Area. SPAs were introduced as the result of one of the European Union's lesser known decisions, the Birds Directive of 1979, which sought to ensure the conservation of wild birds. The Birds Directive lists 180 or so European birds which are considered particularly rare or vulnerable.

In 1992 the European Union agreed the Habitats Directive, which basically picked up all the other issues of biodiversity and nature conservancy that hadn't already been dealt with in the Birds Directive. From this second directive came yet another designation for the South Pennine moors, which now became one of England's 236 Special Areas of Conservation. Confusingly (and, let's face it, it wouldn't be surprising if you were a little confused by now) all the SACs have recently been given formal European status as well, as Sites of Community Importance, SCIs. Another set of initials joins the list.

Let's try to summarise. The government believes these moors need looking after, and the SSSI, SPA and SAC designations are its way of trying to do this. The South Pennine moors may not be in particularly good shape today but they're environmentally important, even if they do still bear the scars of their industrial heritage.

The most radical rearrangement of the Pennine landscape brought about as a result of the industrial revolution was the systematic collection of water into reservoirs. The nineteenth and early twentieth centuries saw major engineering works on the high hills as city and town corporations tried to ensure sources of safe drinking water for their growing populations. Manchester had the Longdendale reservoirs, for instance, Sheffield the Derwent valley reservoirs south-east of Bleaklow. Burnley, Halifax and Keighley had their own reservoirs in the South Pennines. Leeds and Bradford looked north to the Yorkshire Dales.

It wasn't only the reservoirs and dams themselves which changed the appearance of the countryside so dramatically. The gathering grounds for these reservoirs were also often subject to major ground works with the creation of networks of catchwater drains, pipes and channels designed to help pull as much water as possible into the reservoirs. At the same time, concerns about water purity meant that farming was discouraged, and the ruins of former farms are now a frequent sight on the slopes above reservoirs. Finally, there was a need for equally significant engineering works to take the water away from the reservoirs towards the towns where it was needed. Under the Pennine hills hereabouts runs a network of tunnels worthy of comparison with the London Underground.

The string of reservoirs along this section of moor – Blackstone Edge, Light Hazzles, White Holme and Warland – are now used to supply drinking water to United Utilities' customers in the Rochdale and Oldham areas. Unusually, however, that wasn't why they were built in the first place. In the last decade of the eighteenth century, just at the time when the

A stone that marks the county border between Yorkshire and Lancashire, with the ubiquitous pylons.

Huddersfield Narrow canal was getting its first shareholders to agree to build the Standedge tunnel, another group of local businessmen were meeting in Rochdale and Hebden Bridge to plan a rival canal. This, the Rochdale canal, didn't require a tunnel but its construction did pose one particular problem, and that was how to ensure that the upper sections of the canal did not run out of water. An obvious point is that every time the lock gates from the highest section of a canal are opened, water is taken from the summit pound downhill. A dependable source of water to replenish the canal is therefore a necessity.

When the Rochdale canal was first being planned it attracted considerable opposition from local mill-owners who were worried that the canal would effectively poach the water supply which they needed to operate their mills, and it became increasingly clear that a significant number of reservoirs would be necessary to provide the water the canal would need as traffic grew. All four of the reservoirs near Blackstone Edge were constructed as feeders for the canal, but the largest of all was Hollingworth Lake just to the west, which rapidly developed into a sort of inland seaside resort. Incidentally, because Hollingworth was well below the level of the canal, the Rochdale Canal Company had to rely on a system of pumps to take the water uphill to where it was needed.

Somewhere near Light Hazzles and Warley reservoirs, the watershed does an abrupt ninety-degree turn, leaving the northerly line which it has followed since Black Hill to swing around to a westerly direction. There's a stiff climb down the hillside to reach the narrow pass between the headwaters of the Calder and the Roch or Roach rivers. Here is, indeed, the Rochdale canal's summit pound, roughly six hundred feet above sea level. Like the Huddersfield Narrow, the Rochdale was for many years derelict but it too has successfully been brought back to life and connected to the inland waterways network. By the swing bridge at Warland Upper Lock, close to the Yorkshire/Lancashire boundary sign, a little plaque commemorates the restoration work.

Lancashire meets Yorkshire at the summit pound of the Rochdale canal.

8. TODMORDEN MOOR

Summit (A6033) – Hades Hill – Trough Edge End – Todmorden Moor (A681)

Not many people, you suspect, could have been very interested in the twelve acres of ex-industrial land near Todmorden when it came on the market in the early 1980s. Once the home of a large earthenware pipe-making factory, the site had been left derelict when customers began to buy plastic pipes instead. Like most brownfield sites, what was left behind was an ugly legacy of a previous period of economic activity, in this case a heap of old red-brick sheds. Unusually, however, this brownfield site was not in an inner-city area but a thousand or so feet up on Todmorden Moor, a mere hop-skip-and-jump away from the watershed.

Peter Drew, however, decided that this was exactly the land he wanted to buy. He had been living down in Bedfordshire previously, but was planning a move north. He wanted somewhere which was in a good geographical location, relatively easy to reach from the major conurbations, but above all he wanted somewhere isolated, away from houses or street lights. He wanted somewhere dark, really dark.

From Mount Teide in Tenerife to Mauna Kea in Hawaii, astronomers have long appreciated the value of high ground. Albeit on a somewhat smaller scale, Peter Drew saw potential in the Pennines as well. And so Todmorden Moor's former pipe works found itself having a very different second life, as the home for a new amateur Astronomy Centre.

The story of how, since the start of the project in 1982, Peter and a group of like-minded fellow enthusiasts have managed to create their observatory is a tale which combines ample quantities of energy and hard work with, inevitably, set-backs and difficulties. What came first was a small planetarium, for which Peter managed to acquire a second-hand planetarium projector from the University of Bradford. The planetarium quickly proved popular, particularly with visiting children. But the observatory was always the big idea for the site, and gradually the groundwork for it began to get under way. Although Peter and his colleagues called in contractors to dig the foundations and to build the circular observatory walls, they worked themselves on pouring the concrete and also took on the hardest part of the whole venture, the manufacture of the aluminium dome to sit atop the building.

Predictably, the Astronomy Centre's site can get some fierce weather. 'It can be frightening for people. You have to watch that the wind doesn't rip the door off your car,' Peter warns. And it was the wind which was the enemy when the time came round to work on the dome. Constructing it had been a long slow process, with 120 panels cut by hand from aluminium sheet and carefully riveted together. Hundreds of hours had already gone into it, and the dome was laid out on the ground, almost ready for erection. 'Then there was an almighty storm one December which wrecked it. There were bits of twisted aluminium for miles,' Peter says.

A characterful relic of a less frenetic age of travel: the old toll-house at Steanor Bottom.

An observatory dome has a key role to play in allowing the telescope inside to have unobstructed access to the right part of the night sky, and this means that doors are needed in the dome which can be slid open as necessary. Furthermore, the dome itself must be able to rotate around the building, so that the whole construction has to be built to sit on a set of wheels which move on a circular running track on the top of the observatory walls. For a dome to work properly, you have to be sure your measurements are completely accurate.

Fortunately, Peter has long experience of engineering projects which require absolute precision. His interest in the heavens began when he was a child ('As a lad, I remember looking up at the night sky, and wondering what it was all about,' he says), and has continued ever since. After school, he did an engineering apprenticeship and began to work for the Ministry of Defence, while in his spare time he used the skills he had acquired to make telescopes. Increasingly he found that the telescopes he was making were quickly finding customers. In 1972, he made the break from the MoD and started making telescopes full-time, working initially from a garden shed where he installed a lathe. As he puts it, 'It was more interesting making telescopes than weapon systems'.

The observatory on Todmorden Moor bears ample testimony to Peter's work. There are telescopes and parts of telescopes almost everywhere. There's even an outsize pair of binoculars, with a pair of optics each a foot across in diameter, waiting to have their own accommodation built to house them. In pride of place at present is a 30-inch telescope constructed in 1985 in time for the arrival of Halley's Comet but this may be replaced shortly by an even larger telescope, a massive 42-inch instrument which Peter is currently working on and which, when it is finished, is likely to be the largest telescope in amateur hands in Britain. The telescope will be fully computer controlled, so that users will be able to point it in the direction they want and view what comes back via the computer downstairs in the observatory or, if everything works out as planned, via an internet connection from their homes.

For telescopes of this sort of size, you need an observatory built to match and the plans for the Todmorden Moor building called for the dome to be 30 feet across. Nothing daunted by their first experience, Peter Drew and his team of volunteers got to work on a replacement. It was to be another two years' work but the eventual erection of the dome was to be, literally, the high moment of the whole project. It was finally winched in place one weekday in March 2000 with the aid of a 50-ton lifting crane. According to those who were there watching, the dome swung slowly in the breeze, began to twist and pitch and at one stage seemed about to hit the walls of the observatory before steadying itself. And it fitted – well, just about. The dome itself was a perfect size, but the observatory walls turned out to have been built in one place slightly out of truly round. The rogue brickwork was attacked with the aid of a large angle grinder and, a few weeks after the lift, the dome was turning smoothly on its running track, ready for use. It was a superb achievement.

There is, however, one insidious problem for observatories like that at Todmorden Moor which can't be overcome just by volunteer sweat and labour. In the past few years, light pollution has become an increasingly pressing issue for astronomers and, indeed, for anyone who enjoys the sight of the night sky. We live in a world where our evenings and nights are lit up with powerful street lights and floodlights, and the result is that the majority of the British population is now unlikely to be able to look up from where they live to see even the brightest planets and stars. The astonishing sight of the Milky Way and the myriad number of stars to be seen on a very dark night is something only a few now regularly enjoy.

When Peter Drew first visited Todmorden Moor in the early 1980s, this was a dark corner of northern England – perhaps not perfect, but as Peter now puts it, about 75 per cent of a really first class night sky. Even though Rochdale, Burnley and other large centres of population were close at hand, the glow from their lights was a problem only on cloudy days, when there would be little point in getting out the telescopes anyway. Since the 1980s, however, light pollution has grown, at Todmorden as everywhere else. Peter says that, as well as lights on the ground, aircraft emissions dissipating in the night sky are an additional problem. 'It's never really dark any more. Now, on many good nights, we can see the outline of trees,' he says.

It seems deeply ironic that, just at the time that science is revealing secrets of the universe undreamed of earlier in human history, most people now are less familiar with the stars than ever before. For our predecessors, constellations like Orion, Cassiopeia and Andromeda and star clusters like the Pleiades would have been familiar companions to them. They would have looked out for the seasonal rotation of the stars through the night sky and would have been conscious too of the heavenly wanderings of the brighter planets. This knowledge, once held by almost all, is now effectively the preserve only of professional and amateur astronomers.

There are, however, attempts being made to address the problem of light pollution. The British Astronomical Association established the Campaign for Dark Skies in 1989, which since then has been working hard to raise public awareness of the issue. The Campaign has also been talking with lighting manufacturers to encourage the wider use of 'full cut-off' lights – in other words, lights which shine downwards and don't permit any illumination to escape upwards – and some of this work seems to be having the desired effect. The Highways Agency, for example, is now promising that the new lights it erects on trunk roads and motorways will be designed to try to reduce light pollution. Some local councils have adopted policies on combating light pollution in their local strategic plans (unfortunately the majority still have not addressed the issue and may actually be making things worse by continuing to install inappropriate lighting). Some supermarkets are promising improvements in the way they floodlight large out-of-town stores and car parks – though campaigners say that having a good written policy in place doesn't necessarily mean things get better in practice on the ground.

It's clear that there's a long way to go. Many badly designed street and road lights remain in place; security lights are a growing issue; so too are floodlights used to illuminate football pitches and games stadiums. And even in country areas, the view of the night sky can be effectively blocked out by insensitive lighting of, say, a church tower or a historic building. The Campaign to Protect Rural England has published a set of maps of Britain at night-time taken using satellite images which show almost all the urban areas of the country as bright red and yellow blotches of colour, representing very high levels of light saturation. The CPRE claims that only about a tenth of the country now experiences truly dark night sky.

Having met Peter Drew and heard about the problems he was encountering at Todmorden, I checked for myself with the CPRE data and it was certainly true that, for much of the line of the Pennine watershed I had already walked, the maps were a disappointingly light blue colour, a long way from the black used to represent a night sky free of light pollution. Only much further north, in the Yorkshire Dales and beyond, did it appear that I would be reaching areas where the night sky could still be properly described as dark.

Nevertheless, despite the problem of encroaching light pollution, it's clear that the Astronomy Centre is successfully meeting a need. Several hundred amateur astronomers pay a few pounds a year to become members and help in its work, and the centre also opens its doors for members of the public almost every Saturday evening when skies are clear. It may be, for example, that Saturn is in the sky so that visitors will be able to inspect the rings through one of the centre's telescopes. It may be that Jupiter is in view, and one or more of the tiny dots which represent Jupiter's four large moons, first observed by Galileo in 1610, will be visible. Or it may be that the centre's telescopes will be turned towards the moon: 'If it's the first time you've seen the moon's crust, it's pretty exciting. When people come here, they're amazed at what they can see,' Peter Drew says.

The Astronomy Centre, high up on Todmorden Moor.

I had arrived at the Astronomy Centre during the day, however, and was resigned to the frustration of seeing nothing more than the print-outs of past viewing sessions pinned up on the observatory walls. But Peter Drew had a surprise for me. We would look at the sun, he said.

This is, of course, normally about the most dangerous activity possible if you don't want to commit eye suicide. But Peter fished into his car and brought out a pair of specially constructed solar binoculars, designed with what's known as a hydrogen-alpha filter which allows through a very narrow fraction of a wavelength of light from the sun. This is not only safe to use, it also means that there's a chance to observe solar prominences, a fascinating feature of the sun's corona (or, in lay terms, 'atmosphere'). While the corona doesn't emit much visible light, solar prominences are made of slightly cooler ionized hydrogen gas and therefore show up as bright features, reddish in colour. Normally, prominences can be seen with the naked eye only during eclipses of the sun, and indeed it was the solar eclipses of 1733 and 1842 which brought them properly to the attention of astronomers. With the aid of Peter Drew's binoculars, I found myself transported from the Pennine hillside, studying the movement of gases on our nearest star, ninety-four million miles away across space.

9. THE HEADWATERS OF THE CALDER(S)

Todmorden Moor (A681) – Thieveley Pike – Cliviger (A646) – Coal Clough Wind Farm

The Pennine watershed scoops its way around Todmorden, scoring out a semicircular line to the south, to the west and then to the north of the town as it follows – naturally – the high ground which separates the Yorkshire tributaries of the river Calder from those streams that head down into Lancashire. One by one, the hills come by: Stubley Cross Hill and Rough Hill, the curiously named Hades Hill (must be hell in winter), Trough Edge End, Hogshead Law Hill, Slate Pit Hill and Thieveley Pike, where the twelfth trig point of the journey to date is reached.

For almost all the way, the watershed provides the historic border between Yorkshire and Lancashire. In fact, the county boundary has been skipping along close beside us since Standedge, and will continue to do so for several more miles of watershed yet, finally heading off by itself in the vicinity of Boulsworth Hill. The boundary receives physical manifestation not only on Ordnance Survey maps but also on the ground, in the shape of old marker stones. On the hill brow not far from the Astronomy Centre, for instance, I came across one marked on one side with a T and on the other with an S: T for Todmorden and S, I decided, for the little settlement of Sharneyford down below on the Lancashire side of the hill.

The watershed's deviation around Todmorden is because the hills here are the headwaters of the first of Yorkshire's major rivers, the Calder. After Todmorden, the Calder will swell on its way through Sowerby Bridge, Elland, Dewsbury and Wakefield before meeting up with the Aire south-east of Leeds. To the west, another river has its source: the Irwell, initially a trickle from a spring just below Thieveley Pike, will go on to greater things downstream as it demarcates the centuries-old boundary between the cities of Manchester and Salford, before disgorging its waters into the Mersey.

North of Todmorden, the watershed separates the headwaters of the Calder from . . . the Calder, since the smaller, Lancashire, river which runs through Burnley confusingly carries the same name as its Yorkshire cousin. More confusing still, this is one of two major river Calders in Lancashire (the second Lancashire Calder flows south from the Forest of Bowland), and of three in the North-West (another Calder flows off the Lake District fells near Ennerdale and gives the nuclear power plant at Calder Hall its name). If you include in addition Northumberland's Kielder – simply a variant spelling – the tally is an impressive five northern rivers sharing the same name, and there may be others as well. The word is Celtic in origin, meaning a rapid stream.

The moors which nurture the Calder, the Irwell and the Calder have been well picked over by humans for many centuries. Attempts have been made to remove lead from the hills in a series of (generally unsuccessful) mining endeavours which began in the late 1620s on

The Cliviger gorge offers a convenient route – for road traffic and rail – across the Yorkshire–Lancashire border.

Dean Scout near Thieveley Pike. That first Thieveley mine lasted only until 1635, though another attempt was made about 120 years later in the mid-eighteenth century in same location and there were periodically other lead mines sunk. Sometimes a name on the map is about the only evidence left of all this effort: look carefully, and you'll see the name 'Lead Mine Clough' on the Ordnance Survey map north of Todmorden, for instance.

There was iron, too, to be had (across the Cliviger gorge from Thieveley, at Riddle Scout). There was fireclay available for digging out on Todmorden Moor, the reason why the earthenware pipe works on which Peter Drew built his observatory had been constructed here in the first place. There was stone to be quarried from the hillside. But above all there was coal, worked commercially from a number of mines in the vicinity.

There are records of coal mining dating back to the nineteenth century and earlier, and there is the evidence left behind on the ground in the form of subsidence caused by these workings, the trial holes which were dug, and the spoil heaps piled up in places on the moor.

But coal mining was not simply something which took place here in times past. Rather surprisingly, perhaps, right on the watershed at the head of Greens Clough north of Todmorden Moor, is the active – or more-or-less active – colliery at Hill Top.

The National Coal Board developed Hill Top Colliery in the years after nationalisation in 1947. It was a drift mine, which is to say that two drifts were driven into the side of the hill for about five hundred yards until the target coal, a large deposit in the Union coal seam at this point about 4 feet 6 inches thick, was reached. The mine was later linked underground to Deerplay Colliery, another drift mine which the NCB operated just to the north of Thieveley Pike.

In the 1960s, both these collieries were closed. However a local miner later acquired the rights to reopen Hill Top and for several years after 1997 small amounts of coal were dug here by him, effectively as a one-man operation. In 2004 his company successfully applied for planning permission for mining to be permitted until 2010. Any account of coal mining here still, just, needs to be written in the present rather than the past tense.

This exploitation of the moorland has left behind, however, a battered landscape which is open to further abuse. Flower Scar Road, a historic track across Todmorden Moor which long pre-dates the modern road near by, became for many years little more than a linear open-air rubbish dump. Word got around the neighbourhood and anyone who had household or commercial waste and who was looking for somewhere to fly-tip it knew exactly where to make for. Unmarked vans would regularly pull up and unload their contents. One Todmorden police officer still recalls the time on Flower Scar Road when he came across a lorry piled high with old tyres, with a couple of men in mid-act of emptying it. (The men tried the best argument they could think of: Actually, officer, we're collecting the tyres. 'Interesting,' came the reply from the law, 'Any idea why the tyres in your van are dry when the ones outside are wet?').

Perhaps the saddest thing about the state of the moorland here was that nobody seemed to care and nobody seemed to take responsibility for sorting out the mess.

Except that it turned out that some people did care. I came across members of the Todmorden Moor Restoration Trust early one Sunday morning, on the highest part of the moorland where Flower Scar Road meets the A681 to Bacup. It was drizzling and the cloud was down, so that visibility was restricted to a few yards. But that hadn't discouraged them. A parked car or two showed I'd come to the right place, and in the next few minutes several more members of the group turned up, equipped with warm jackets and Wellington boots and carrying a range of garden tools.

This Sunday had been put aside for yet another practical session of voluntary work to try to improve the state of Todmorden Moor. This time, the work was going to consist of reseeding a small strip of bare ground with moorland grasses. The group got out their garden rakes, opened the sacks of grass seed they had purchased from a specialist agricultural supplier, and started the slow work of broadcasting the seeds on to the ground below.

It was about as far removed from the reseeding I'd seen being undertaken at Black Hill as you could imagine: no helicopter, no prilled seed or fertiliser, no bags of geojute, just a few committed individuals trying to make a difference on a damp Sunday. But nevertheless, their aim of moorland restoration was exactly the same as that of the professionals at Moors for the Future further south.

They began as a protest campaign called Todmorden Moor Action Group. Back in 1989, a mining company had put forward plans for the remaining coal hereabouts to be extracted through a new open-cast mining operation. The proposed pit would have gouged out a large chunk of the moor, including parts of Flower Scar Road itself, and not surprisingly attracted local opposition. 'It was indignation all round. People were saying, they can't do that,' recalls Sarah Pennie, now the chairman of the group. Well-attended meetings were held and the Action Group established, bringing together both a group of local farmers who had commoners' rights over the moor and townsfolk. Sarah herself was, in local parlance, an off-cummed 'un, meaning that she had moved in from outside the area to Todmorden in 1989 with her husband to run a second-hand bookshop. Usefully, as it would turn out, her training back in the 1970s had been in agriculture, however.

The Action Group, together with other voices raised against the open-cast proposal, was successful and the mining company withdrew their proposal. The same thing happened a few years later, in 1991–2, when another open-cast mining proposal was knocked back. Sarah Pennie and her colleagues had also seen off a couple of attempts to extend quarrying operations up on the moors. But in 1991, the group took an important decision – rather than simply being there to oppose things, they would reconstitute themselves as a group pro-actively working to improve the state of the moors. The Restoration Trust was born.

'Todmorden Moor is an urban common, which is supposed to be there for people as well as animals to use, but for years – for decades – people have abused it. We thought to ourselves, everybody knows Todmorden Moor is a mess, but it's a mess because we've made it a mess. We can restore it,' says Sarah Pennie.

What followed was a classic example of a volunteer-based community organisation at work. The group's members turned out regularly for working parties, their first success being the reclamation of a small quarry which, as on the moor, had been used for tipping. There were also many sessions on Flower Scar Road itself, trying to shift the accumulated rubbish. This was, by all accounts, both hard dirty physical labour and – on occasions – soul-destroying work. Sarah recalls the mass working party which had been organised one time which had successfully cleared a small moorland pool of all its flytipped waste. They'd turned their attention to another area further up on the moor, before coming back down the road at the day's end. 'We couldn't believe it. While we'd been away, a whole bedroom had arrived in the pool. Somebody had been up and left two beds, a wardrobe, a chest of drawers and bedside tables. We'd only just cleared it,' Sarah says.

It was obvious that volunteers couldn't be expected to carry on like this. The only sustainable solution, the Trust felt, was for Flower Scar Road to be deregulated as a highway and gated. Their local authority, which they had been lobbying hard for support for a number of years, eventually agreed with them. By 2006 the work had been done and two solid locked gates now bar the way for vehicles to get access to the moorland track. There is a chance now, perhaps, for Todmorden Moor to have a new start.

'The curlews are back again, having disappeared for several years, and the twite is back, too,' Sarah Pennie says with pride. But nevertheless there is one difficulty facing her group's attempts to improve Todmorden Moor. When the boundary was drawn for the South Pennine Moors SSSI, and with it the Special Protection Area and the Special Area of Conservation, the line stopped on the other side of Todmorden. 'Over there,' – Sarah points in a broad easterly direction – 'all that moorland is protected. This is not protected at all. It's a joke. And it means we have problems: people say, oh well, if it's not in the SPA, then it's not a priority,' she says.

The lack of official designation for these moors means that the efforts of the Restoration Trust to re-establish the area as a recreational resource for local people to enjoy (the slogan is 'more use, less abuse') may yet come under renewed pressure from the commercial exploitation of the land. The current controversy concerns wind farms, with proposals under way to erect a number of wind turbines here. It's an issue which has split the local community, with some strongly supportive of further development of wind farms and others critical of the environmental consequences involved. The Todmorden Moor Restoration Trust has come out against the turbines, arguing both that a wind farm here would militate against public enjoyment of the moorland and that – and there's something just a little ironic about this – past mining activity here has left the land riddled with underground workings and therefore unsafe for the siting of turbines.

This book isn't the place to rehearse the arguments for and against wind farms. But there is an opportunity, as the watershed crosses the Cliviger gorge between the two river Calders, to decide at least on the aesthetic aspect of windfarms, since a short distance up the hillside the twenty-four turbines of the Coal Clough Wind Farm are reached.

Coal Clough windfarm in its moorland setting.

The first commercial wind farm in Britain was erected in 1991 in Cornwall which makes Coal Clough, which began generating electricity in December 1992, one of the very early pioneers. When it first opened parking was provided for what it was felt might become a local visitor attraction, though it has to be said that this never happened and the car park has since closed.

Since the average lifetime of a wind farm is about 20–25 years, Coal Clough is definitely well into its middle-age and its turbines (at 400 kilowatt capacity) are effectively old technology. Modern turbines tend both to have much greater capacity (the average for an onshore turbine is currently about 2 megawatts, five times that at Coal Clough) and to be significantly higher above the ground.

But are they a blot or a welcome addition to the landscape? It's a question which relates directly back to the similar one I posed on Blackstone Edge. Are turbines a modern-day version of a landscape feature like Stoodley Pike obelisk, now a focal point of the countryside? Or the equivalent of a line of pylons?

10. BOULSWORTH HILL

Coal Clough Wind Farm – Hoof Stones Height – Black Hameldon – Boulsworth – Crow Hill – Watersheddles

We are approaching the highest ground on the watershed since Black Hill. Pre-metric maps give the height at Lad Law stones on the summit of Boulsworth Hill as 1,699 feet, so the extra height of the trig point here – my fourteenth so far – must be enough to push the hill above the 1,700-foot line. Nowadays Boulsworth's height is given more mundanely as 517 metres.

When Tom Stephenson, Edwin Royce and their fellow ramblers were first plotting the line of the Pennine Way they considered bringing the route this way, over the top of Boulsworth and then down to the attractive hamlet of Wycoller below. Wycoller, where the main features of interest are the old stone bridges which span little Wycoller Beck, was one of those places along the route which Stephenson and Royce thought Pennine Way walkers would particularly appreciate. (Indeed, Wycoller is now one of Lancashire County Council's country parks and has become a popular weekend visitor attraction.) Tom Stephenson's original 1935 *Daily Herald* article actually mentions Boulsworth by name, as one of the route's suggested staging posts: the 'carefree youngsters' undertaking the walk, he wrote, having steered themselves between the industrial blackspots of this part of the Pennines 'would stand on Boulsworth, and behold, on the one hand, the level brow of Pendle . . . and, on the other, the dark moors which inspired the Brontës'.

Pennine Way walkers today, young, carefree or otherwise, are routed further to the east of Boulsworth and Wycoller, to avoid what was, until very recently, private moorland. In fact, it was a dispute about access rights to the moors around Boulsworth in the 1950s that helped reinforce ramblers' suspicions that the 1949 National Parks and Access to the Countryside Act might not have given them quite as much as they originally had hoped. The 1949 Act was supposed, according to the government of the day, to establish a 'comprehensive charter of rights for all lovers of the open air'. What the Act didn't give was the automatic right of public access to open country, the central demand for which the outdoor ramblers' movement had been battling since the first Access to Mountains Act of 1884. Nevertheless, the Act gave local authorities powers to establish access agreements with landowners, and to impose access orders where agreement could not be reached. In each case, suitable compensation was payable.

If the letter of the law did not grant universal access, the spirit of the times in the late 1940s was such that many ramblers must have felt that public access to the mountains and moors of England and Wales was just around the corner. In practice, however, it was really only in the Peak District national park where, not coincidentally, the battles for access had been hardest fought that major efforts were taken to make use of access agreements. Nine

More gritstone outcrops on the watershed – known as the Gorple Stones.

square miles on the northern side of the Kinder plateau – including the land over which the 1932 trespassers had passed – were opened to the public through an agreement which the landowner the Duke of Devonshire signed in December 1952, and a separate agreement with the Duke four years later gave access to over thirty square miles of Bleaklow. The National Park Authority also negotiated an agreement to open the southern approaches to Kinder Scout, a deal which involved fifteen landowners and which – after some initial resistance and difficulties – was eventually completed in 1958.

Even in the Peak District, however, some moorland areas remained legally out of bounds behind private signs, and elsewhere the 1949 Act powers didn't seem to be making much difference at all. In the Yorkshire Dales national park, for example, only about 6 per cent of the open uncultivated countryside was legally accessible by the public until very recently, when the 2000 Countryside and Rights of Way Act – the 'right to roam' legislation – finally opened up the remaining 94 per cent.

Even where the local authority was prepared to contemplate making an access order, things didn't necessarily always end up the way ramblers would have wanted. In 1955, Lancashire Country Council introduced two access orders which together were intended to open up about 4,000 acres of moorland on Boulsworth Hill to the public. But the order was contested, not only by grouse shooting interests but also by the water authorities which used the land as collecting grounds for drinking water. The case went to a public enquiry in March 1956 when Tom Stephenson himself was the main representative of the Ramblers' Association. It took fifteen months for the result of the enquiry to emerge from Whitehall, but when it did the verdict went against Lancashire and the ramblers: concern about drinking water purity meant that walkers would be kept off Boulsworth, said the ministry. Indeed, it took over twenty more years before even a short loop of concessionary footpath could be negotiated to allow walkers the opportunity to stand on Boulsworth's summit and enjoy the view. It's perhaps not surprising if, in the 1990s, this area was the focus of an active Access to Boulsworth Campaign, set up by a new generation of local walkers to carry on the battle lost in the 1950s.

The chance to admire the view from Boulsworth may have been a long time coming, but it is certainly one to appreciate. For the first time, the Pennine watershed offers a panorama spreading out to the north, which means that the hills of the Yorkshire Dales are now before us, as a visible reminder of what is to come. On a decent day Ingleborough, Pen-y-ghent, Fountains Fell and the high ground of the moors near Malham can all be seen, away across the lower ground in the foreground. Much nearer to hand, just across the valley which holds the mill towns of Nelson and Colne, is the great landmark which is Pendle hill.

Come up here on a very clear day, ideally late in the afternoon when the setting sun is low in the sky, however, and there's something else which can also occasionally be seen. Blackpool Tower is forty miles away almost due west from Boulsworth, and in the right weather conditions it appears against the horizon like a tiny black pin, framed between the fells of Bowland to the north and the West Pennine moors to the south.

I've seen Blackpool Tower a handful of times from here, and when you see it there's no mistaking what you're looking at. What I've never seen from Boulsworth, however, is what the nineteenth-century Halifax bookseller and antiquarian Francis Leyland apparently saw once, one afternoon in early June. It has to be said that Leyland had a telescope with him but apparently the weather was so clear that day that he could make out – so he claimed in an article he wrote later in the Halifax Courier – the houses on Blackpool beach, the steeple of the Catholic church in Blackpool's Talbot Road, nearby windmills, and even the Horse Bank, a prominent sandbank off-shore from Lytham. It must have been a good telescope: Leyland added in his article that he could also identify shrimping and fishing boats out at sea, as well as a paddle-steamer which was passing along the coast at the time.

So Boulsworth is a pleasant place to be in fine weather. But sometimes the weather isn't like it was for Francis Leyland that day. Sometimes it's raining. Sometimes, as we say in these parts, the clag is down, reducing visibility to a few yards. Sometimes the wild wind can be blowing straight along the hill-ridge between Boulsworth and neighbouring Crow Hill. Or it may be storming – indeed, on my last visit before writing this chapter, I found myself directly underneath a sudden electric storm which blew up out of nowhere and left me hurriedly escaping the lightning and the hail stones which were accompanying it in my rush to reach lower ground.

But maybe this is the way it should be up here, since – to quote Tom Stephenson from that original *Daily Herald* piece – beyond Boulsworth lie the dark moors which inspired the Brontës. And that surely must mean an expectation of a wild, hostile, savage landscape, a place of foreboding, perhaps even of terror, which is fit to match the storylines of the Brontë sisters'

The 'beached whale' outline of Pendle hill, viewed from Boulsworth.

works, and most particularly the passion of Heathcliff and Catherine in Emily Brontë's *Wuthering Heights*.

It could be said that the Pennine landscape in *Wuthering Heights* has as key a role to play in the novel as that of the main characters. From the opening pages onwards, when the ingenuous narrator Lockwood receives a frosty welcome on his first visit to Heathcliff's house and — a day later — is caught in an appalling snowstorm on an ill-advised second visit, the moorland landscape and weather matches the mood of the storyline. The novel's title itself reinforces this. The narrator is called upon to explain it very early in the novel:

> Wuthering Heights is the name of Mr Heathcliff's dwelling, 'wuthering' being a signif-
> icant provincial adjective, descriptive of the atmospheric tumult to which its station is
> exposed in stormy weather. Pure, bracing ventilation they must have up there at all
> times, indeed: one may guess the power of the north wind, blowing over the edge, by
> the excessive slant of a few stunted firs at the end of the house; and by a range of gaunt
> thorns all stretching their limbs one way, as if craving alms of the sun.

Emily Brontë endows the moorland landscape she knew well with almost as much personality as the human actors of the story, and that personality is, in part at least we feel, a

malevolent one. It is inconceivable to imagine the action of Wuthering Heights unfolding in a different, gentler, country setting – say, in the Cotswolds or Sussex. Heathcliff's brooding presence throughout the book goes with the brooding wildness of these moors.

Because of this, the moors around Haworth are a magnet for those who have read the Brontë sisters' novels and want to experience this landscape for themselves. By long (if possibly erroneous) tradition, the location of Wuthering Heights itself is taken to be the isolated and now ruined farmhouse of Top Withens, even though the actual farm building doesn't resemble that of the house described in the novel. The walk out to Top Withens, about four miles south-west of Haworth, has become a regular pilgrimage route. A small number of Brontë lovers want an even wilder experience and venture further, on to the boggy and isolated moorland beyond Top Withens to the rocky outcrop known as the Alcomden Stones and on, even further, across the badlands of Stanbury Bog to Crow Hill.

I have used a number of highly subjective adjectives in the last few paragraphs in my description of the moors – words such as wild, hostile and savage – which, frankly, should not be allowed to pass without comment and challenge. We have become so familiar with this way of viewing moorland landscape, however, that the likelihood is that their use did not seem striking or inappropriate. We have accustomed ourselves to the idea of the moors do indeed possess a sort of innate wildness about them. We also unconsciously incline towards anthropomorphising this landscape, or in other words attributing to it human characteristics and attributes: that it is, for example, a 'hostile' or 'unfriendly' land.

In doing so, we tend to forget that this approach to moorland landscape is a learned one, a product of a particular cultural and historical approach which has only been prevalent in relatively modern times, say for the past 250 years or so. We still today view the landscape through the prism of what's called romanticism, the artistic and cultural movement which began to develop during the eighteenth century (and which we most obviously associate with, for example, the poetry of Wordsworth or Coleridge or with the art of Turner or Constable). Romanticism emphasises the imagination, feeling and intuition, as a counterpoint to a more overtly rationalist approach to nature, art and life.

Emily Brontë's Wuthering Heights is written with an approach to the landscape which is suffused with romanticism and it is no exaggeration to say that her novel couldn't possibly have been written before the cultural changes which developed romantic sensibility had taken place. Readers in an earlier period of history would have found her approach incomprehensible.

Since much of this book is going to be dealing with northern moorland landscape, this may be the time to say a little more about this theme. Before romanticism taught us a particular way of responding to this type of landscape, moorland areas which were unsuitable for productive agricultural use tended to get categorised simply as 'waste'. The small numbers of people in the metropolitan élite who had the leisure to travel for pleasure tended to view moors and mountains as places best avoided, an approach which continued until well into the eighteenth century. There was little or no attempt to engage emotionally and aesthetically with landscapes like this.

But by the mid-eighteenth century, the old approach was changing. Travellers were beginning to interpret the natural landscape in a new way, and in particular to enjoy the frisson of excitement which came from experiencing the call of the 'wild'. Mountains, at least, began to attract tourists, even if less dramatic moorland still remained largely ignored.

There was, for example, the fashionable trend to seek out features which were deemed to be 'picturesque', a term which (although capable of various interpretations) was in eighteenth-century parlance rather more precise in meaning than its modern catch-all usage. Making a tour of areas of Britain such as the Lakes, the Wye valley, North Wales and the highlands of Scotland in search of the 'picturesque' became something many well-heeled travellers undertook. The trend was popularised particularly by the Cumberland clergyman and artist William Gilpin who wrote of his own travels, encouraged others to follow in his footsteps, and also helped lay down exactly what it was that searchers for the picturesque should be looking for.

There was a particular sort of landscape which was sought after. Rocks and rugged places, precipices, waterfalls, shattered trees, ruins, caves and grottoes, even the hovels of shepherds, all these could fit this new aesthetic and attract the attention of the picturesque tourist. In fact, this fashion was carried over into the world of gardening, where efforts were often made during this period to introduce picturesque elements to a garden by creating fake ruined buildings or grottoes.

The committed searcher for the picturesque was aware that their journey could be uncomfortable, or even difficult or dangerous, but that in a sense was the point. Here, for example, is how the poet Thomas Gray, best known for his *Elegy Written in a Country Churchyard*, describes with an obvious sort of relish the 'horror' of Gordale Scar near Malham, which he visited on his way back from the Lakes in October 1769:

> The rock on the left rises perpendicular, with stubbed yew-trees and shrubs staring from its side, to the height of at least 300 feet; but these are not the thing: it is the rock to the right, under which you stand to see the fall, that forms the principal horror of the place. From its very base it begins to slope forwards over you in one block or solid mass without any crevice in its surface, and overshadows half the area below with its dreadful canopy; when I stood at (I believe) four yards distance from its foot, the drops, which perpetually distil from its brow, fell on my head; and in one part of its top, more exposed to the weather, there are loose stones that hang in air, and threaten visibly some idle spectator with instant destruction. . . . The gloomy uncomfortable day well suited the savage aspect of the place, and made it still more formidable: I stayed there, not without shuddering, a quarter of an hour, and thought my trouble richly paid; for the impression will last for life.

The idea that we can be moved and attracted by things that cause fear or dread was a concept considered by philosophers during this period, as for example in Edmund Burke's *Philosophical Essay into the Origin of our Ideas of the Sublime and Beautiful*, published in 1757 when he was still in his twenties. As the lengthy title suggests, Burke was concerned to try to distinguish between what humans found conventionally *beautiful* and what attracts another, more powerful, response, to which he gave the term *sublime*. (He was borrowing a term first discussed by Longinus, a Greek writer living during the years of the Roman empire; the word sublime itself comes from the Latin, where its meanings include high, exalted.)

Burke saw the sublime and the beautiful as mutually exclusive and his essay, which rambles around the subject at some length, tried to identify what it was that causes something to be sublime – or, in his words, 'productive of the strongest emotion which is

Haworth Moor, with Top Withens in the background: a landscape very familiar to the talented Brontë sisters.

the mind is capable of feeling'. The feeling of danger or terror was an important element, he felt: 'Whatever is in any sort terrible, or is conversant about terrible objects, or operates in a manner analogous to terror, is a source of the sublime,' he claimed. Another cause of the sublime was vastness. Another was obscurity, another a sense of power, and there were others as well.

Burke was writing in general terms and was by no means only concerned with approaches to the natural world, but he did give some examples of what he felt to be sublime elements in the landscape. One example was Stonehenge: 'Those huge rude masses of stone, set on end, and piled each on other, turn the mind on the immense force necessary for such a work. Nay the rudeness of the work increases this cause of grandeur . . .', he wrote.

Writings like Burke's helped provide the intellectual framework on which the new romantic aesthetic could develop and are perhaps worth bearing in mind as we look at our own reactions today to the upland landscapes. I suspect, for example, that not many people would describe the peat groughs of Kinder Scout or Bleaklow, or the less-frequented areas of the Brontë moors such as Stanbury Bog, as 'beautiful'. We respond to these landscapes in a different way, and though it would be a highly unusual walker who peered across an empty moor and proclaimed, 'This is so sublime,' it's possible to argue that our response is closer to Burke's idea of what constitutes the sublime – a sense of distance, of grandeur and with it a slight whiff of danger.

In case there's any misunderstanding, I don't want to suggest that we shouldn't respond emotionally to the landscape when we are out in the countryside. Such an approach would diminish our pleasure – and, anyway, a romantic approach is now culturally so deeply embedded that it would be close to impossible. We're hardwired with a romantic sensibility.

But it probably helps to be aware of how our emotional response has been formed, and it's surely good to seek to understand the landscape in ways which go beyond the purely emotional.

There's another point which should perhaps be made before we leave Boulsworth Hill, Crow Hill and the Brontë moors behind and head north. There is, I'm aware, a popular sense that in some way moorlands constitute a residual element of wilderness, an area of countryside which has remained untouched by human activity. It's an approach which has been utilised for tourist potential: the North Pennines, for example, markets itself as 'England's last wilderness'.

The idea that this landscape is a primeval one is a deeply appealing one for the romanticist within each of us, but unfortunately it's one which is historically completely inaccurate. The moorlands have been shaped by human activity from the earliest days, and continue to be shaped in both minor and major ways.

Observant walkers in blanket bog moorland are aware that the moors were previously much more afforested than today, because it's a relatively common sight to see tree root systems preserved inside peat banks. But scientific knowledge of the way the moors looked centuries and millennia past is much more advanced than many people might imagine. Peat, which has built up over thousands of years, preserves within it pollen, seeds and spores, and these are important clues which can be decoded through careful analysis to tell us exactly what types of vegetation formerly covered these hills. (This branch of science where archaeology meets botany is known as palynology). We can tell, for example, the periods of history and prehistory when particular types of tree grew on the moors, the extent of heather cover and the prevalence of particular types of moorland grass.

We'll come back to the story of the changing moorland landscape later. At this point it's enough to make a general point, and for this I'm calling in Professor Ian Simmons of Durham University, whose comprehensive work *The Moorlands of England and Wales* offers a survey of environmental history from right back in 8000 BC. Simmons writes, 'If a 'natural' environment is one in which there is no human interference at all, then the moorlands of England and Wales have not been 'natural' for much of the last 10,000 years.'

11. BEYOND WATERSHEDDLES

Watersheddles – Combe Hill

Far and away the most important influence on the appearance of the upland countryside is agriculture. The Pennine moors are the workplaces for hill farmers, and it is their activities that determine to a large extent the form of the landscape: the type of vegetation, fences and walls, the buildings, the tracks, and, above all, the presence of livestock on the high ground. Today's countryside looks the way it does, in large measure, because it is being farmed.

Put in this way, these remarks may seem so obvious as to be superfluous, but I'm not sure that's really the case. It seems to me that very large numbers of people visit the countryside and enjoy the landscapes without properly comprehending the nature of the farming activities which are going on around them. Sheep and cattle will be noticed, but the context which explains why they are there (or, at certain times of the year, not there) somehow eludes the grasp of even the most committed walker or lover of the outdoors. It can sometimes seem as if recreational users are occupying a countryside which is slightly detached from and parallel to the one occupied by farmers.

This seems a curious state of affairs, if you accept that the pleasure which we derive from enjoying the countryside and relishing the landscape is deepened and augmented by being able to interpret what we see. But if this lack of comprehension exists it doesn't seem to attract comment. If you flip through the pages of the outdoor press, for example, you'll be hard-pressed to find any articles discussing – say – the implications for the countryside of the reform of the Hill Farm Allowance, or the operation of the Environmental Stewardship scheme. You'd certainly fail to discover that British agriculture is currently going through a major period of change, the most radical for at least a generation.

Perhaps there's criticism to be levelled, too, at the other side. Farmers, or at least some farmers, may feel that the presence of the general public on their land is nothing but trouble, liable to make their work more difficult to achieve. And communication skills aren't necessarily taught at agricultural college. So there can be a gap of understanding, on which suspicion and mutual mistrust develop. Non-farmers consider farming an esoteric activity which they neither understand nor want to understand. Farmers miss the opportunity to explain the value of their work they do.

That's not a criticism which I would want to level at David Airey. David, who farms a very large swathe of the Yorkshire moors on the far side of the Haworth–Colne road from Crow Hill, just to the north of Watersheddles reservoir, was more than helpful when I first rang him up. Yes, he'd be happy to make time to meet me and to talk about his farm, he said. When did I want to come?

We sat round his kitchen table in the farmhouse on a by-road near the village of Cowling. It was David's father who had first started farming here forty years or so ago, he told me, taking up originally the tenancy for a farm of just 120 acres. Since then, the size of the undertaking has grown considerably, and David is now the tenant farmer of a whopping 2500 acres in total. All of the land is over a thousand feet in height and much of it is open moorland, though the farm also has some better-quality enclosed grazing land lower down nearer the farmhouse, the in-bye land. (This, as we'll see, is important.) Like most Pennine hill farms, David's business is based on sheep, and he currently keeps a flock of seven hundred ewes.

There are more than eighty breeds of sheep recognised by the UK's National Sheep Association, as different in appearance and characteristics from each other as, say, a whippet is from a cocker spaniel. If you're farming on high exposed moorland with poor vegetation, you want to ensure that you have a type of sheep which – over generations of breeding – has been bred for the uplands, and David chooses pure-bred Swaledale sheep for his farm. Swaledales are one of the more easily recognisable breeds, with their curly horns and distinctive 'black' and 'white' markings on the face. (It probably helps recognition, too, that the Yorkshire Dales national park has chosen a representation of the Swaledale as the park's logo.)

Which breed of sheep you choose comes from the experience which is gained from past trial and error, and the key factor is the nature of the land you are farming. David Airey says that he, and his father before him, previously experimented with two other hill breeds, the Lonk and the Derbyshire Gritstone, both associated particularly with the southern Pennines and Peak District, before deciding to stick to Swaledales. It's not that Swaledales are necessarily hardier, he told me, it's a question of which breed is right for the particular moorland vegetation on which they'll be feeding. 'I have neighbours with Lonk and Gritstone who do better with them than they would with Swaledales. But our moorland is 70 per cent heather, and Swaledale sheep are good at going up and rummaging through it,' he says.

Like most Pennine farmers today, David Airey relies on a quad bike for getting around his land.

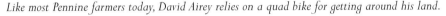

So you need to know your own land intimately to be able to farm it efficiently. 'It took my dad years to learn this farm,' David says. 'I couldn't go and farm in, say, Malham – the winters are different, I wouldn't understand that, I'd have to have help.' (Malham, it perhaps should be added, is barely fifteen miles away from Cowling and at roughly the same height above sea-level.) So it's not surprisingly that sheep breeds continue to be very strongly focused on particular parts of the country, the breeds changing with the landscape and the farmers' accents. Further north on the Pennine watershed, there won't be Lonks or Gritstones on the moors, there will be Rough Fell or Dalesbred sheep instead.

Each year is different, but nevertheless there is a well-established pattern to the sheep hill-farming calendar. David's stock will be brought down from his moorland around the end of October and will stay off until the New Year. The weeks before Christmas are tupping time, the one period in the year when the services of the tup (the ram) are required. Tups are kept busy, with typically forty or fifty ewes being serviced by a single male. In fact, there's a balance to be struck here: generally, the numbers of lambs you'll get will increase if you limit a single tup to, say, forty ewes, but on the other hand this means that you will need to have invested overall in more tups for your farm.

Selecting a good tup is essential if you want to improve the bloodline of the flock and maximise the chances that your lambs the following spring will be strong and healthy. The Swaledale Sheep Breeders Association keep a detailed flock book recording bloodlines (it's the same principle as that followed for pedigree dogs by the Kennel Club), and there are a handful of Swaledale breeders who are well known for the quality of their tups. Astonishingly, a few years ago a Swaledale tup was sold at auction for £101,000.

This is exceptional, but the best animals will be bought and sold for prices in excess of £20,000 and these will end up with the premier Swaledale flocks. For the more typical hill sheep farm, you'd be planning to pay a few thousand pounds; David says that his most recent acquisitions have cost him £2,000–£3,000 apiece. There is real skill in being able to size up a tup in the auction pen, so that you maximise the chance of getting your money's worth. 'You look for a big, tall, sturdy sheep with good shoulders and a good back end, to improve the ewes and to breed strong sheep. The hair should be hard – that's a sign that the sheep is a hardier animal,' David told me.

The tupping time over, the ewes will be put back on the high ground after Christmas. The next key event takes place around the middle of February, when the sheep get their equiva-lent of an antenatal check-up. In fact, the ultrasound scan which is used is identical technology to that in place up the road at the maternity wing of the local Airedale hospital, David Airey says. 'We have a contractor who goes round everyone. He sits at the side of a crate, and pulls up the sheep up on its belly. He's very accurate, he'll mark the sheep which have twins or triplets,' he explains. At this point, the ewes carrying single lambs will be put back on the moor, while the others will be kept closer to hand. This is one of those occasions when it's invaluable to have a farm with enough in-bye land. Allotments (larger enclosed fields, taken in from moorland) provide a halfway house between the in-bye and the open moor.

Lambing at David Airey's farm takes place in April, the busiest time of the year in a Pennine sheep farmer's calendar. The lambs take their chance immediately on the upland moors, and the whole flock will then remain on the moorland until July, when it is time for clipping (shearing) and dipping. As the late summer and early autumn arrives, after the lambs are weaned, the decision is taken as to which of the ewes and lambs will be going to market.

There is a traditional structure to sheep farming in northern England, whereby pure-bred ewes are typically kept on the high hill farms for three breeding seasons (or, in other words, until they are five years old) and then sold on to farms lower down the hillside. Thereafter, again traditionally, they will be mated with longwool breeds of sheep to produce half-breeds. Swaledale ewes are frequently crossed with Bluefaced Leicester to produce a type of hardy sheep known logically (if somewhat confusingly to those of us who aren't farmers) as mules. David Airey tells of a misunderstanding several years ago with his bank manager who couldn't work out why a sheep farmer would want to have several hundred mules on a single farm.

But this is getting ahead of the story. Each new spring brings several hundred new lambs to David Airey's farm; taking into account lambing time losses, you'd expect about to end up with around 130 lambs for every 100 ewes. The male lambs, the wethers, unfortunately don't have much of a future ahead of them. Once weaned, they will be taken to market, and either sold to lowland farms to be fattened up or taken abroad. The export market accounts for about 45 per cent of hill lambs in Britain, with southern European countries such as Greece and Italy traditionally important. But there's also a significant market for hill farmed lamb from Britain's Muslim communities; Pennine lamb from the watershed moors farmed by David Airey and his neighbours may well end as the prime ingredient in Bradford's celebrated curry houses, for example. Hill-bred lamb may not be particularly meaty, but it's considered tasty.

The female lambs have a different future marked out for them, and here it helps to learn a little extra vocabulary. While the rest of us normally make do perfectly well with two words to describe beasts of the ovian variety (lambs and sheep), farmers have their own terms. Ewe lambs are known universally as gimmers. Adolescence lambs (roughly from their first Christmas to the following summer, when they are clipped for the first time) are hoggs (another word which could confuse an urban bank manager). After the first clipping, they are likely to be known as shearlings. They will be put to the tup for the first time the following autumn.

In the traditional way of hill sheep farming, hoggs would be sent away from their home farm for the first winter to lowland farms, to be brought back at the end of their winter holiday hopefully nicely plumped up and healthy. David Airey himself used to have arrangements with lowland farms in Uttoxeter. More generally, overwintering Swaledale hoggs from Pennine farms can be found in large numbers in places like Carlisle and Stockton-on-Tees. But sending hoggs away costs money, and again it's a question of assessing value for money. In recent years, David Airey has chosen to keep his hoggs at home. They don't grow as quickly during the winter months, he says, but they quickly catch up the following spring.

There's a lot of tradition in hill farming, but there's also continual experimentation and change. Although sheep farming predominates on the moorland hill farms of the Pennines, upland cattle farming is also carried out and indeed David Airey himself kept a small herd of suckler cows for a time. Once again, a farming system has developed so that hill farms have their particular role to play in an overall production cycle which also includes lowland farms.

Usually cattle farming in upland areas is based on rearing beef calves which are suckled by their mother for about six to ten months (it's a low intensity approach: one calf for each cow). Once weaned, the calves are sold on to other farms in lowland areas, where the animals will be 'finished' (in other words, fattened up, ready for the meat trade). Unlike sheep, calves can be born throughout the year, and there are advantages and disadvantages of each season. Hill calves born in the spring will be put to grass over the summer months and normally sold at the autumn sales. Calves born in the autumn tend to be heavier, and therefore likely to fetch

A typical Pennine landscape, with fields 'taken in' from the moorland, and delineated by dry-stone walls.

more when they eventually go to auction. On the other hand, they have to be kept over the winter. This may entail buying in considerable quantities of supplementary feed and it's also likely to mean having housing available near the farmhouse. Again, it's a question of getting the balance right, and choosing the best solution for your own farm.

As with sheep, so hill farmers look to choose breeds of cow suitable for the tough outdoor life. Crossbred cows are most often used for the suckler cow system of farming, since this is felt to be the best way of getting strong, vigorous stock. Dairy crosses tend to be the usual choice.

Incidentally environmentalists and ecologists with an interest in the condition of the Pennines' blanket bogs, although they have a general concern about overgrazing, tend to welcome the presence of cattle as well as sheep on the high moors. Cattle graze in a different way to sheep, and in particular tend to keep the tussocky mat-grass and purple moor grass (molinia) under better control. Cattle are also good at tackling rushes, which sheep tend to spurn and which may otherwise need to be kept under control through the use of pesticides.

Just to complete the agricultural picture for upland areas, there is also a small amount of dairy farming taking place. The overall trend in dairy production in recent years has been towards larger farms with sizeable herds of dairy cows (Friesians and Holsteins) and this has had its effect on smaller operators in marginal areas. It's several years now since David Airey and his father last kept a dairy herd, for example. It's more usual to find dairy herds on farms that are slightly down the hillside from the open moorland.

The year-round task of looking after livestock, trying to produce strong, healthy animals, is, of course, what farming is all about. Except that, in reality, it's not – or at least it's only one half of the job of running of a successful farm business. The other part of the job couldn't be more different, but it's equally important. This is dealing with the various government subsidy schemes, and making sure you've got your paperwork adequately up to date.

Governments over the last thirty years in Britain, whatever party has been in power, have been concerned to trumpet the importance of market forces in the economy. We have been given to understand repeatedly that there is no place for businesses and sectors which aren't commercially viable. It was on this basis, for example, that Britain's traditional manufacturing base was decimated in the 1980s, as was coal mining. So it comes initially as something of a shock to find that farming is still happily living in a different era, one where this hard-headed emphasis on commercial viability and market forces does not hold sway.

The way that farming as an industry is structured is heavily dependent on the system of state subsidies which exist. Hill farming in particular would be a non-starter in terms of viability if it had to pay its way entirely on the income generated from sheep and cattle production. There are reasons why things are arranged in the way they are, however. One is that Britain, through its membership of the European Union, is a partner in the EU's Common Agricultural Policy, which has historically had the objective of promoting a strong agricultural sector and of protecting against food shortages by encouraging farmers to maximise production. Whether they recognise it or not, farmers have reason to be grateful that Britain's membership of the EU has protected them from full exposure to market economics.

And though agriculture seems to take a disproportionately large share of the overall European Union's budget – it was at one stage over 70 per cent, and it is still about 45 per cent of the total – there are understandable reasons why the CAP was established as it was. Governments above all have to ensure their peoples are fed, and the CAP was developed during a period when memories of war and post-war food shortages and rationing were very fresh. The imperative seemed to be to ensure that land was farmed in the most productive way possible. Furthermore CAP in its historic form not only delivered food, it delivered affordable food.

However, as is relatively well known even among non-farmers, CAP is currently going through a period of major reform. Over a ten-year transition period up to 2012 the main system of subsidies is changing so that what you get will no longer be based on the levels of livestock you hold or the amount of farm production you achieve but will be fixed solely in accordance with the amount of land you farm. There will no longer be the same incentives to maximise farm returns at all costs, including maximising utilisation of marginal land, the sort of approach which led to the so-called European wine lakes and butter mountains.

It's not yet clear how the CAP reforms will affect farming, but it's widely accepted that change is inevitable. And with the move to the new 'single payment scheme' under CAP where, unkind observers might claim, farmers are rewarded simply for *being there*, attention inevitably becomes focused on why public money is being invested in agriculture. These are questions which become particularly insistent in relation to the least commercial parts of agriculture, or in other words hill farming.

As long ago as 1975 the European Union recognised that some farmers had to cope with more difficult terrain than others when it came up with the concept of 'less favoured areas' of agricultural land, LFAs, and agreed to what led to the Hill Livestock Compensatory Allowance, later replaced by the Hill Farm Allowance. All the Pennine watershed, perhaps not surprisingly, is classified as an LFA. Within this category, there is a further distinction between 'disadvantaged areas' (DAs) and 'severely disadvantaged areas' (SDAs). Again, almost all the watershed moors are designated as SDAs. (As with the medley of initials we looked at earlier in relation to environmental classification of the moors, there are plenty of new abbreviations and acronyms to get to grips with, when it comes to agriculture.)

The government estimates that upland farmers in England typically receive a total of about £117 million in public money through the CAP single payment scheme. In addition they are eligible for the Hill Farm Allowance, which in recent years has been set at about £27 million a year. About 10,000 hill farmers currently benefit from this allowance, which can represent a significant boost to overall income. Figures suggest that for sheep farmers in SDA areas the Hill Farm Allowance can work out at 20–30 per cent of the total family income.

But the government talk in recent years has been for the Hill Farm Allowance in its current form to be abolished and replaced by something else. Inevitably, this has led to a wider discussion about why, and whether, hill farming should attract extra public money. The government commissioned a number of studies to provide background research, including one by a consortium of researchers led by the Institute for European Environmental Policy who were told to look at the economic, environmental and social implications of hill farming.

Their report was pretty unequivocal in terms of the economics: 'The argument for public support for hill farming based on its agricultural output is weak; basic commodities of beef, milk and lamb can be produced more cheaply and efficiently elsewhere.' Instead, the report pointed out the non-economic public benefits which could be said to come from farming in the uplands:

> The continuation of hill farming appears critical, in particular, to maintaining and enhancing the environmental quality of the uplands. This environmental quality is important in its own right, for example in terms of soil, air and water resources. It also appears to underpin a range of economic activity, particularly tourism, which provides

jobs and benefits to the local economy and more widely. . . . Hill farming is also strongly associated with the cultural identity of upland areas . . .

The government itself has dealt pretty firmly with any idea that hill farm grants should continue to be paid just to keep livestock production levels up. Its 2006 consultation report put it like this: 'Government does not believe that there is a role for public expenditure in subsidising food production. . . . The Government is not minded to maintain a hectare-based payment for the uplands which is not tied to the positive provision of public goods'. What these 'public goods' might be is made clear a little further on: 'In looking at the options for a new system of payments in the uplands, the Government believes we should use the public funds available in order to encourage the provision of landscape and environmental benefits'.

In other words, the Hill Farm Allowance in due course will be reborn as what's called, in the jargon, an agri-environmental scheme. Farmers are to be rewarded for their role as custodians of the environment.

This is the very strong message which the government has been trying to send out to all farmers, not all of whom necessarily like what they're hearing. As well as the new CAP single farm payment, all farms can already sign up if they choose to what's called the Entry Level Scheme (ELS) of a new Environmental Stewardship initiative. It's designed to be relatively straightforward process for farmers and the government hopes that, before long, the majority of agricultural land will have been signed up. Farmers who choose to join ELS normally receive £30 per hectare per year; farmers in Less Favoured Areas like the Pennines receive £8 per hectare. (A hectare is 100 metres squared, or approximately 2½ acres.)

What's the point of Environmental Stewardship? The government has identified four objectives: to conserve wildlife (or in other words encourage biodiversity), to maintain and enhance the landscape, to protect the historical environment and natural resources and, last but not least, to 'promote public access and understanding of the countryside'. To be eligible for ELS you need points (8 points per hectare for a hill farmer), and to earn points you have to commit to a range of undertakings, for a period of five years. In the southern Pennines area, for example, you might get points by agreeing to maintain field boundaries, to keep any existing woodland, to manage rough grazing in order to provide habitat for wading birds, and to try to reduce soil erosion and to improve water quality. Looking after any archaeological features is also another possible way of earning ELS points.

As well as the Entry Level Scheme, the overall Environmental Stewardship initiative includes a Higher Level Scheme, which involves a much greater degree of commitment to environmental objectives, focused around a farm management agreement to which other agencies such as nature conservation bodies may contribute their recommendations. The actual work of putting in an HLS application is time-consuming, involving the preparation of a detailed Farm Environment Plan, so normally farmers bring in agents or consultants to help them cope with the paperwork. HLS is also discretionary: the pot of money is limited and not everyone who applies is accepted.

For moorland areas, the objectives identified for an HLS agreement are likely to be similar to those for the ELS, though the requirements will be much more rigorous. You might agree, for example, to take measures to restore or maintain moorland, to provide rough grazing for nesting birds, to control gorse by burning or cutting, and to rewet dry moorland, for instance by gully-blocking. You sign up to the HLS for a ten year period and – provided you meet your side of the farm management agreement – receive much more generous grants than those payable under the Entry Level Scheme.

The last few paragraphs seem to have been invaded by yet another set of initials, and by this stage you may be wondering how four nice simple objectives for environmental farming can end up producing quite complicated arrangements. By the time you read this it may have got still more complicated, for it's very likely that the subsidy currently paid through the Hill Farm Allowance will be redirected shortly into the new Uplands Entry Level Stewardship Scheme specifically targeted at hill farmers.

David Airey turns out to be something of an old hand when it comes to agri-environmental schemes. He and his landlord signed part of his farm into Countryside Stewardship, an early precursor to the current Environmental Stewardship schemes, shortly after the idea was first introduced in 1991, and more recently David has extended his involvement by agreeing to put all of his 2,500 acres into the scheme. Although the Countryside Stewardship initiative is no longer operating, he'll be able to stay in until the end of his ten years, though the likelihood is that in due course he may migrate across to the HLS.

Joining Countryside Stewardship has involved work to improve heather cover and reduce purple moor grass on one area of moorland. It's meant avoiding fertiliser and agreeing to muck the fields instead at particular times of year. But the most dramatic change, encouraged by Natural England, has been to David's stocking levels. The 700 ewes he farms today are less than half the livestock he once ran on his farm: there was a time when he had 1,000 pure Swaledales and 600 mules. Fortunately, having fewer sheep fits well with what he wants, making the job slightly less frantic and also saving on the need to employ casual labour.

Anyway, David Airey is happy to ensure that the moorland birds have their nesting ground. 'We like to see the birds – at certain times of the year, birds are the only things we do see up on the moor. The curlew is a brilliant bird. You can see the chicks running, and the mother going crazy overhead. And we get snipe, and a lot of partridge as well,' he says.

David Airey is concerned, though, about the future of hill farming. He followed his father into the family business in the traditional way, but his two sons have chosen to make their careers outside farming, an increasingly common story. The overall average age of farmers is creeping higher and higher: one recent survey suggested that the average age of farmers in the Dark Peak area of the Pennines was fifty-eight, for example.

The problem as David Airey sees it is that the key farming skills aren't necessarily getting passed on to the next generation, so that – regardless of the policies and strategies on agriculture which governments may choose to have in place – the old hill farming traditions could die anyway. 'I went with my dad to the Swaledale tup sales – all my age group were there with their dads. The problem now is the young lads aren't there. I liken it to mining: if we had to open up the mines we closed, we'd find that we couldn't because the skills have gone. Exactly the same will happen in the hills – the skills won't be there.'

Hill farming has evolved over a very long period of time, and today's farmers build on the ideas and improvements which have come in over generations. The worry for farmers like David Airey is that they just may be the last in this long chain.

'Part of my father went into this farm, and part of me has gone into it as well. I've done a lot of work on it. If I had to leave what I do here, well I'd be sad, but I hope I'd leave in good enough heart if I knew that another young lad was coming in to farm it,' he says. But leaving the land unfarmed, allowing it (in the phrase which is currently receiving much attention in policy circles) to be rewilded, would be a different matter. 'We'd lose a valuable asset. We'd lose the land as it is.'

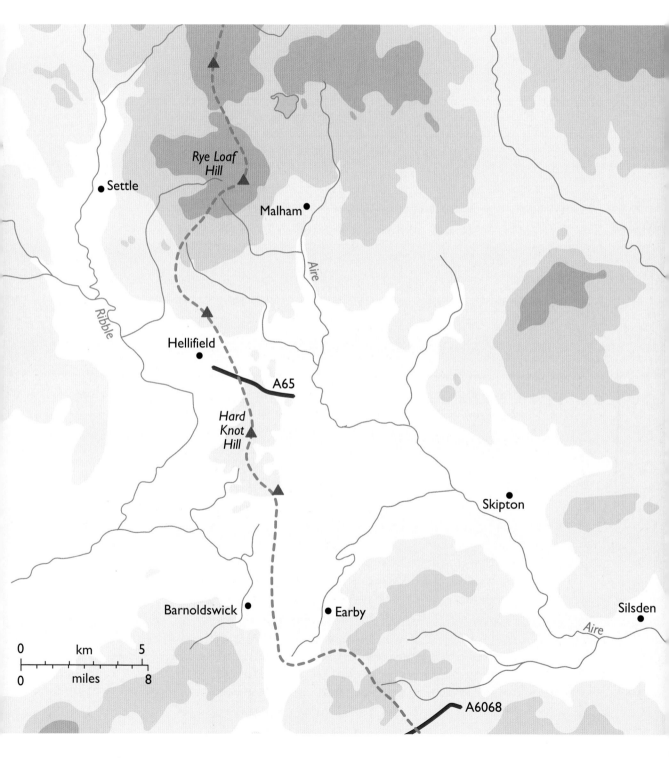

12. EMMOTT MOOR

Combe Hill – Emmott Moor – A6068 – Spring Green – Bleara Moor – Earby (Sough) (A56)

Emmott Moor is still recovering from a serious fire which swept it in the summer of 2006. When I came this way, the moor was a terrible sight: a desert of bare soil, with vegetation burned down to ground level. Walking across it was like walking across sand dunes.

The fire burned solidly for two days and nights and took out hundreds of acres on the Lancashire side of the watershed. David Airey at his farm just across on the Yorkshire side was lucky: the fire was stopped just at the edge of his land. If it had crossed the ridge, the consequences would have been even worse, he told me. 'The heather was dry and crisp and the wind was coming out of the west. It would have gone whoof!' he says.

Wild fires like these tend to be tackled not just by the Fire Brigade but by the efforts of local gamekeepers and farmers. Word goes round the area. For the fire at Emmott Moor, for example, keepers turned up from the shooting estates on Ilkley Moor to lend a hand. Then they had to rush back to their own moor: Ilkley, too, suffered from serious moorland fires in 2006.

As we saw on Bleaklow, moorland fires can be a major factor in creating peat erosion and moorland degeneration. Most obviously, they damage the fragile moorland vegetation and the ecosystem that is based around it. Rather less obviously, they can damage the area's hydrology and the quality of the water coming off the moor. And there's another serious problem: peat is a carbon store, packed full of greenhouse gases which have been successfully trapped in the ground rather than being released into the atmosphere. A moorland fire releases carbon into the air.

Some wild fires start from natural causes, for example from lightning strikes. Most however are caused directly or indirectly by humans, and unfortunately the finger points primarily at visitors to the countryside who are either being careless or are deliberately starting fires. A survey of thirty-six wild fires in the Peak District national park blamed cigarettes for thirteen, arson for ten and camp fires for a further three (the remaining ten had been started through the carelessness of gamekeepers or farmers).

The fact, too, is that fires are more likely to start at weekends and bank holidays than mid-week. According to an academic study from the University of Manchester, a typical British bank holiday is almost five times more perilous than seven days of dry weather: 'It is human impact rather than meteorological pressure that emerges as the main villain of the piece,' the report stated.

However careless a day-tripper may be, they're unlikely to start a fire on a day which is cold and damp, but what worries environmentalists is that climate change looks set to increase the sort of weather conditions which make moorland fires more likely. In other words, this could be a growing problem in the future.

The law allows for open access country to be closed to the public temporarily when there is deemed to be a high risk of fire, and this has been implemented in some areas on a number of occasions since the introduction of the access provisions of the Countryside and Rights of Way Act. But actually, there's some suggestion that this may not necessarily reduce the risk. Roads across moorland areas remain open – and cigarettes are perhaps more likely to be tossed from a speeding car window than deliberately discarded on to the moor by a walker. And if the moors are closed there are fewer people about to spot fires and to report them. Moor closure in the Peak District made no significant difference to the prevalent of wild fires, according to the Manchester researchers.

As well as the sort of devastating wild fire which swept Emmott Moor, however, the Pennine moors also see each year a host of deliberate managed fires. Heather and grass burning has long been a feature of the moorland management regime undertaken by the shooting estates or, more precisely, by the gamekeepers who are employed to look after them.

From the Peak District to Northumberland the Pennine moors provide the backdrop for grouse shooting. Almost all the moorland areas have shooting rights attached to them. Large (and smaller) holdings of open moors may be privately owned and held primarily because of the shooting, and for these areas the normal arrangement is for agricultural tenancies to be given to those who are farming the land. In other areas – for example, in the case of land held by the water companies and used as catchment for reservoirs – both agricultural tenancies and shooting tenancies will be offered. Shooting tenancies may be acquired by individuals, by shooting clubs or perhaps by a small group who come together as a syndicate. Whatever the arrangements, in the days and weeks immediately after 12th August when the red grouse shooting season officially opens, the moors become busy. Beaters are employed to push the birds towards the grouse butts where the party of 'guns', and their guns, will be waiting. Typically a shooting party will be made up of eight 'guns'.

Hunting has taken place on the upland moors for centuries. In late medieval times, large tracts of moorland were dedicated specifically as hunting areas. Royal hunting grounds were known as 'forests', the term not referring to the amount of tree cover they had but rather to the fact that they were established outside the normal laws of the land, *foris* being the Latin for outside. It is in this sense that the New Forest in Hampshire got its name, as did the Forest of Bowland in Lancashire, though visitors to Bowland's open fells today still puzzle about where all the trees have gone. The area around Trawden (just to the north of Boulsworth Hill) was a forest, and close near by were others: the Forest of Pendle is one example, the Forest of Rossendale another.

Forests and other areas dedicated for hunting (technically, 'forests' were royal hunting grounds, while the term 'chase' was applied to hunting estates owned by the nobility) were managed carefully for the game, with measures in place to discourage poaching or illegal grazing of livestock by local people. The prize animal for the hunt was the deer, specifically the red deer, though wild boar made good sport as did sometimes the hare also. The anonymous poet of the medieval poem *Sir Gawain and the Green Knight* recounts in graphic detail a deer hunt and a boar hunt in an upland northern area.

So the use of the high moors today for 'field sports', while an activity which probably invokes incomprehension or active hostility on the part of the bulk of the English population, has at least got history on its side. Red grouse shooting as practised today developed in the middle of the nineteenth century, one important innovation being that of driven grouse

A substantial farmstead, with Emmott Moor in the background.

shooting: in other words, you drove the birds towards the guns, rather than simply going up to a moor with a gun and seeing what you could find. There were also technological improvements in gun design.

Red grouse are wild birds, unlike other game birds such as pheasant, for which breeding pens can be used to increase the numbers available for sport. But nevertheless, grouse moors are carefully managed in order to try to maximise each year's harvest and in this sense grouse could be said to be farmed as actively as livestock. If the last chapter stressed the primary importance of agriculture in determining the appearance and condition of the uplands, it's perhaps time to add a codicil: close behind farming as a factor in how the Pennine landscape looks is the moorland management undertaken for grouse shooting purposes. It's difficult to understand the moorland landscape without being aware of the work which goes on round the year on the shooting estates.

It probably helps the field sports lobby that the sort of moors which are ideal for grouse are also the landscapes which the general public regards with most affection. Cameras come out in great numbers every autumn to capture the sight of the great swathes of purple heather; given the choice between looking at, say, a degraded 'white moor' dominated by mat-grass or molinia grass or a dry moor with heather, the vast majority of people would naturally opt for the latter. What they perhaps don't realise is that heather moors are very definitely the result of human activity. Indeed, the emphasis on heather to the exclusion of other types of vegetation is, in reality, a form of monoculture which – if it failed to tune with our aesthetic preferences – might come in for criticism.

During the second half of the nineteenth century it was discovered that greater numbers of grouse seemed to be found in places where there was younger, shorter heather. As a consequence, the principle of burning patches of heather on a rotational basis became established as a key element of estate management, particularly after an influential report from a committee chaired by Lord Lovat in 1911 recommended the practice. The idea is for a mosaic of heathers of different ages and heights to be created across a whole grouse moor. Older heather provides cover for grouse, but it is the young succulent shoots of new heather which grow on land that has been recently burned which grouse and their chicks find particularly attractive.

How often a particular area of heather is burned depends on the particular practices of each estate and its head gamekeeper, but it is also strongly influenced by the nature of the ground. Some estates burn as frequently as every five or six years, but a cycle of burning over

The moors are carpeted, every summer, with cottongrass.

eight or ten years for dry heather moor would perhaps be more typical. Left to itself, a heather plant has a life cycle of around thirty years, growing into a mature plant after about 20–25 years and then degenerating into old age. Current best advice is to wait until heather is between eight inches and twelve inches in height before burning, and to allow some heather to grow even higher. This means, if heather takes say eight years to reach eight inches, logically a grouse moor would be burned in blocks, each year burning one eighth of the total area under management.

This is a typical scenario for a dry heather moor. On blanket bogs, however, some people say that once every twenty years is enough – and there's also a strong feeling from environmentalists that wet blanket bog shouldn't be subject to controlled burning at all. There are also issues about moors which are designated as Sites of Special Scientific Interest.

The more you probe into this subject, in fact, the more scope for controversy there seems to be. Little embers of disagreement are lying waiting, potentially ready to be fanned into a full flare-up. If environmentalists tend to want to ensure that sufficient measures are in place to minimise what they see as the negative effects of burning, organisations representing the shooting industry think differently. Their position can be précised very easily: leave it to us, trust our gamekeepers. The Country Land and Business Association (CLA), for example, in a submission to a recent government consultation on the subject put it like this: 'It is the experience and practical knowledge of those burning that will ensure moorland continues to be managed in an effective and responsible way.' Perhaps the CLA allowed its irritation at being forced to defend traditional practices to show through a little too clearly, for another part of its submission was slightly less diplomatic:

> There is a grave risk that we are heading towards a culture of over-prescription and micromanagement underpinned with petty enforcement . . . Ten years ago keepers could get local help to go burning; now there is hardly anybody available. However they can ring dozens of desktop conservationists who have recently 'found' the moors that will come out to do a report and take months or even a year to make a decision. We feel that officials who are drafting possible changes in the control of heather and grassland burning should be made to undertake burning so they truly understand the rigours of the job . . .

Defra, the government department responsible for countryside issues, holds the ring and, not surprisingly, points to both advantages and snags to controlled burning:

> Burning in general provides improved accessibility for grazing animals and increased availability of suitable habitats for game and wildlife at all stages of their life cycle. . . . However if this management technique is not planned carefully, burning can be counter-productive, destroying valuable grazing, plants, animals and birds; altering the physical structure, the chemical composition and even the hydrology of the soil.

Heather and grassland burning is, in fact, already controlled, at least in theory. Break the Heather and Grass Etc (Burning) Regulations of 1986, and you could find yourself committing an offence and hauled off to face a fine of £1,000. In practice, gamekeepers probably don't need to have too many sleepless nights. As Defra itself has candidly admitted, 'Enforcing the current Regulations is the responsibility of the police, local authorities, and statutory agencies. However, the remoteness of many burning sites presents difficulties in terms of enforcement.' Perhaps the most significant restriction under the Regulations are the time limits imposed for burning, which cannot normally take place in upland areas between 16th April and the end of September.

Recent debate has focused on whether the Regulations, and an accompanying code of good practice, need changing. Should the law be strengthened, or by contrast are the Regulations actually unnecessary? The CLA, for example, claims that there are already enough alternative measures in place to protect SSSIs and other sensitive areas: rescind the Regulations altogether, they argue. There's also been debate over the issue of so-called 'no burn' areas, such as the edges of watercourses, steep ground, and wet blanket bog. Should burning these areas be proscribed, discouraged or simply left to the discretion of the people on the ground?

Perhaps inevitably, the way forward will be a compromise between shooting interests and environmentalists, with everyone agreeing on the importance of creating controlled cool burns which move rapidly across the heather and don't burn deep into the peat. What's not disputed is that moorland burning will carry on. Little coils of smoke rising up from the heather will continue to be a winter sight on the high Pennine moors.

Shortly after Emmott Moor is crossed, the moors abruptly stop, however. Indeed, for the next fifteen miles or so it seems as though the Pennines themselves have disappeared. The high ground is further west, in the distinctive shape of Pendle hill, and further east, where Rombalds Moor separates Airedale from Wharfedale. But for the watershed itself the direction is definitely downhill. In fact, this frequently doesn't feel much like a watershed, or at least not *the* watershed dividing northern England in two. In places the height above sea level falls to around 130 metres, or little more than 400 feet. This is a big change from Kinder Scout and Black Hill and rather different from what is waiting ahead, once the Yorkshire Dales begin.

For the first time, too, as I mentioned in my introduction, the follower of the watershed can't rely on the route being on open access land. North of the A6068 between Colne and Cowling I had to make the best use I could of rights of way, trying to stick as close to the line I had marked on my map but inevitably in places having to deviate. The route I chose took me along footpaths past hill farms, playing peek-a-boo with the long-distance Pendle Way which for a time was going broadly my way but which had its own mind about the route it was going to take. Briefly there was the heather-clad handkerchief-sized moor of Bleara to cross, before I headed down to the main A56 road close to Earby and then around the back of the town of Barnoldswick to find the third trans-Pennine canal, the Leeds and Liverpool.

13. EARBY

Earby (Sough) (A56) – Barnoldswick (Skipton Road)

Any story of the Pennines has to acknowledge that what now seem resolutely rural areas were once important industrial centres. For many centuries, lead mining was a major feature of life from Derbyshire to Northumberland, playing a key role in the local economy, heavily influencing social and working life and, in many respects, dominating the appearance of the landscape as well. Even today, though a century or so has passed since the industry effectively came to an end, the physical remains which lead mining left behind (both under- and overground) are there to be found in all the major mining areas of the Pennines. But increasingly the knowledge of this history is passing: many visitors to Swaledale, for example, once a key lead mining area, now enjoy the beauty of the valley oblivious of its industrial past.

Not all the areas of the Pennines were affected. There were three main regions where lead was found. The first was the North Pennines, a large geographical area which included upper Weardale, upper Teesdale, Allendales and – particularly relevant for us, since it included mining directly under the watershed near Cross Fell and Great Dun Fell – the moorland around Alston. Secondly, there was an important centre of mining in the Yorkshire Dales, focused on Swaledale, Arkengarthdale and upper Wensleydale in the north and, further south, around Greenhow Hill (between Nidderdale and Wharfedale) and Grassington Moor. Finally, there were major lead mining areas in Derbyshire, from the High Peak down to Ashbourne.

There were also other, less significant, areas where lead mining took place. There were mines at Cononley south of Skipton, for example, and on Malham Moor. And as we have already seen in Chapter 9, there was a seventeenth-century lead mining effort at Thieveley in the Cliviger gorge near Todmorden.

So there are several places in this account where it might be appropriate to say a little more about the lead industry. But the village of Earby, you'd think, would not be one of them. Earby, on the road from Colne to Skipton, was not a centre for lead mining; the nearest major focus of the industry, on the moors above Grassington, was some distance away to the north. But it is at Earby, nevertheless, that today you can visit the Museum of Yorkshire Dales Lead Mining.

Of course in an ideal world you might want to magic the building away from Earby, which is a pleasant enough place but, frankly, a tourist-free zone, and put it down in a Dales honeypot like Grassington. In fact, as Peter Hart from the voluntary trust which runs the museum told me, there had been discussions a number of times in the past about moving the collection away from its current home. But recently a firm decision had been taken: 'We're here, and we're going to stay here. We want people to come to Earby to find us,' he told me.

And there is a reason why the lead mining museum is where it is. Earby has had for many years an active Pothole Club. As well as exploring the natural limestone caverns and potholes of the Yorkshire Dales' limestone country, its members also took an early interest in making their way through the tunnels, shafts and levels left behind from the region's lead mines. As early as 1945 the Earby Mines Research Group had been established, set up as an offshoot of the Pothole Club, and over the following twenty or thirty years its enthusiasts had spent a great deal of time visiting former mines, recording, measuring and photographing the remains and, where possible, recovering tools and machinery which had been left by the miners underground. All these items had to be stored somewhere – and, according to Peter, they were given temporary homes in a range of unsuitable places, including members' coalhouses.

In 1970, however, a much more satisfactory solution became possible. The county council vacated Earby's old grammar school, a beautiful old stone building dating from around 1594 which had more recently been used as a clinic, and the local charitable foundation which was responsible for looking after the property offered it to the Mines Research Group. After a year spent cleaning, decorating and arranging the exhibits, the group opened the doors of its new museum in May 1971.

The history of lead mining in northern England goes back at least to the Romans, and possibly to pre-Roman times. The Brigantes are known to have been skilled metal workers and may have excavated the most easily accessible lead where the mineral veins broke the surface. The Romans, who had considerable expertise gained, for example, in extensive mining operations in Spain, certainly exploited the lead deposits of the north of England. Pigs, or ingots, of lead have been found with Latin inscriptions in Derbyshire and in the Yorkshire Dales, and there are also some suggestions that the Romans worked the lead mines in Weardale, Co. Durham and in the South Tyne valley.

This was the start of a story which lasted for almost two millennia. Already by medieval times, miners in the North Pennines and Derbyshire were able to undertake their work under the protection of a set of codified laws and customs which helped regulate the operation of the mines and resolve disputes. At this stage, miners would have been independent workers using relatively basic tools (the pick was the key tool necessary for prising out the 'bouse', the mixture of ore and rock taken to the surface) and perhaps combining their mining activities with farming or running a smallholding. How well they did would depend on how hard they worked, and how lucky or unlucky they were in finding a rich vein to exploit.

Lead ore is found in mineral veins which run through the Carboniferous rock, normally in a broadly vertical direction. This meant that, once the ore on and close to the surface had been removed, it was a question of sinking shafts in order to chase the ore-rich veins as they snaked their way down through the rocks. Even in relatively early times these shafts could be to a significant depth, of a hundred feet or more. Because of the weight problem of pulling up a rope from a deep shaft, one technique was to build a series of shorter staggered shafts, linked by cross passages. In this way, veins could be followed vertically down for several hundred feet. (Later, a way was found for ore to be pulled directly up deeper shafts, using the power of horses linked to pulley arrangements: the animal would spend their working day walking round and round, and round and round, the shaft head.)

But the deeper the mine workings went, the more problems there were likely to be with ventilation and particularly with flooding. Arthur Raistrick, the university lecturer and local historian who was one of the first to give the lead industry the attention it deserved, put it like this:

In every way water was the miners' common enemy. He would as often as not arrive at the mine wet or at least wetshod; he might change into mine clothes at the 'shop' but at the smaller mines his clothes would be cold and damp and plastered with clay. Underground, water would be dripping from the roof, running on the level floors and in deeper workings threatening always to drown him out and sometimes succeeding. There are records of mines where, failing the capital or skill to install powerful pumps, the miners have spent as much as six hours out of eight in lifting water from the shaft in buckets to get to a working place.

Raistrick went on to say, 'Add to the wetness the frequent foulness of the air in the levels and drifts, the oppressive darkness relieved for a few dim feet by the light of a tallow dip, and the complete isolation far underground and it will soon be realised that mining conditions were extreme in their demands upon the strength and endurance of the men who wrought in them.'

From the 1600s onwards, it became increasingly common in Pennine areas to try to sort out ventilation and flooding problems at the foot of shafts by digging horizontal drainage tunnels or adits into the hillside from lower down the hill. Provided you got your direction and slope right, your adit would meet up with the shaft and provide an escape route for the water accumulating at the bottom.

By the beginning of the nineteenth century these 'levels' were being engineered to a very high standard, not simply for water drainage but as a way of actually reaching and removing lead ore. In the North Pennines, for example, much of the lead mining began to be undertaken from levels rather than from vertical shafts. The levels were constructed large enough for horses to pull waggons of bouse on rails to the surface and they could easily extend for a mile or more into the hillside. Indeed, in some areas of the Pennines, interlinking levels and shafts make up a very extensive labyrinthine network of underground passages.

The task of constructing new levels was slow and to a large extent unproductive 'dead' work, and therefore required access to adequate capital resources. So too did other techno-logical innovations, such as the use of steam or hydraulic engines to provide ventilation or remove water. From the end of the 1600s the structure of the industry began to change, therefore, with the growth of larger commercial undertakings, which might be established either as joint-stock companies or by major local landowners. One major enterprise, the Quaker-run London Lead Company, was established at the end of the seventeenth century and from the late eighteenth century focused its attention entirely on the North Pennines, where it became the dominant player in the industry.

In areas where lead mining has taken place it's a relatively common sight to see the entrances to levels, often with elaborate portals, still in place. If you are so inclined, you can get a glimpse of what lies beyond this threshold by joining a group such as the Northern Mine Research Society and going along on one of their specialist guided tours underground. Or, less arduously and more easily, you can visit the Earby museum, where Peter Hart or one of his colleagues will be pleased to show you their reconstruction of a Yorkshire Dales level, complete with a very lifelike (if fibreglass) horse pulling a string of waggons. This tableau is probably the museum's most impressive feature, and is suitably dimly lit – though not as damp or dirty, and certainly not as dangerous, as the real thing.

It ought to be said that, as well as shafts and levels, there was another rough-and-ready method of getting at lead ore which lay close to the surface, by using water power to scour away top soil and rocks and to expose the mineral veins beneath. This technique was known as hushing. In order to form a sufficient force of water, a temporary dam would be created at the head of a valley to build up a reservoir of water. The dam would then be deliberately breached, to allow the water to rush out. Once the mineral veins were exposed, they could then be worked through open-cast excavation, with the hushing process repeated if necessary to clear away debris. Because hushing tended to involve a fairly substantial rearrangement of the landscape, the remains of past hushes are still very much in evidence in places such as Gunnerside Gill in Swaledale.

The mining of lead ore was only one aspect of the process. Once the bouse had been brought out by one means or another to the surface, it had to be sorted or 'dressed' to remove the worthless rocks. Typically this work was undertaken by women and girls and by boys too young to begin working underground, and it too was hard labour. The main task was to separate out the lead ore which could then be taken for smelting, and until the intro- duction in the larger mining areas of water-powered roller crushers which mechanised the process it was human labour which had to undertake the task of hammering away at the ore until it was down to small enough pieces, often as small as peas. Flat-faced hammers were used for this labour.

Lead ore particles are heavier than those of other minerals and therefore they sink to the bottom in water, a fact that was used to advantage on the dressing floors. (The process was similar to that employed when panning for gold.) Moorland streams were particularly valuable if their flow could be regulated and their course diverted to pass across the area where the ore was being dressed.

The dressing floors were out on the moors, close to the shafts or levels from which the bouse was removed and, since they would not necessarily be protected from the weather, the work of hammering away at the rocks had to be carried out in whatever weather happened to come over the hill top. The voices of the women and children who worked in this way have faded, but there is one memory of work on the dressing floor which has survived, in the song 'Fourpence a Day'. This was collected shortly after the second world war from John Gowland, who was a retired lead miner living in Middleton-in-Teesdale, but is usually attributed to an earlier Teesdale miner and poet called Thomas Raine. The song packs a powerful message and is still sung in folk circles today. The first verse is:

> The ore is waiting in the tubs, the snow's upon the fell
> Canny folk are sleeping yet, but lead is reet to sell.
> Come, my little washer lad, come let's away,
> We're bound down to slavery for fourpence a day.

Earby's museum is another way of trying to remember the lives and labours of those who once earned their living from lead. For Peter Hart, it's become a major part of his life. As we sat and chatted in the small café area by the entrance he told me how he had first got interested in the history of lead mining. He had been working as a telephone engineer in the Yorkshire Dales, he said, a job which involved travelling throughout the Dales area. 'I wondered what all the holes in the ground were,' he explained. 'A lad who was a potholer and interested in geology got me involved. He kept asking me, "Do you know about this?"'

Earby Mining Museum, housed in a handsome building that used to be a grammar school.

Eventually Peter signed up for an evening class on geology being run by the Workers' Education Association in Skipton, and got his potholing friends to initiate him into the underground world of the mines. And, inevitably, he found himself getting involved in the museum, too. This was back in the early 1970s, shortly after the museum first opened. But it's been over the past few years that the task of looking after the museum and of trying to find funding for it has loomed ever larger in Peter's life.

The Earby lead mining museum has gone through major changes. In fact, from 2000 to 2005 the museum was closed altogether, and some may have wondered whether it would ever open its doors again. Initially the closure was needed to enable major structural work to be undertaken to the building, including a complete new roof. But the closure was an opportunity, too, to reassess what the museum was for – was it simply going to remain a collection of

Few motorists notice this old roadside milestone between Earby and Barnoldswick.

artefacts built up over the years by the Earby Mines Research Group members and other industrial archaeologists, or could it be developed into something more? Could it be redesigned to try to tell the story of lead mining more effectively to visitors?

It's a debate which museums far better resourced than Earby's have also been having in recent times. Back in Victorian times when museums first began to be a feature of civic life, you could say that their prime function was seen as simply ensuring that physical objects from the past were saved indefinitely for the future. The main work of a curator was to record provenance and ensure the physical preservation of an artefact. The needs of the public (if they were admitted at all) were something of an afterthought. But these days we require more from our museums. We look to them for a role in explaining the past, and we demand that the physical objects are not simply passively displayed but are adequately interpreted. We want education. We also want entertainment, since a visit to a museum increasingly has to compete with other leisure-time pursuits. An adequate museum experience has to be on a par with that on offer, say, in an out-of-town shopping centre or multiplex complex.

This poses a practical problem for those running museums, particularly a small one run by voluntary effort like the lead mining museum at Earby. But there's also a philosophical, or if you prefer an ideological, issue to address. It's not so much *how* we should structure a museum like this, but *why* we want to do it. What's the message about the past which we are trying to communicate?

With considerable effort, Peter Hart and his committee tried to find the grant funding they thought was necessary. It was, by all accounts, quite a task. 'It took over my life for two years. I wrote letter after letter after letter, and was very disappointed by the responses I got,' he recalls. But eventually his luck turned: the Heritage Lottery Fund had decided that the museum at Earby did deserve support, and a grant of about £200,000 was forthcoming. The museum could be properly designed. The collection was weeded out, and care taken to devise an adequate series of interpretation panels to explain to the public the purpose of the displays. Space was left downstairs for the reconstruction of the level, and the fibreglass horse was commissioned.

It's a good effort, and the Earby museum deserves to pull in visitors. But even so there's only so much a building can do in trying to recreate a lost industry. Outside the museum, for example, are the remains of a very large waterwheel. It's certainly an impressive sight, but try as I might I found it hard to visualise it earning its keep powering the ore crushing machine at the Providence mine at Kettlewell in Wharfedale. The wheel has become separated from the context in which it once was operated and the loss of this contextual setting has simply turned it into a relic of the past, stripped of its economic and social attributes.

The problem, in other words, is that museum displays can become the modern equivalent of medieval saints' reliquaries. And even interpretation can be problematic, because however good and well-written the information panels and display boards may be, they tend to offer only a single way of approaching the past. History is not necessarily quite so tidy or uncontroversial.

The Pennines lead industry headed into recession during the final years of the nineteenth century and one by one the mining companies closed their operations. Although some lead mining continued into the twentieth century, the focus primarily switched to two other minerals, fluorspar (calcium fluoride) and baryte (barium sulphate). Any account of the lead industry is, effectively, a tale of the past, not the present.

So what should we remember of this past? Do we honour the memory of the engineers who pushed forward the technological frontiers of the industry, and of the surveyors who ensured that the shafts and levels found the veins? Do we commemorate the entrepreneurs who created wealth from out the earth? Do we focus on the ordinary men and women who found work in this industry, in often appalling conditions, like the washer lads earning fourpence a day in 'slavery' on the dressing floor?

It's surely important to remember the lead-miners themselves and to acknowledge their contribution. But even here we have to be careful: 'Fourpence a Day' is certainly a fine song with a strong message, but if we sing it today, are we simply engaging in an exercise in nostalgia?

14. TO THE DALES

Barnoldswick (Skipton Road) – Flambers Hill – Hard Knot Hill – Hellifield Brow (A65) – Newton Moor Top – High Langber – Rye Loaf Hill – Black Hill – Fountains Fell

Once you're north of Barnoldswick, thoughts inevitably begin to turn towards the Yorkshire Dales, waiting just a few miles to the north.

I picked out the line of the watershed around Earby and Barnoldswick on the map with some difficulty, the task complicated (or so I told myself) because of the rearrangement of the water catchment systems here which had accompanied the creation of the Leeds and Liverpool canal. This celebrated Pennine canal differs from the Huddersfield Narrow and Rochdale canals further south in being built to take wider boats: the locks were able to accommodate boats 60 feet long and 14 feet wide. But, like the other canals, it had its origins in the period of enthusiastic canal construction at the end of the eighteenth century. In fact, if the canal company hadn't run out of money in the late 1770s, the Leeds and Liverpool would have been the first trans-Pennine canal to open. As it was, the final linking section through Foulridge and Barnoldswick to Gargrave had to wait until more money became available in the 1790s, and the whole 127-mile link from Leeds to the sea at Liverpool was finally completed in 1816.

As you'd expect, it is the summit pound which the watershed meets at Barnoldswick, the canal relying on reservoirs near Foulridge just to the south for ensuring an adequate supply of water. North of the canal, my task of plotting the watershed line seemed a little easier. I traced it on the map, crossing a series of small hills: Copy Hill, Ransa Hill, Flambers Hill, Hard Knot Hill. On the ground, though, it wasn't easy at all: I had to deviate, making do with whatever by-roads or footpaths I could find which headed in approximately the right direction. I took the lane to West Marton, carried on along another stretch of tarmac north to Gledstone Hall, and then finally picked up a poorly waymarked footpath which ran close to the watershed near Flambers Hill – the first trig point since Boulsworth Hill, by the way, and therefore number fifteen. Beyond, there was another frustrating road section from Swinden Moor to Brightenber before another path ran off in roughly the right direction northwards.

By past standards this part of England's backbone is low ground, and for the first part of the journey north of Barnoldswick there's little sense of distance or drama in the landscape crossed. But gradually the horizon opens up and by the time Hard Knot Hill is approached just before the A65 trunk road there are 360-degree views to enjoy: over the nearby Ribble valley with the Forest of Bowland beyond and Pendle behind. And ahead, to the Dales.

The Yorkshire Dales national park is entered just to the north of Hellifield. The park itself was established in 1954, an obvious candidate for designation following the passing of the 1949 national parks legislation. It is, as the park authority itself points out, an area of England which is special for many: 'the interaction of people with nature through history has produced, in the Yorkshire Dales, a landscape or remarkable beauty, distinctive character and immense

The Leeds and Liverpool canal near Barnoldswick: the most northerly of the three waterways that cross the Pennine watershed.

interest that is cherished and enjoyed by the nation'. There is, the authority says, a 'spirit of place' that is unique to the Dales.

Geology is important here, especially limestone. The spectacular limestone landscape known as karst is unlike that created by any other rock, and the Great Scar limestone of the southern Yorkshire Dales offers the finest karst landscape in Britain. Above ground are extensive limestone pavements, such as those at Malham Cove or on the flanks of Ingleborough: above ground, too, are the limestone outcrops and scars, the deep gorges and the dry valleys (dry, because the streams have disappeared underground through sink holes) which together are a striking feature of the landscape. But underground things are just as impressive: under the grass of Dales fields and moors lie complex systems of caves and potholes, created over the millennia of geological time by the action of water on rock. Much of the famous Gaping Gill system, for example, is more than 350,000 years old.

It would be wrong to think that the Dales landscape is simply a story of limestone, however. Millstone Grit is here too, breaking out often above limestone layers to form high plateaux comprised of the sort of soggy moorland which is already so familiar to us from gritstone country further south. Away from the valleys, the Yorkshire Dales can offer wild moorland as remote as anything found in the Peak District or South Pennines: try walking in the countryside near Meugher between Wharfedale and Nidderdale, for example, to get a real taste of blanket bog isolation, Dales-style.

Rolling farmland around Hellifield: some of the lowest-lying country on the watershed.

So it is misleading to assume that the images of the Dales which appear most often on postcards and guide books – that is to say, a tapestry of green valleys crisscrossed with drystone walls, of numerous small stone barns scattered through the fields and of pleasant stone-built cottages in pleasant stone-built villages – represents the full extent of the landscape to be found in the national park area. Nevertheless, entirely accurate or not, this 'classic' Dales landscape is one which is held very dear and very deep by many people.

So far in this chapter the word 'landscape' has already appeared eight times. Up to now in this book I haven't felt the need to define exactly what I've meant, proceeding on the basis that it's a common word which most people will immediately understand. Nevertheless perhaps now is the right time to look at this term a little more closely.

Landscape is clearly more than just 'the view'. It's more, too, than an approach which an ecologist might take, focusing exclusively on the vegetation, plant and animal life of the land. Landscape is shaped by geology, but geological factors by themselves are not the only determining factors. When we talk of the landscape, we also have to take into account human engagement with the land, going back over centuries. Perhaps the following definition will do for the time being: 'landscape means an area, as perceived by people, whose character is the result of the action and interaction of natural and/or human factors'.

That's the definition which was chosen in 2000 when the official text of the European Landscape Convention was formally adopted. It may be, of course, that this particular international treaty has passed you by, and that you have been unaware that Britain signed the Convention in February 2006 and ratified it in November 2006, or that since March 2007 it has been binding on our government. It may even be that you have a sliver of suspicion about whether international documents like this have any real value. And you may by now have slipped into a Europhobic mode and be about to blame Brussels bureaucrats for intervening into things that don't concern them – though if you have, you've jumped to the wrong conclusion for this is a product of the Council of Europe, the much broader European body which was set up in 1949 and which represents every part of our continent from Russia and Turkey to Iceland.

My own view is that it would be a shame to let scepticism triumph. It's true that the official text of the Convention is not immediately front-page material. It starts: 'The member States of the Council of Europe signatory hereto' and then goes into a series of hanging clauses beloved of legal documents which begin in turn 'Considering that . . .', 'Concerned to achieve . . .', 'Noting that . . .', 'Aware that . . .', 'Acknowledging that . . .', 'Noting that . . .', 'Wishing to . . .', 'Believing that . . .' and 'Having regard to . . .', before eventually arriving 500 words later at what amounts to the end of the first sentence and the bit we've all been waiting for: '. . . have agreed as follows:'

But international treaties probably have to be written like this. What the Convention is saying, if I can be allowed my own précis, is something as follows: Landscape is important to us all. It's about the relationship between people and place. Whether it's ordinary or outstanding, urban or rural, it's about the way human activity has interacted with the natural world. It's a facet of human culture. And it's vital both that governments look after the landscape and that ordinary people are engaged in this work, too.

This last point is something which the Council of Europe tries to stress: as one of the background documents supporting the Convention puts it, 'The landscape is important as a component of the environment and of people's surroundings. . . . The public is accordingly encouraged to take an active part in landscape management and planning, and to feel it has responsibility for what happens to the landscape. . . . Landscape is the concern of all and lends itself to democratic treatment.' So the Convention, among other things, encourages the development of good practice in relation to things like consciousness raising about the landscape.

A Council of Europe Convention like this one comes into force provided ten countries sign up to it, and there was never any doubt about this. Seventeen landscape-loving governments endorsed it the day that the Convention was open for signature: Belgium, Bulgaria, Croatia, Denmark, Finland, France, Italy, Lithuania, Luxembourg, Malta, Moldova, Portugal, Romania, Spain, Switzerland and Turkey. Oh, and San Marino. And the UK? Well, more than four years on, in July 2005, Defra published a report which looked into the pros and cons of signing up, and on balance, after eleven pages, considered that it was a good idea. Nevertheless, just in case anyone might accuse the government of a certain rashness here, Defra's website is anxious to reassure: 'Signing the Convention commits the UK to honour the obligations set out in the text. However, the Council of Europe has no legal powers over the UK and could not apply any set of international sanctions if the UK failed to meet its obligations. Council of Europe Conventions depend for their effectiveness on the compliance of the member states and domestic scrutiny.'

So let's offer a little domestic scrutiny. Work on landscape issues in England has been undertaken in recent years by the Countryside Agency, passing in 2006 under the remit of the new body, Natural England, and although it may not have been particularly high profile some of this work is to be commended. I particularly liked a little pamphlet which came my way, entitled *Landscape: Beyond the View* and produced by the Countryside Agency in 2006, which seemed fully attuned to the thinking behind the Convention: 'The interaction of natural components and cultural patterns creates the rich diversity of England's landscapes, with their own distinctive features and sense of place. Landscape is a human concept and as such encompasses how we view the land; how we hear, smell and feel our surroundings; and the feelings, memories or associations that they evoke. In short, people's perceptions turn land into landscape,' it said. And then: 'Landscapes are not static; their constant evolution is a result of changing natural processes, as well as the changing needs of our society.'

One major piece of work undertaken by the Countryside Agency/Natural England has been the mapping of the whole of England into distinctive landscape areas, which have been given the name of Character Areas. In total, there are more than 150 of these, ranging from number 1 (North Northumberland Coastal Plain) to 159, which has been allocated just to the little Bristol Channel island of Lundy. As part of this work some rather cheerful maps of the country are now available, showing all these Character Areas in sets of bright colours. As far as our journey along the Pennine watershed is concerned, there are four landscape Character Areas identified: the Dark Peak, the southern Pennines, the Yorkshire Dales and – coming in a few chapters' time – the North Pennines. The watershed also dips briefly into a fifth Character Area ('Lancashire Valleys') around Earby and Barnoldswick.

Accompanying this work are detailed published accounts of each Character Area's features. For the Yorkshire Dales, for example, thirteen key attributes are identified, which include 'Striking contrasts between wild, remote moors and sheltered dales, each with its own distinctive character', 'Visible evidence of historic land use arising from conservation of features from all periods' and 'Widespread remains of historic mineral working, especially lead mining'.

You might say that Landscape Character Assessment, the name given to what is rapidly becoming a new mini-industry with its own network of professional practitioners and academics, is little more than codified common sense. But if landscape is to be planned for, managed and protected as the European Convention requires, then it seems to be necessary to work out exactly what is distinctive about each area. Furthermore, on the basic foundation of England's 159 Character Areas can be built other initiatives: for example, in several parts of the country parish councils and local community organisations are being encouraged to undertake smaller-scale landscape character assessments for their own particular areas. This research can be linked to other issues as well: one recent piece of work identifies 123 specialist 'locality foods' in England which have a particular relationship with the parts of the country where they are produced.

Landscape, as the European Convention stresses, is a dynamic rather than a static concept, changing as social and economic factors change. For regions such as the Yorkshire Dales, which agriculturally-speaking are classified as Severely Disadvantaged Areas, this raises the implications for the landscape of current and future changes in agriculture.

We've seen already that there are potentially difficult times ahead for traditional hill farming in England which without continuing public support is highly unlikely to be commercially viable. The hill farming debate in recent years has led some people to raise the prospect of what is called 'rewilding' of the countryside. Rewilding is already a feature of the countryside in some parts of Europe, where it is associated with a shift from rural to urban areas. Is this a likely prospect for Pennine areas in Britain?

In reality, land reclamation and abandonment has historically been a cyclical feature in relation to land at the edges of the main moors. Ian Simmons, in his historical study of the English and Welsh moorlands, talks of a central core of unimproved moor which may have

The emblem of the Yorkshire Dales national park is a curly-horned Swaledale ram.

been cultivated in prehistoric times or marginally in medieval times but which had laid unimproved for several centuries before 1800. He writes: 'During the years 1800–2000, some of this core may have been converted to farmland and stayed that way; some of that land may subsequently have reverted to moorland, yet a small proportion may have been taken in again. This may have happened (exceptionally, it must be stressed) up to four times.'

So there is nothing necessarily new about some land given over to agriculture reverting back to moorland vegetation, or the boundary of improved land being subject to a process of ebbing and flowing over the years. But talk today of rewilding means something rather more that this: it could mean a significant shift in the way that the upland landscape looks.

Initially the idea of rewilding sounds very appealing, relating back to those ideas we have of wilderness and 'natural' landscapes which we explored in relation to the Brontë moors. But farmers tend to argue that rewilding is just a polite word to describe land abandonment, a term which frankly is much less attractive. They maintain that a landscape which is not actively farmed will rapidly go, almost literally, to seed.

I talked to David Airey briefly about this when we met at his farm near Cowling. He was concerned about the risks of leaving land unattended for a period of time. 'Gaps can start in walls which I can put right in an afternoon, but if you leave it for twenty years the whole wall falls down,' he pointed out. 'At the moment if a field drain breaks I go and repair it. If you go away and let it rewild, eventually the drains will fail, and it costs thousands of pounds to drain a five-acre field.'

Rewilding would be likely to mean, therefore, the eventual removal of aspects of the rural landscape such as dry-stone walls which are linked to current farming practice. It

An isolated farm between Stainforth and Malham, against a backdrop of Malham Moor.

would also have implications for vegetation. Ultimately, it would mean more land would be likely to become forested, or at least scrubby woodland, and in the shorter term it might mean more areas of bracken. This is not necessarily what the public wants when it heads off to the Yorkshire Dales.

But talk of rewilding may be misleading. Agricultural land prices in upland areas have in general stayed buoyant, suggesting that there is still a general confidence that farming will continue. If traditional hill farms do disappear, farmers say, what's rather more likely to take their place are much larger operations who engage in large ranch-style livestock farming: thousands of sheep on many thousands of acres.

So what sort of landscape do people want for the Dales, and – perhaps more to the point – how much public money should be put into achieving it? These were the questions tackled by two academics from the University of Newcastle, in a study which although it took place back in 1990 still seems relevant today. Their research involved interviewing 300 Yorkshire Dales residents and 300 visitors to the national park, accosted at visitor car parks in Malham, Kettlewell and Grassington. In each case, they were asked to look at pictures of eight possible future Dales landscapes and asked to say which they preferred. One option, for example, was the 'abandoned' scenario, another a deliberately created 'wild' landscape and a third that associated with intensive ranch-style agriculture. And there were other choices: one possibility was described as a 'conserved' landscape, where efforts would be taken to ensure, for example, that there were more hay meadows and that new broadleaved woodlands were planted. Another option was simply the continuation of today's Dales landscape.

People are, it seems, a conservative lot when it comes to landscape matters, for the first choice of around half the people surveyed, both Dales residents and visitors, was for the existing landscape to be maintained. A further 30 per cent or so preferred the 'conserved landscape' option. Only about 2–3 per cent plumped for an 'abandoned' landscape as their first choice, and absolutely nobody chose the intensive agriculture option.

These results are perhaps what you might expect. But the survey went further, using a scientific model to try to put a monetary tag on different landscape preferences, by finding in each case people's 'willingness to pay' value. *How much*, in other words, do we really value wild flower meadows or broadleaved woodland or dry-stone walls? According to the survey (and using 1990 prices), visitors thought that their preferred landscape was worth about £27 a year, while local people gave a figure of about £25 a year. This doesn't mean that these are the amounts that could actually be deducted directly from taxes, or at a toll booth at the entry to the Dales. But exercises like this do help the government and public agencies decide whether the large public subsidies being put into agriculture and countryside preservation are being spent in accordance with people's broad wishes. The research study suggested that they were: 'The benefits of some form of intervention to maintain today's landscape, or even spending more public money to create a conserved landscape, outweigh the benefits to be generated if government subsidies were withdrawn and an abandoned, sporting or wild landscape developed,' the researchers wrote.

That seems reassuring. But nevertheless landscapes do change, sometimes quite strikingly, over time and it could just be that we become so familiar with the way things look today that we decide that we prefer this to any other alternative. Some people think we should be more welcoming of change: 'perhaps we need to challenge the inherent conservatism that seems to be apparent . . . and encourage both professionals and public alike to be more willing to think the previously unthinkable', one leading landscape academic suggested recently.

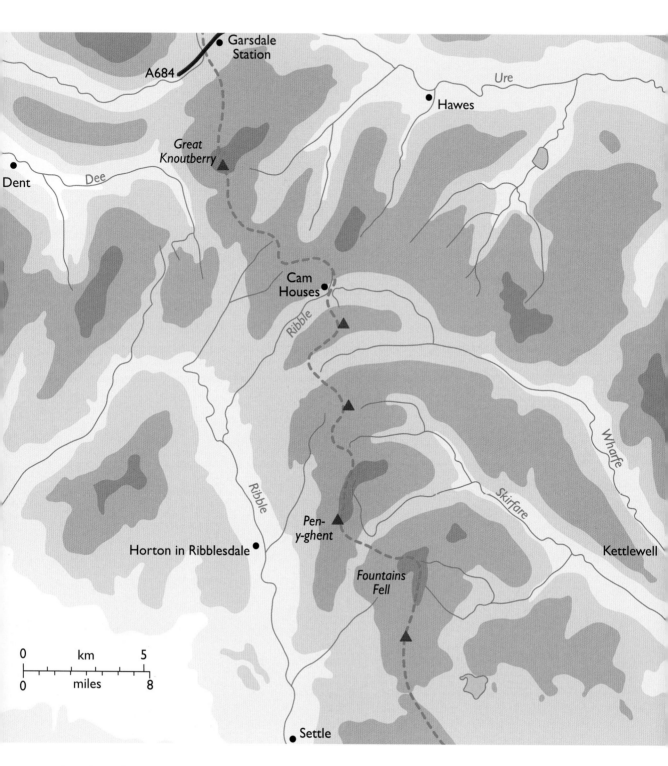

15. PEN-Y-GHENT

Fountains Fell – Pen-y-ghent – Plover Hill – Green Haw Moor – Cam Rakes

Whernside, Ingleborough and Pen-y-ghent collectively comprise Yorkshire's Three Peaks. Whernside is the highest at 2419 feet (736 m), Ingleborough a touch lower, and Pen-y-ghent a little lower still. So it is perhaps perverse of the Pennine watershed that, of the Three Peaks, only Pen-y-ghent lies on its route.

From the crossing of the A65 trunk road at Hellifield and our entry into the Yorkshire Dales national park onwards, we have been climbing steadily. One by one, the trig points can be marked off, each higher than the last: Newton Moor Top, Rye Loaf Hill, and then Fountains Fell, the hillside taking its name from Fountains Abbey which prior to the dissolution of the monasteries was the landowner here. After Fountains Fell, there's a short drop down into Silverdale before the stiff climb up Pen-y-ghent.

Pen-y-ghent's rugged profile is a distinctive landmark. Over the years its name has attracted a variety of spellings and these days there's still an element of discretion about what you do about the hyphens: Wainwright in his usual opinionated way was strongly against them ('hyphens here, as elsewhere, are an irritation') but on the other hand the hyphens seem to better reflect modern Welsh orthography and to remind us that the name is a legacy of the days when Celtic people populated the Dales.

There are two Pen-y-ghent mountains in Britain, the other (in the Scottish borders south-west of the town of Hawick) admittedly carrying the variant spelling Pennygant. The 'pen' part of the name is straightforward, meaning a head or top in both medieval and

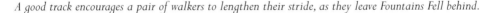

A good track encourages a pair of walkers to lengthen their stride, as they leave Fountains Fell behind.

The profile of Pen-y-ghent: one of the most distinctive landmarks in the Yorkshire Dales.

modern Welsh. The 'ghent' part of the name ('y' being simply the definite article) is more obscure. One possible recent suggestion is that is may mean 'edge' or 'border', which might mean that Pen-y-ghent some time in the deep past marked the boundary between two tribal or political areas.

Pen-y-ghent may be junior to Yorkshire's other two Three Peaks in terms of height but at 2273 feet (694 m) it's the highest ground yet encountered on the backbone of England. And one of the busiest, in terms of footfall. The Pennine Way – very briefly – rejoins the watershed here, so that any through-walkers from Edale to Kirk Yetholm will be coming this way.

The Three Peaks themselves make up a much loved Dales circuit for walkers. Tackling the Three Peaks involves a twenty-four mile walk with about 4,500 feet of climbing. If you complete it within twelve hours, you become eligible to join the Three Peaks of Yorkshire Club, and can if you so wish buy the badge. To be admitted, however, you have to notify the café in Horton-in-Ribblesdale when you leave and have to clock in again as you arrive back (when I first walked the Three Peaks with friends several years back we apparently failed to leave all the necessary information when we started out and were disqualified). Or you can run the Three Peaks, every spring when the annual fell race is being held. This is one of the classic northern English fell races, run regularly since 1954 and attracting some of fell-running's best athletes (the course record is currently just over two hours forty-six minutes).

Or, of course, you can just scramble to the top of Pen-y-ghent from Horton and stroll back down, taking as long as you like. One of the most striking statistics to emerge from the latest government survey of our leisure time activities is just how important walking is for so many people. For example, of the forty-two million or so leisure visits made each year to England's national parks, more than half are made for the main purpose of going for a walk. The opportunity to have a walk (and walking here includes everything from strolls to hill walks) is far and away the most important factor when it comes to deciding to make for a national park, far more important than anything else (the next four reasons reported, to eat/drink, to go for a drive, to play sport or to visit an attraction, even taken together, are much less significant as motivating factors). For the Yorkshire Dales area itself, the National Park Authority says that 81 per cent of its visitors go walking.

When you visit the countryside to go for a walk you may feel as though you are just, well, doing that. But economists know that you are also participating in the tourism industry, and analyses of the economy point to the overall significance which tourism plays, particularly in country areas. The Lake District national park has estimated that 48 per cent of the employment within the national park area is associated with tourism (agriculture by contrast was responsible for 1 per cent). In the Dales, one early survey pointed to tourism supporting the equivalent of 1,000 full-time jobs in the national park and perhaps another 250 outside. Tourism is a multi-billion pound sector: for England as a whole, the latest comprehensive government survey suggests that 'tourism visits' are worth approximately £48 billion, though admittedly the term is used broadly to describe any leisure trip lasting more than three hours.

Tourism brings benefits but also disadvantages. The Dales National Park Authority talks of its 'difficult role' in balancing its legal duties of conserving the special qualities of the area and of promoting opportunities for the public to understand and enjoy the country-side: 'while the benefits of tourism to the area are obvious, unchecked growth in visitor numbers could place the special character of the Dales at risk and destroy those things that make it such a desirable place to spend time,' it says.

You could say the same much more specifically about the pressures brought to the most popular paths by walkers' feet. As Peter McGrory's survey of footpaths in Peak District made clear, pressure from walkers can leave some footpaths needing remedial work, and this has been the case in the Three Peaks area as well.

Except when path repair work has been undertaken in a particularly unsympathetic fashion, walkers are often oblivious of the work which has been undertaken on their behalf. Over the past few decades, the skills of repairing upland paths have been slowly acquired and shared – or perhaps reacquired, for particularly in the southern Pennines there is a legacy of earlier path-building left behind in the paved causey paths across the moors, originally built for the packhorse trains carrying cloth and goods. The modern story of footpath construction and repair goes back to the 1960s, when it started becoming increasingly obvious that some footpaths (including the peatier sections of the Pennine Way) were becoming loved to death. Over a period of just ten years, some popular paths had quadrupled their width, particularly where the ground was boggy and walkers were taking ever-wider diversions to try to stay on solid ground. In the Lake District and other mountainous areas, there were problems of soil washout and rock slip where paths went across scree slopes.

But at that stage footpath erosion hadn't yet been recognised as an issue needing management attention or budgeting, and in any case no-one really had a clear idea of what to do about the problem anyway. The first modern attempt to tackle path erosion was, it's said, the determined efforts made by two National Trust wardens in Langdale in the Lake District in 1970, but it was the coming of the job creation programmes associated with the Manpower Services Commission in the 1980s which helped build up the body of expertise which now exists in relation to upland footpath repair.

What you can do depends on what sort of ground your path is covering, with peat probably the biggest challenge. With peaty ground, there are now reckoned to be three techniques you can try. For example, you can copy the causey paths put down in earlier centuries by using large flagstones, laid so that each abuts on to the next. This is the technique which has been used on Black Hill and in several areas of the South Pennines where the Pennine Way crosses blanket bog. There is a pleasing element of recycling involved, since many of the flags which now line the Pennine Way were taken from old mills in the Manchester area which were derelict and being demolished. Laying flags has advantages: it's relatively easy to put the path down, it's a durable solution, and it requires relatively little maintenance. Except in very wet areas, the flags can be put straight down on the vegetation. But there are disadvantages, too: one is that lines of flags can look offputtingly uniform. Flagstones are considered appropriate only in Pennine districts, particularly the southern Pennines, and look out of character in other parts of the country.

A second alternative is to create what's called a floated aggregate path. Here you create a shallow trench lined with a layer of geotextile matting, the matting helping to prevent parts of the path sinking into the peat by spreading the pressure over a wider area. On to the matting goes a coarse base of aggregate, with smaller stones put on the top. This solution can be effective, though once again there are snags. One is the fact that the end result can look unpleasantly like a road if it's not been constructed with sensitivity. Another is that creating aggregate paths is labour-intensive, and that the aggregate needs regular renewing.

You can also choose the technique called soil inversion or soil reorganisation (or, sometimes, Hymac, taken from the brand name of the excavator often used). This idea was developed in the late 1980s and has been used widely since then, including in the Three Peaks area. It involves excavating peat along the line of a path right down to the mineral soil below (if necessary, several metres down), and then swapping the layers of peat and minerals around so that the mineral soil ends up on top of the peat.

In mountainous areas or places where paths have steep gradients, there's a fourth alternative, and that is to use stone pitching. This is an old technique which has been brought back into use in recent years: stones are laid in a random manner, so that a series of irregular steps are created which – hopefully – blend into the landscape and don't look like a uniform set of stairs. The recommended approach is to use stones which are gathered on or near by the site, so as not to bring in anything alien to the local geology.

In the Three Peaks area all these techniques, and a few others as well, have been put to the test. By the mid-1980s the National Park Authority recognised that path erosion had become a major problem; for example both the northern and southern approaches to Pen-y-ghent on the Pennine Way and the main route from Ribblehead on to Whernside were becoming badly worn. In 1987 it launched the Three Peaks Project, a practical five-year initiative to try to rectify things.

The Pennine Way up to Pen-y-ghent is a case study in how different techniques can be chosen for different terrain. The short stretch of track from the Silverdale road to Dale

Head is a traditional farm track, but beyond this is a section which was constructed using black limestone aggregate placed on a geotextile mat. On the steep final approach to Pen-y-ghent stone pitching has been used, while on the summit area and beyond, on the Pennine Way descent to Horton by Hunt Pot, the path is made from soil inversion (a 'Hymac' path).

The watershed goes a different way from Pen-y-ghent summit, however, carrying on to the north to nearby Plover Hill, then down to the col between Foxup Beck and Swarth Gill Sike, and up again to the trig point on the hillside known as Cosh Outside. Much of this ground has only become open to walkers with the introduction of open access and so far not many people, it seems, are taking up their new-found rights here. Even on days when Pen-y-ghent is packed with visitors, the crowds can quickly be left behind. Whatever time of year you come, this area of the Dales will almost certainly be quiet.

Duckboards on the route to Pen-y-ghent help walkers to negotiate a boggy stretch.

16. CAM HIGH ROAD AND BEYOND

Cam Rakes – Cam High Road – Widdale Head – Arten Gill Moss – Great Knoutberry

The infant streams of two major rivers share the watershed close to the high Dales hamlet of Cam Houses. One is the Ribble, Lancashire's river, which will eventually join the Irish Sea beyond Preston. The other is the Wharfe, destined to traverse a large swathe of North Yorkshire until – having joined the Yorkshire Ouse – it ends its days in the Humber estuary. In watershed terms, therefore, this hillside is significant.

In all other respects, however, Cam is – if a water metaphor can be used without incongruity – well out of the mainstream. Even when there was a settlement here (there were, reportedly, thirteen households at the end of the eighteenth century), Cam Houses was known as one of the most remote farming communities in the Dales. The place was frequently snowed up for several weeks in winter and families would make sure they had enough oatmeal stored to tide them through.

Today most of the cottages have gone, though there's still the opportunity for walkers coming this way on the Pennine Way or the Dales Way to stop for bed and breakfast at Camm Farm (two 'm's: there seems to be a certain flexibility about spelling hereabouts). The Dales Way passes the front door while the Pennine Way – crossing the watershed on its way from Horton to Hawes – is at this point just up the hillside, following what's known as the Cam High Road. As even a cursory glance at the map shows, Cam High Road was originally a Roman road. Its route can be traced, as a series of almost straight alignments in one direction to the Wensleydale town of Bainbridge (Roman Virosidum), where the Romans constructed a fort. In the other direction, the line the Roman road engineers chose is equally easy to follow, down through Chapel le-Dale to Ingleton. Beyond that, the line is less clear-cut but the ultimate destination seems to have been Lancaster.

So there is considerable history at Cam, which might help to explain the ghosts. Local writers Ella Pontefract and Marie Hartley in their 1938 book *Wharfedale* tell of two ghosts associated with the place, one that of a noisy but apparently friendly 'owd joiner' who could sometimes be heard at work hammering in one of the house. The other ghostly presence, according to the authors' account, seems to have been less well-motivated:

> A furry animal something like a dog, and known as Jerry, used to haunt the path from the Roman road. If a man was riding, his horse generally saw it first, and would shy off the path, and as often as it was driven back it would shy again, though a Cam man seldom tried the path more than once. He would make a wide detour if he knew the ghost was about, struggling frantically through bogs and peat, and often leaving his horse to its fate.

A sheep poses obligingly near Cam Houses, against the silhouette of Pen-y-ghent

It is to be hoped that Jerry has decided to move on, for many more horse riders are likely to be coming this way in the years ahead. The route of the Pennine Bridleway, the latest official National Trail and the only one designed specifically for riders and cyclists to enjoy, comes along Cam High Road from the south to Cold Keld Gate, where it turns westwards, following close to the watershed for the next four miles or so.

Tom Stephenson has already been given credit earlier in this book for the idea of the Pennine Way, so it's only fair to tell at this point the story of Mary Towneley, the woman whose vision led to the realisation of the Pennine Bridleway fifty years and more later. Both shared the determination to ensure that their ideas were taken up by the authorities and brought into being. In almost every other way, however, they were poles apart. Tom Stephenson, as we've seen, came from a Lancashire working class background and as a young man became active nationally in the Labour Party. Mary Towneley was from the upper classes (she was born into the Derbyshire family of Fitzherbert). As a young woman she became the wife of Simon

The Pennine Way, going north from Cam Fell, looking ahead to Garsdale.

Towneley, later Sir Simon Towneley and Lord Lieutenant of Lancashire, with whom she was eventually to have seven children, six daughters and a son.

The Towneleys were until the nineteenth century one of the foremost landowning families in central Lancashire, with holdings in Burnley and Bowland (as well as an estate in County Durham) and with the large country house Towneley Hall just outside Burnley. A dearth of male heirs, however, led to the Towneley estates being split in the late 1880s between different sides of the family and in 1901 Towneley Hall itself was sold to Burnley council; the house and parkland is now open to the public. One part of the Towneley lands, the Worsthorne estate, became in the 1920s the property of the daughter of the Earl of Abingdon and Caroline Towneley, and it was this which passed to her grandson Simon Towneley Worsthorne in 1952. Simon assumed the Towneley surname in 1955 by royal licence.

By her marriage, therefore, Mary moved from one distinguished surname to another (she also incidentally acquired the journalist Peregrine Worsthorne as a brother-in-law). She was, in the words of her daughter Cosima Towneley, 'an experienced organiser, consummate horse-woman and dogged promoter of countryside access but above all a visionary'. As a horse rider living in the South Pennines close to Burnley she was in the heart of the area crossed by old packhorse trails and causey paths. Frustratingly for her, however, the majority of these were no longer easily available for riders to use: many routes once used by horses had been classified as footpaths rather than bridleways when definitive maps for rights of way were originally drawn up, and others had fallen off the rights of way maps altogether.

Further afield, in the Yorkshire Dales, North Pennines and the Peak District, it was a similar story so that, while walkers wanting a challenge could tackle the Pennine Way, horse riders looking for long-distance routes had to piece together short stretches of bridleway as best they could, or take the risk of traffic on roads. And yet, as Mary Towneley knew, once there had been networks of droving lanes across the uplands of northern England, used by drovers bringing cattle south from Scotland.

By the middle of the 1980s her efforts to encourage the authorities to do more to improve the bridleway network seemed to be bearing little fruit and it was time for a change of tactics: 'I would research, and if possible prove by riding, that a continuous linkage of old drove and driftways still existed down the Pennine spine of England,' she wrote later. Mary Towneley found inspiration in the tales of early travellers Celia Fiennes and Daniel Defoe, and in the diaries of the formidable Lady Anne Clifford, who in the later seventeenth century regularly journeyed across country between the castles she owned in Westmorland and Yorkshire. Because of her background, Mary Towneley was also able to gain access to private estate records, helping her in her researches.

The project took over the house. 'Tables disappeared under the weight of books on drove roads, packhorse trails, byway and highways, and maps which took over so many walls of the house that we began to look like an outward bound centre,' recalls Cosima. But by 1986 Mary Towneley had successfully worked out what she called a 'fragile chain' from Hexham in Northumberland to Ashbourne in Derbyshire. It was time to test the route in practice.

She was accompanied on this journey by two horse riding friends, while a third provided necessary back-up by car, with a horsebox in tow. They began in September 1986, making their way from Hexham across the moors to Nenthead and then across an old bridleway known as the Tynehead Road to Great Dun Fell. The Tynehead Road, she was told at the time, had probably not been ridden for the best part of a hundred years: 'We picked our way with difficulty and considerable anxiety between the crumbling banks, hock high in the fast flowing stream, up the boulder strewn bed of a small tributary to the great Tyne itself until a final steep haul brought us to the summit of Great Dun Fell. There, spread beneath us like the promised land and flooded with light lay the Eden Valley.'

On the third day there was a set-back: Mary was riding a young pony when somewhere in Cumbria rider and mount fell victim to 'a deep, black peat bog': 'Although we extracted ourselves from its greedy embrace without serious damage it knocked the stuffing out of the young fellow. The days were long and hard and the going tough so I made a quick overnight exchange for our faithful cob, Bambino.'

Mary, Bambino, and her two friends on their own horses pressed on into the Dales, coming into Hawes along the High Way, an old road once ridden by Lady Anne Clifford, and then south along the Cam High Way into Wharfedale. The going became a little easier. Day by day, they pressed on, eventually arriving in Ashbourne after nine days' riding. They had completed, they reckoned, 249½ miles.

The ride, however, was simply a means to an end, the end being Mary Towneley's determination to see a Pennine Bridleway actually brought into being. Fortunately the Countryside Commission, as it then was, quickly took up Mary's idea. An early feasibility study in 1987–8 led to a comprehensive consultation report in 1990 which included detailed proposals for the line of the route, at this stage envisaged from Hexham to Wirksworth in Derbyshire. But there were also problems, most notably in Cumbria and Northumberland, where objections from local residents as well as opposition on nature conservancy grounds saw the original line challenged.

When government approval for the Pennine Bridleway was given in 1995, it was only for the southern section from Derbyshire to Kirkby Stephen. The so-called northern extension later got the green light in 2002, but with a much changed route: instead of Hexham, the

The view to the north, from the Coal Road linking Dentdale and Garsdale, with Wild Boar Fell in the distance.

northern destination of the Pennine Bridleway was changed to Byrness near Otterburn, increasingly the overall length to around 350 miles. However, government approval is only one part of the process, because funding also has to be secured. An £1.8 million lottery grant in 1999 from Sport England enabled the route to be developed to Kirkby Stephen, but funding for the northern section is still, at time of writing, being pieced together. Horse riders and cyclists planning the full journey to Byrness may have to be a little patient.

To open a new national trail like the Pennine Bridleway requires two sorts of work to be undertaken. There is the work which has to be done on the ground, ensuring that an firm track is laid down even in wet areas of moorland, with the track wide enough, where possible, for two horses to travel side by side. But long before the contractors are called in, there is first the necessary legal work to be put in hand. The whole Pennine Bridleway project, when it is completed, will have involved the creation of about 130 miles of new bridleway, sometimes achieved by reclassifying existing footpaths but also in places brought about by creating brand new rights of way. One example of the latter is the mile or so from the Cam High Road just north of Cam Houses westwards to Gavel Gap, where the Bridleway follows the line of a path which previously existed on the ground but which was not a recognised footpath. The plans for the Bridleway south-west of Cam Houses required an even more ambitious outcome: the creation of a new stretch of bridleway across Far Moor and a new single span bridge over the Ribble.

The legal preparations for the Pennine Bridleway have also involved negotiating with, and paying compensation to, the landowners whose land is being crossed by the route. This sort of work is not always plain sailing. When both sides are happy, the outcome is what is known as a Creation Agreement; if negotiations break down however (and they did in a number of places in this part of the Dales, when landowners disputed the amount of compensation being offered), compulsory Creation Orders are the last resort.

It took thirty years from Tom Stephenson's original article about the Pennine Way before the route was formally opened and it may ultimately take a similar period of time before Mary

Great Knoutberry Hill dominates the eastern end of Dentdale.

Towneley's dream, the Pennine Bridleway, is finally completed. Sadly Mary herself will not be there to enjoy it: she died in February 2001. By the time of her death, however, she knew that her 1986 ride had been the success she had hoped. Appropriately enough the first section of the Bridleway, a 47-mile loop through the South Pennines countryside near her home which was opened in 2002, carries her name.

Beyond Cam High Road, the watershed has been making its way steadily northwards, with the Pennine Bridleway tagging along close at hand. Until the local government reorganisation of 1974, the watershed here marked the border between Yorkshire's West Riding and the North Riding, and there's a reminder of this history in the old county boundary stone still in place beside the Hawes to Ribblehead road at Widdale Head. The West Riding was an astonishingly sprawling territory, stretching down beyond Sheffield to the edge of Sherwood Forest, and Widdale Head was not even the furthest point north, for Sedbergh and the southern half of the Howgill Fells, now in Cumbria, also formed part of the county.

The Pennine Bridleway finally decides to make its own way north at Arten Gill Moss, leaving the watershed to head straight for the top of Great Knoutberry. The hill gets its name from the cloudberry plant which, although associated particularly with the semi-arctic areas of northern Scandinavia, can also be found in Pennine blanket bogs, its little yellow-orange berries a special sight in summer.

Here's a place which seems hardly troubled by walkers, who are perhaps all busy walking up Pen-y-ghent instead – a shame for, weather permitting of course, the hill offers great views. Directly to the west the whole of Dentdale lies spread out like a long green ribbon, while just to the north the parallel valley of Garsdale comes peeking into view. To the south are the Three Peaks with, even further to the south, Pendle hill while over to the north-east lies Wensleydale and Great Shunner Fell beyond. But it is the view to the north which is perhaps the best of all, with the distinctively craggy profile of Wild Boar Fell dominating the valley of Mallerstang. This is the way ahead.

17. NORTH OF GREAT KNOUTBERRY

Great Knoutberry – Garsdale Station

Many miles back, while I was talking of the burnt acres of Emmott Moor, I discussed the ways that the heather moorlands are managed to provide a better habitat for red grouse. I commented on the fact that most of the Pennine upland moors come with shooting rights attached. I pointed out the implications for the landscape. But grouse shooting is a significant feature of the moors and it is time to take another pop at the subject.

Nick Parker offered to talk to me about his job. Nick is the head gamekeeper for the Mossdale estate and therefore responsible for 5,000 acres of moorland, rising up to well over 2,000 feet above sea level, between Great Knoutberry Hill and the upper Wensleydale valley. This means that for Nick the Pennine watershed and the land surrounding it are his place of work.

I'm aware that up to now gamekeepers have played only a minor role in this narrative, and when they have appeared at all, as in the account of the Kinder Scout trespass, they have tended to be cast as the villain of the piece, guarding the countryside on behalf of their masters. Even more than seventy-five years on from Kinder, there is still a deal of mutual suspicion between keepers and walkers and I'm fairly sure that Benny Rothman, were he still alive, would not be Nick Parker's best friend. I'm also conscious that many people, walkers or not, find the idea of shooting wild birds for sport anathema.

But it also has to be said that gamekeepers have a unique knowledge of the moors they look after and anyone who wants a better understanding of the Pennine countryside needs to take their experience into account. So I appreciated the fact that Nick was prepared to spend a morning of his time showing me round his moors and describing to me a little of the work he does.

When I met him, Nick was approaching the end of his fifth season at Mossdale. He is in his late thirties, comes originally from Hertfordshire and still speaks with a southern accent which isn't necessarily what you are expecting of a gamekeeper in Yorkshire. In fact, Nick's career as a gamekeeper has involved a number of moves around the country, building up expertise in very different types of terrain. Before moving to upper Wensleydale, he worked for several years on the Isle of Bute in Scotland, on an estate where deer were as important as grouse. He started, however, close to his home, on a low-ground estate where partridge and pheasant were the game to be looked after.

It is clearly a job he has always loved. He describes how, when he was about eleven, he started helping out the keepers on a nearby country estate, turning up on weekends and holidays to see what he could do. After he left school, he started what amounted to an informal apprenticeship in gamekeeping, learning his skills on the job by shadowing the more experi-

Nick Parker, head gamekeeper for the 5,000 acres that comprise the Mossdale estate.

enced keepers as they went about their work. While these days you can study gamekeeping at some agricultural colleges, Nick thinks the old way of learning on the job is the best.

With his move to Yorkshire, Nick has taken on the task of keeping an estate which – although a few fields lower down are reserved for pheasants – is primarily managed for red grouse. Gamekeepers like Nick have one overarching objective which influences everything they do, and that is to maximise the number of grouse which are up on the moors when the shooting season begins each year on 12th August. A good year for Nick will see his 5,000 acres produce a harvest of over 2,000 grouse (or, following the shooting convention as we probably should, more than a thousand brace: one brace, two birds). A poor year may mean that no grouse shooting at all can take place.

Grouse, in other words, can be unpredictable. The glory-days for grouse shooting (glory, that is, for those wielding the guns, if not for the grouse themselves) were back in the early twentieth century. The record for the most birds taken during a single day's shoot is held by the Abbeystead estate in the Forest of Bowland in August 1915 when 1464½ brace of birds were brought down by a party of eight 'guns'. More than 2,950 brace were shot during the first three days of shooting at Abbeystead that year. Another peak was in the 1930s, but there have also been lean periods when the bags were right down. What is clear is that there appears

Nick Parker retrieves a stoat from one of his traps.

to be a natural cyclical trend to grouse numbers, which in the north of England tends to come round about every four years.

To an extent, keepers have to accept this cycle as just the way nature does things. But only to an extent. Because of the importance of grouse shooting, there is now a very considerable body of scientific knowledge about the life-cycle of this bird, and from this research – as well as from generations of trial and error by gamekeepers on the hills – come the measures which Nick Parker and his fellow keepers try to put into practice on their estates.

Given that red grouse are likely to be a familiar companion to anyone exploring the Pennine moors, I think at this point it could be appropriate to say a little more about the general state of health of the birds, and in particular to probe into the subject of the red grouse's guts (sensitive readers please skip the next few paragraphs). Grouse have a real problem with a parasitic intestinal threadworm called *Trichostrongylosis tenuis* or, more simply, the strongyle worm. These worms live and mate inside the part of the gut known as the caeca, with the female worm producing more than 100 eggs a day. The eggs are then excreted, hatch and turn into minute larvae, which eventually make their way up to the growing tips of heather plants. The heather tips, complete with larvae, are eaten by grouse, the larvae passing down into the gut where they develop into adult worms. At this point the cycle starts over again. This cycle, incidentally, may take no more than two weeks to complete.

This means that there are a lot of strongyle worms about. A healthy bird may have a few hundred inside it. Beyond about 3,000 worms, the bird's digestive system begins to be affected and its general state of health starts to decline. Birds suffering from high 'worm burden' can be found sitting in heather, unable to get up and fly away when disturbed and dead birds may be seen particularly near streams, having been too weak to escape. At the extreme, a single grouse may be carrying over 30,000 worms.

(How do we know? We know because estates are encouraged by the Game Conservancy Trust to carry out spot checks of the guts of freshly shot grouse. This involves using scissors to make an incision just above the bird's anus and reaching in with your fingers past the gizzard to find the two caeca. At this point, you carefully cut the caeca . . . but no, I think this is getting a little too specialised for a general book.)

As a grouse moor gamekeeper, your task would be to try to ensure that the parent birds are as healthy as possible in the run-up to the nesting season. You have two weapons in your armoury. One is to place at regular intervals around your heather moors little heaps of grit medicated with a chemical called fenbendazole which kills the worm eggs. Small piles of quartz grit have been left by gamekeepers on heather moors for many years, since grouse naturally try to look for grit which they can ingest to help their digestive processes; the idea of medicating this grit developed in the 1980s and has since become widely used. Nick Parker says he gets through two tons a year, each ton costing about £1,200. The grit is placed in specially constructed grit trays which he cleans out and refills every autumn and then tops up a second time in the spring.

The second way of deworming your grouse is to slip a dose of medicine straight down their throats. First, of course, you have to catch the birds and you do this at night by 'lamping' them. A dark night is best, one with no moon, which means of course that gamekeepers can become almost as familiar with their moors at night as by day. You temporarily paralyse the grouse by shining a bright light at their eyes, catch them in a net and as quickly as possible carry out the dosing before releasing them. The basic idea is to quarter the moors as systematically as possible, looking for the give-away light from the grouse's eyes shining back at you. If you're efficient and know your trade, you should be able to lamp up to ten grouse in an hour.

A recent study from the Game Conservancy Trust seems to demonstrate pretty conclusively that this work is worthwhile: estates which dosed grouse and also put down medicated grit had consistently higher numbers of grouse available later in the year for shooting. But unfortunately *Trichostrongylosis tenuis* is only one of the things ready to cause grouse harm; another is *Ixodes ricinus*, the sheep tick. Sheep ticks have been in Britain for eight hundred years and have been on the heather uplands probably since the nineteenth century. The ticks transmit a viral disease known as louping ill which mainly affects sheep but which can hit other farm animals. Red grouse also catch louping ill, and if they do the effects are very serious: one study found that four in five chicks with the virus die. The best solution is to keep down the sheep tick population and this is done by vaccinating the sheep regularly. Some shooting estates pay sheep farmers to undertake extra dipping against ticks, and also engage in regular aerial spraying of bracken where the ticks have a tendency to lurk.

But trying to ensure that the grouse keep in good health is only one aspect of Nick Parker's work. Grouse, and particularly their chicks, make tasty meals for other creatures living up on the moors and this means that gamekeepers carry on an endless struggle to reduce the number of predators on the land they manage. Nick stopped the landrover in which we had been bouncing our way along one of the shooting tracks up towards the higher moors in order to show me the tunnel traps he had put down to catch stoats, rats and weasels. Traps like these operate a little like extra-large mousetraps, and the usual technique is to position them close to walls or field boundaries, half-buried under soil or turf. The theory is that the animals are looking for attractive and apparently safe runs which they can run into and out of, so that they aren't lingering unnecessarily in the open. It helps therefore to create an inviting entrance to the run in which the trap has been placed. Another strategy is to place traps on animal routes over streams, for example on little wooden boards.

Nick lifted the slate with which he had covered the trap to check whether it was occupied. This time it was empty. With a stick he demonstrated the trap's mechanism which snapped back noisily, and then, with care, he reset it. It was clear that this was not a place to get your fingers trapped.

Nick also aims to remove foxes from his estate, typically taking around eighty to a hundred each year. There are various ways you can catch foxes: you can lamp them at night in the same as grouse are lamped (the difference is that you don't release later), or you can wait for snowy days and follow their tracks back to their dens. You can also buy fox traps. But the technique widely used to catch foxes on grouse moors is to snare them. Fox snares are simple: a loop of wire roughly a foot wide and seven inches high which is attached by a swivel to the steel support anchored firmly in the ground.

We stopped the landrover again further up the hill, and Nick showed me the fox snare he had positioned just alongside an animal track. The loop hung just above the ground, ready to catch and hold the head of any fox careless enough to come this way. I looked at it glinting in the sunlight and wondered how many fox snares I'd passed so far on the watershed and failed to notice.

People think that the foxes are garrotted but that's not the way they work at all, Nick said. Instead, the snare swivels as the animal enters it, bringing it to a halt nine inches or so further down the track. The live animal is then held until Nick or his fellow gamekeeper visit, at which point it is dispatched with a shotgun. The law says that snares have to be checked at least once a day.

If you're trying to catch foxes, it helps to know where to put your snare and for this your skills as a gamekeeper are invaluable. You'll be looking out for fox tracks and for long fox-coloured red hairs caught on brambles or twigs. You may also be able to detect the strong musty fox smell, which suggests that a fox frequents the area. You'll also be concerned not to inadvertently snare other animals, although fox snares should be set in such a way that creatures such as deer can free themselves.

It's perfectly legal to trap or snare stoats, weasels and foxes in this way, and it's also legal to use cage traps to take certain birds which are deemed to be pests, including carrion and hooded crows, jackdaws and magpies. You can use a so-called Larsen trap, a small metal trap

The rounded contours of Widdale Fell, towards the western end of Wensleydale.

with two compartments, or you can use a much more substantial crow trap, which is roughly a cube about six feet in length and height made of metal grill, and with a funnel in the top through which the birds you are trying to trap come tumbling through.

To catch crows requires normally the use of a decoy bird. 'I keep a live crow as the decoy. It's fed and watered, and I keep it over the winter,' Nick says. It would be wrong to describe this in any sense as a pet, however; Nick says he finds crows 'horrible' birds. The decoy, which is placed in one of the chambers, attracts other crows towards it and these are caught and later destroyed.

It's the use of traps and snares, and particularly of large crow traps which are prominent objects on any moor, which can bring gamekeepers into conflict with the general public. Keepers complain that they regularly lose traps to theft and vandalism from people who don't like the idea of animals being caught but who, keepers feel, are ignorant of the reasoning behind the work they do. If keepers didn't kill foxes and stoats, Nick argues, it wouldn't only be grouse numbers which declined, it would be other moorland birds as well. And he recounts the time he found a couple with their son beside his crow trap, just about to release the decoy bird. 'I crept down and caught them red-handed. I told them what crows do – how they can

The Mossdale estate: green fields and traditional barns beneath the moors that echo to the call of the red grouse.

peck out the eyes of lambs. It's the only time I've bollocked someone and tried to educate them at the same time,' he says.

Nick Parker doesn't like the right to roam. He thinks that, since the land is privately owned, the landowner should be allowed his privacy, and he argues that the footpath network should be adequate for walkers. He's particularly annoyed at the problems which loose dogs can cause on grouse moors (though in fact dogs shouldn't be on his moors, since a dog exclusion order has been arranged using powers available to landowners under the Countryside and Rights of Way Act). But he also accepts that gamekeepers should perhaps try to explain the work they do a little more actively. Rural kids tend to understand, he tells me as later on we talk back in his house down in the valley, but maybe he should invite school parties from cities like Preston?

The start of the red grouse shooting season, 12th August, and the days of shooting which follow are the culmination of his year's activity. It is on his advice that the decision will be taken on how many days' shooting can take place. This advice will be based on his assessment of how many birds there are, and this in turn is based on the two counts he has organised, one in the spring before the nesting season and one in July. Pointers and spaniels are used for the counting, which involves several patient days spent quartering the moors. In choosing how many grouse to 'harvest', the aim is to maintain a sustainable and self-balancing population. Too many grouse left for the winter can actually be counter-productive by encouraging disease, he argues.

Nick Parker as head gamekeeper also runs the show during the days when shooting takes place, arranging to have enough people on the moors to act as beaters and flankers (normally this work goes to local lads) and, if there are plenty of birds, to be the loaders there to help the eight 'guns'. Typically, there will be five drives of grouse during a day's shooting, three before lunch and two in the afternoon. Luncheon is an important part of the day's proceedings, which is probably just as well because, unless you are the landowner's family or friends, you will be paying a substantial amount of money for your day out. Some shooting estates charge as much as £20,000 a day for a party of eight 'guns'. On Nick Parker's moors, the arrangement might be to pay for what you shoot: a typical bag for a party of eight could be about 100 brace of grouse, which are charged for at £120–£130 a brace.

In other words, we are talking serious money. Some estates are run primarily for their owners' pleasure, but some are intended to operate as profit-generating businesses. Either way, organisations which represent shooting interests argue that their sport contributes significantly to the rural economy. (One recent claim is that, in total, the whole shooting industry is worth £1.6 billion. When you look more closely, however, grouse shooting turns out to be a relatively small part of the whole picture, with an estimated 59,000 individual 'gun days' a year.) What isn't in doubt is the significance of shooting for upland land management and the landscape. Take gamekeepers like Nick Parker away and the appearance of the moorlands and the type of habitats the moors provide would be very different indeed.

Warcop

Brough

Eden

Kirkby
Stephen

Mallerstang

High
Seat

Garsdale
Station

Ure

A684

B6276

Great
Knipe

A66

High
Greygrits

Nine
Standards
Rigg

Swale

Keld

Greta

Bowes

0   km   5

0   miles   8

18. GARSDALE STATION

Garsdale Station – Grisedale Common – Aisgill Moor Cottages – Ure Head – Hugh Seat – Gregory Chapel – High Seat – High Pike – B6270 – Nine Standards Rigg

Leaving Great Knoutberry Hill (I marked the trig point there as number twenty-three since Mam Tor), the watershed heads firmly downhill and bumps into the Settle to Carlisle railway close to Garsdale station at Dandry Mire. This, it's clear, is a mire of some repute. It became notorious when the railway was being built in the early 1870s since each time the navvies tried to construct the embankment which the plans said would be crossing the ground here the material simply slid away into the bog below. Eventually the decision was taken: give up on the embankment, replace it instead with a viaduct. Make sure the foundations of the piers are dug down deep into the solid ground below.

You could say that the whole story of the Settle to Carlisle was one of triumph against the odds. In the history of railway building in Britain the line was a latecomer, constructed to enable the Midland railway to compete with its rival the London and North Western Railway on traffic north of the Border. As such, it was built to be an important main line, not simply a rural branch line serving local communities. However, it nearly wasn't built at all. The tale is that the Midland obtained the necessary Act of Parliament in 1866 because of its increasing frustration with the way the LNWR was preventing it getting access to Scotland. Journeys which might have begun at the company's magnificent architectural masterpiece of St Pancras, just in the process of being completed, petered out at Ingleton where the Midland met the LNWR line. Beyond here, despite its efforts, the Midland had been unable to negotiate the right to run its own trains.

So the plan to build a line between Settle and Carlisle, linking the Ribble and Eden valleys, was the Midland railway's solution to this problem. Or at least, this is what the company claimed – some railway historians suspect that the whole idea was an elaborate bluff devised by the Midland to bring the LNWR back to the negotiating table. If it was, the bluff worked very well for by 1868 the LNWR told the Midland that it was ready to agree terms for shared use of its lines beyond Ingleton up to Carlisle and beyond. But, by then, it was too late. The Midland needed Parliament's approval to abandon its proposed Settle–Carlisle route and Parliament declined, leaving the Midland with no choice but to build the line anyway. The first sod was cut in 1869 and the line was completed in 1876. It was a tough engineering assignment which came in 60 per cent over budget and two years behind schedule. As well as the enormously impressive Ribblehead viaduct the work also included the construction of the 2,600 yard Blea Moor tunnel, the viaduct over Dandry Mire and several other significant tunnels and bridges. There is a modest monument to the navvies and their families who lost their lives (to smallpox as well as to accidents) in the little chapel at Outhgill just to the north of Garsdale, in Mallerstang.

Nick Chetwood on the steps of his signal box at Garsdale station, on the Settle–Carlisle line.

And then, a century or so after the Midland railway's Parliamentary effort, the Settle to Carlisle faced a second attempt to abandon it. The Beeching report in 1963 had identified the line as one which could be closed, with traffic instead to be concentrated on the west coast main line. Stopping trains were withdrawn on the line in 1970 with only Settle and Appleby stations remaining open for the residual passenger service on what became a very slow way indeed to travel between London and Glasgow. Freight traffic was in decline, too. In the early 1980s, it became clear that the time was rapidly approaching when British Railways intended to go ahead with the Beeching recommendation and close the line altogether.

But at this point came the fight-back. The Friends of the Settle–Carlisle Line Association was set up at a meeting in Settle Town Hall in 1981 and rapidly developed into a powerful community organisation with considerable skills in campaigning and lobbying. There was some encouraging news to celebrate five years later. Although occasional trains had since the mid-1970s been stopping at some of the closed stations these had been special charter services run to enable walkers to get easy access to the western part of the national park. In 1986 British Railways acknowledged this demonstration of a latent demand and agreed to reopen the stations properly, once more running a stopping service on the line. Even so, the axe continued to be poised above the line as a whole until 1989, when the formal reprieve finally arrived.

Since then the line has become busier and busier. As well as the restored passenger services (these days often equipped by refreshment trolleys run by volunteer Friends of the Settle–Carlisle), freight has also grown in importance. Well over a hundred fully loaded coal trains a week have been using the line in recent years, each taking up to 1,600 tonnes of coal south from Scotland to English coal-burning power stations (the coal comes both from an opencast source in Ayrshire and from coal imported to a deepwater terminal on the Clyde). The coal trains then return empty, rattling their way back slightly faster over Ribblehead

The Moorcock Inn, one of the very few pubs on the watershed, marks where Wensleydale meets the Mallerstang Valley.

viaduct and through Blea Moor tunnel than they did on the way down. The other important freight traffic is in gypsum, a by-product of the way that emissions from power stations are cleaned, which is taken to Kirkby Thore near Appleby to be turned into plasterboard.

This means that there is a night life on the Settle–Carlisle line as well as the daytime passenger experience. Long after the last passenger trains have sidled out of Garsdale station on their way to Leeds or Carlisle, the lights will be burning in the signal box at Garsdale station and the signaller will be waiting to pass the freight trains on their way. Depending on the shift arrangements, it may be Nick Chetwood who's on duty.

I'd talked briefly about the work I was undertaking for this book with Nick, and in exchange he told me a little of his work. Nick, it quickly transpired, had a natural interest in a book about the countryside: long before applying for the job at Garsdale he'd been a outdoor education instructor, both at the well-known Plas y Brenin centre in North Wales and later, in Kendal, at a centre run for people with disabilities. He'd also for three winters running undertaken what is, in the outdoor movement at least, one of the most celebrated jobs in Britain: it involves making your way up Helvellyn each day to take weather readings at the summit, regardless of whatever blizzard conditions may be coming at you. Your report is then available to anyone pondering a day winter walking or climbing in that part of the Lakes: as Nick says, it's a simple way to improve safety in the mountains.

Working in Garsdale signal box is obviously a rather different experience. It's perched up some steps on the station's down platform (the side for trains to Carlisle: 'down' as in down from London, even if it's also 'up' to Scotland) and is so close to the line of the watershed that I decided it definitely merited its place in this book. Once upon a time, signalling here required a team of two: the signalman himself, who had a set of forty levers to control, and a clerk, whose task it was to record all the trains as they passed together with their times. That's when Garsdale station was known as Hawes Junction, and the job involved managing train movements not only on the Settle–Carlisle main line but also on the little Wensleydale branch line which headed off just to the east of the station on its way down to Hawes, Aysgarth and eventually Northallerton.

Most of the forty or so levers are still there in the signal box but now the majority of them are out of service and painted white, a ghostly memento of a line which lost its passenger services in the 1950s even before the Beeching report came along. Now Garsdale is what Network Rail calls a Grade II box, the simplest you can get, with just three signals apiece on the up line and down line, as well as a cross-over and siding for occasional use. But Garsdale's role in ensuring that trains are making their way safely on their journey is as important as any.

Much of the signalling on the Settle to Carlisle would have been familiar to a Midland railway employee, in that the system is still based around pulling off signals by hand and communicating by bells. The job, Nick tells me, is a little like the game of pass the parcel, with the train cast in the role of parcel. The Garsdale signal box takes trains on from the sections controlled by the neighbouring boxes at Blea Moor to the south and Kirkby Stephen to the north, who in turn are in touch with the next signal boxes, those at Settle and Appleby.

What happens is this. The first indication that there's a train on its way from the south will be a single bell sent through from Blea Moor, a wake-up call to the Garsdale box which requires a similar response. 'I send him one bell back, which means I'm listening,' Nick says. Then Blea Moor in turn responds by identifying the type of train that's coming. There are a number of possible combinations: five bells for a full coal train, four for an express passenger train and 3–1 for a stopping passenger train, for example. Nick is at this point being 'offered' the new train, which provided all is well he will accept by repeating the bell code back to Blea Moor. He'll also release a safety device at Garsdale which permits the Blea Moor signaller to pull off his own signal lever, allowing the train to proceed.

At this point, however, the train itself will be a long way away, having barely left Settle. For a laden freight train making its way up the long drag, as the climb from Settle was known back in the days of steam locomotives, it may take as long as fifty-five minutes for it to emerge eventually into sight at Garsdale, pass the box, and disappear off northwards over the viaduct across Dandry Mire. First, however, it will reach Blea Moor and cross into Nick's own section. Again, bells communicate when this happens. 'When it gets to Blea Moor I will be given two bells. Blea Moor is telling me 'It's passed me, it's in your section'. I give two bells back in acknowledgment,' Nick tells me. This is the point where Nick has in turn to offer the train onwards to Kirkby Stephen, sending on the correct bell code for the train, waiting for the bells to be returned, and waiting too for Kirkby Stephen to release their safety lever so that he can release his own signals.

Thus do all the trains on the Settle–Carlisle line progress on their journey. Normally there is a reassuring regularity to the routine of life in the box. Bells ring, and are repeated. Levers are pulled off and on. Periodically, the trains themselves appear, stop or pass straight by, and disappear onwards. At night, particularly in the early hours, there is a profound calm (albeit definitely a wakeful one) about proceedings. But a high-level route like the Settle–Carlisle requires constant vigilance, particularly when the weather turns bad. Ever since the line was first constructed landslips have been a recurring problem, and it was a landslide on the line close to Ais Gill summit, at 1,169 feet the highest point of the line, which caused two

The Mallerstang Valley, looking towards Hugh Seat.

passenger trains to crash in January 1995. Flooding had already closed the line south of Ribblehead, and a southbound sprinter train had been turned round to return to Carlisle when it was derailed by the landslide. A few minutes later another train ran into it. One of the train conductors was killed and thirty people were injured.

The story was very nearly repeated four years later in 1999, again in January and again in very bad weather, when an evening train from Leeds was derailed by a landslide, this time on a section of the line a little further north. The driver managed to run half a mile back to place a detonator on the track, which was enough to warn the following coal train of the problem ahead. Though the freight train collided with the derailed train, crew and passengers escaped with only minor injuries.

Sadly one of the worst accidents in the history of the railway, very early in the morning of Christmas Eve 1910, was the result of a simple mistake by the signalman at what was then the Hawes Junction box. He allowed the northbound Scotch Express on to the section of track north of Garsdale already occupied by two pilot engines. The express ran into the engines and derailed, six of its eight coaches caught fire and twelve people died. (I was relieved to be told by Nick Chetwood that the safety measures in place would prevent anything like that being possible today.) But it probably didn't help the signaller's concentration that day that, yet again, the weather was reportedly very bad, with torrential rain beating on the signal box windows.

It is not surprising therefore that in times past the instructions issued to railway employees included the following sentence: 'Stationmasters and signalmen between Hellifield and Carlisle must carefully watch the weather during the winter months . . .' In fact, in very bad winters such as the infamous big freeze of 1947 the line was something of a lifeline for the Dales communities along the route. During the eight weeks in February and March 1947 when the country was gripped by deep snowfalls, food supplies were brought up by train and collected by local people along the trackside, or (as at Selside) stored in the signal boxes. There is a tale of the time that year when a thousand loaves were baked in Skipton and sent to Horton, where the stationmaster himself (this still being the age of stationmasters) took on the task of distributing them.

There are no station staff left these days at the intermediate stations along the line, but the stations themselves are probably better looked after than at any time in their history. Volunteers from the Friends of the Settle–Carlisle Line regularly tend the flower beds and hanging baskets. Garsdale itself boasted a fine display of bizzy lizzies when I was there, and I was later to admire photographs of the petunias at Horton, the sweet williams at Settle and the red hot pokers at Langwathby. Many of the station buildings themselves have been restored to their prime, the work of the Settle and Carlisle Railway Trust which was established in 1990 to preserve the line's built heritage and which, like the Friends, taps into the great depth of community support which exists for this much-loved line. It's now recognised that what's been done for the Settle–Carlisle line since it was up for closure in the early 1980s is a model for community involvement in other railway lines elsewhere in the country.

It is almost time to bid farewell to the Yorkshire Dales. Having crossed the railway at Dandry Mire the watershed continues for three miles or so along the western edge of Mallerstang towards Swarth Fell and Wild Boar Fell before seeming to change its mind, deciding to drop straight down to the valley and making a second crossing of the railway, this time logically enough at the summit at Ais Gill. High up once more, this time on the eastern flank of Mallerstang, is another important watershed divide. As the name Ure Head suggests, this is the source of the Ure, the river which runs through Wensleydale, through Hawes and Ripon, to turn itself into the Yorkshire Ouse at York. Little more than feet away to the north on this featureless hillside is the source of the Eden, which will carve out the Eden valley and eventually emerge into the Solway Firth.

Mallerstang is magnificent, and there's plenty of interest for the next few miles north. Lady Anne Clifford, the seventeenth-century aristocrat whose Dales journeys were one of Mary Towneley's inspirations for the Pennine Bridleway, regularly came through Mallerstang and one of her five castles, Pendragon, lies just beside the Eden here in a beautiful setting north of Outhgill. There is a souvenir of her life even closer to hand, however, for the tall stone at Hugh Seat a short distance on the watershed from Ure Head carries the name Lady's Pillar and was erected, at least according to local memory, on Lady Anne's orders to mark the extent of her landholdings. Or perhaps she intended to commemorate her ancestor Sir Hugh de Morville, after whom Hugh Seat gets its name. The story of Lady Anne's involvement appears to be vindicated by the carving of the letters A.P. (Anne was at this stage of her life Lady Pembroke) and the date of 1664 on the pillar, both clearly visible today. The stone was restored in the nineteenth century, and the reverse side bears a slightly less visible date: 1890, or perhaps 1880. I looked carefully but couldn't be quite certain.

And then from Hugh Seat on to High Seat, crossing briefly the 700-metre contour for the very first time on this journey. And here, for the first time too, the North Pennine hills come into view. There, it seems now not so very far away, is the last great section of the Pennine watershed ahead. There is the radar station on Great Dun Fell, and just beyond it Cross Fell, the highest point of all, and now only a few chapters away.

After several miles where the views have been dominated by Pen-y-ghent, Ingleborough and Whernside, there are new horizons. Beyond High Seat at High Pike there's a first glimpse westwards towards the Lakeland fells. Even further away is Scotland, and the Galloway hills visible across the waters of the Solway Firth. But it's worth pressing on, from High Pike over the minor road into Swaledale to Nine Standards Rigg, because close to the trig point is a properly constructed viewing stone, what's officially known as a toposcope, here to help identify exactly what can be seen. Here's the place to pause, perhaps, to look across to the Lakes and make out Blencathra to the north, Coniston Old Man to the south, Scafell Pike and all the other great Lake District mountains. And to look eastwards as well. I can't vouch for the story, but I've heard it said that in exceptional weather conditions you can see right across northern England from here, from Irish Sea to North Sea.

The nine standards themselves, the grouping of large cairns which dominate the horizon above Kirkby Stephen, are the first major example encountered yet of the stone pillars and cairns, given the local name curricks, which will increasingly be a feature of the North Pennines hilltops. Why the curricks were built is something of a mystery. Certainly, the history of the nine standards themselves seems obscure, though Wainwright recounts a good tale of how they were originally built to frighten off any Scottish invaders tempted to explore the Eden valley by giving them the false idea that an army of English was waiting for them up on the hills. Well, perhaps.

Driving sheep to higher ground, near the watershed above Mallerstang.

19. STAINMORE

Nine Standards Rigg – High Greygrits – Stainmore (A66) – Great Knipe – B6276

Just as peat accumulates from the remains of living organisms, so figuratively too the Pennine moors have soaked up centuries of human history. Mostly this history is unwritten and unremembered, tales of unknown lives lived in times gone by which are now beyond recall. Sometimes, however, there is evidence remaining to remind us of past lives.

The evidence can be in documentary form. For example, I can find out quite a lot about the events on 12th October 1663 on Kaber Rigg moor just to the north of Nine Standards, about how a small group of men came together there as part of what they hoped was a national plot to overthrow Charles II and to bring back the days of the English Commonwealth, because written records of their uprising remain and because modern historians have researched the story and written up their findings. I know the name of their ringleader, Captain Robert Atkinson, a yeoman from Mallerstang who had had an illustrious career in the Parliamentary army during the years of the English Revolution and the Commonwealth, rising through the ranks to end up as the commander of the troops in Westmorland and, for a time, Governor of Appleby town. I know how he had been in contact with others planning the uprising elsewhere in the North, and how they had tried to coordinate their actions with rebels in London and Scotland as well. I know that the plotters had a Declaration already drafted, *A Door of Hope Opened in the Valley of Achor for the Mourners in Sion out of the North*. I know also that they were betrayed to the government authorities, who probably used agents provocateurs to encourage the rebels into action. And I know that, when 12th October arrived, the planned spontaneous uprising across the country turned to fiasco. Only about twenty or so horsemen met up with Robert Atkinson on windswept Kaber Rigg, waiting to be joined by other forces from the North-West which never materialised, and after a cold evening spent on the moor they dispersed to their homes hoping, unsuccessfully, to have escaped detection. (Robert Atkinson was later to be hanged for his treason in the town he had once governed, Appleby.)

This, in abbreviated form, is the Westmorland part of the story of what is today called the Northern Risings of 1663. It was, according to one modern historian, a potentially large-scale insurrection at the end of an unprecedented period of radical activity in England. But it failed, and history moves on.

Sometimes the evidence from the past is there in the landscape. There's no shortage of remains of past industry at Kettlepot Gill, for example, three or four miles along the watershed beyond Nine Standards Rigg, where coal was for many years removed from the ground. In fact, the task of following the watershed line through this tumbled landscape can be a potentially hazardous undertaking, for not all the shafts left behind from the days of the

The road between Kirkby Stephen and Swaledale rising, through the mist, to the watershed.

Kettlepot Colliery have been capped or filled in. On the day I came this way I progressed with great care and caution, remembering the story told me by a former landlady at nearby Tan Hill inn of the dog which had disappeared suddenly down an old unmarked shaft only a short distance away.

Though lead mining was important not far away in Arkengarthdale and Swaledale, it was coal which was taken from the ground at Tan Hill. Tan Hill coal was widely used in medieval times, reportedly burning in the hearths of Richmond Castle in the fourteenth century, and mining continued until recent times, the last coal being taken from these hillsides in 1938. But the last of the generations of coal miners from Tan Hill have now gone, taking their experiences with them. Just the evidence of their labours remains, dismissed by us as scars on the landscape.

The further back we go in time, the more work we have to do to interpret the evidence left behind. Nevertheless, as archaeologists know, there's real satisfaction when the land can be persuaded to reveal a little of the secrets it holds. There are few places in the Pennines where more work has been done in trying to tease out an understanding of the past from the evidence left behind than at Stainmore, just ahead of us now on the watershed route.

The Stainmore gap marks the geological divide between the two great blocks of Carboniferous rock which make up the high ground of the Dales and of the North Pennines.

Walking in pale sunlight on the path up to Nine Standards Rigg.

It's because of this that the A66 between Scotch Corner and Penrith is such a valuable cross-Pennine route for cars and lorries, and it's not surprising to find that this route through the hills was also used by nineteenth-century railway builders. The Stainmore railway predated the Settle–Carlisle by over twenty years, being constructed in 1861, and its primary role was to convey coal and iron between Teesside and the North-West, though later it also proved a valuable way to transport Newcastle people to Blackpool for their summer holidays (the line closed in 1962).

The A66's direct ancestor, the first modern road through Stainmore gap, was the turnpike which was constructed in 1743. But Stainmore has been a key trans-Pennine route for very much longer than this. For example, though only its stump remains today, Rey Cross has been standing on almost the highest point of the crossing since pre-Norman times. There was a long-lived legend locally that the cross was erected over the bones of Erik Bloodaxe, who was king of Norway from 930–4, ruled Northumbria briefly in the years around 950 and who is reported to have met his death in 954 in Stainmore. Not surprisingly, there was considerable local media interest in August 1990 when, as part of road widening work for the A66, the cross had to be relocated to a nearby site, allowing the ground underneath it to be excavated. Sadly for romantics everywhere, no bones were found. The body of the last Viking king of Northumbria may, of course, be in another corner of the moorland in Stainmore, but if so his resting place remains as yet undiscovered.

The A66 widening provided the opportunity for a very significant archaeological study of Stainmore, looking at far more than simply the Rey Cross site. Fieldwork was undertaken over a three-year period, from 1989 to 1991, and one of the key focuses for the researchers was the Roman period. The Romans, as you'd imagine, were fully aware of the value of the Stainmore gap and their road through it cut straight through the heart of the Brigantes' territory. There were forts built at Bowes and Brough at either end of the pass, a substantial camp close to where Rey Cross now stands (just to the east of the watershed), and a small 'fortlet' now known as Maiden Castle (just to the west of the summit). Both the Rey Cross

Four of the cairns that comprise the Nine Standards, showing their differing designs.

and Maiden Castle sites were the focus of archaeological attention during the 1989–91 digs, and from this work some sense of the Romans' use of the Stainmore area has emerged.

What came first, it's clear, was the fortified camp at Rey Cross. This predated the construction of the road through the pass and was probably put up at the time when the Romans were first pushing into the north of England, in the early 70s AD. To quote Pip Robinson, the archaeologist who supervised the 1989–91 project, 'It is probable that the Roman army in its initial campaign into unoccupied and potentially dangerous territory built the marching camp first for overnight security and constructed the road at a later date, when resources were available and the region was more secure.' The road may date from the period when Agricola was governor of Britain, in the years after AD 78.

Despite the extensive excavations, however, it is by no means easy to put together the jigsaw and build up a comprehensive picture of the Roman times here. Why was the smaller fort at Maiden Castle built, for example? It dates from a later period of Roman occupation, being used probably from the mid-second to the late-fourth centuries. One theory is that it functioned as the Roman equivalent of a motorway toll booth, or more accurately a customs post, controlling trade as it passed on its way through the Pennines.

There's also uncertainty about why the Romans built a series of small towers through Stainmore. One idea which had previously been advanced has now been challenged, even though Ordnance Survey maps continue to label each site as that of a 'Roman signal station'. (The one closest to the watershed, just south of the A66 crossing, bears the impressive name of Roper Castle.) The signal station theory was first advanced by an archaeologist in 1951 and was tried out in practice in 1977 when a group of army apprentices spent a couple of days in Stainmore trying to send messages to each other using a variety of signalling techniques which the Romans might have employed. But today archaeologists are more hesitant about this idea. What meaningful signals could have been passed between the towers? Why couldn't despatch riders carry messages more speedily along the road? Where is the accommodation which teams of signallers would have needed at each site? Why was Roper Castle built so far off the

Roman road? So it seems we will have to admit that here's another problem still to be solved, another case where we can't properly interpret the evidence left behind in the landscape.

What's interesting about Stainmore is that the story doesn't begin with the Romans. The current archaeological view is that the Stainmore gap has been an important east–west link perhaps from the Bronze Age onwards (generally regarded as starting about 2000 BC in Britain) or even earlier, and certainly from Iron Age times. The marching camp the Romans built at Rey Cross turns out to have been put up on the site of an earlier circle of stones, which has been tentatively assigned to the early Bronze Age period, and other Bronze Age sites have also been identified elsewhere in the Stainmore area.

We can push our knowledge even further back in time. The Stainmore archaeological project at the time of the A66 widening made use of palynological techniques (palynology, you may recall, is the study of pollen and grains), as well as the related science of pedology (the study of samples of soil). During 1989–90, five samples taken from peat were extracted from the Stainmore area and what they contained was then subject to careful analysis. The researchers were looking for pollen which could reveal the types of vegetation which had been growing at the time the peat was being formed, including any evidence that early arable culti- vation of cereal grasses was being undertaken.

It might sound to a layperson extraordinary that the soil can be made to give up its secrets in this way, but in fact palynological analysis is a well-tried method in the Pennines, going back to at least twenty-five years. The results can be impressive. In the case of the Stainmore research, for example, the gradual replacement of woodland cover with blanket peat could be deduced from increasing evidence of heather and the fall in the pollen count found from trees like birch, oak, elm and lime as the more recent layers of peat replaced the deeper layers.

The Nine Standards, silhouetted against the skyline, as seen by walkers on Wainwright's Coast-to-Coast path.

We can conclude, it seems, that peat began to build up from the fourth millennium BC, before which there was widespread post-glacial woodland cover. Some of this woodland was cleared in prehistoric times, during the late Mesolithic and early Neolithic period, and there appears to have been another period of woodland clearance during the second millennium BC when crops were being grown on the Pennine uplands.

We can also get an idea of how the climate changed over the centuries and millennia from similar research techniques. The last ice age is considered to have ended about 10,000 years ago, and there was a rapid warming over the first thousand years after that, of perhaps 1°C per century. From about 6800–2500 BC average annual temperatures were warmer than they are at the moment, by about 1–2°C. Sea levels were rising, the land bridge between Britain and continental Europe disappearing about six or seven millennia before our own. After about 3000 BC, the climate got slightly worse as cooler and wetter weather set in, though the Romans were able to enjoy a relatively warm and dry interval when they were in Britain, particularly during the last two centuries of their occupation.

So climate changes had a direct impact on the way that the uplands were utilised and the type of vegetation which was growing. The peoples living here in the centuries before the Romans seem to have gradually switched from arable agriculture to livestock grazing, perhaps as the peat started building up on land which had previously been cultivatable, so by the time the first Roman troops made their way through Stainmore the land probably looked not dissimilar from the way it does today. There'd have been no modern field boundary fences or walls of course. And there'd have been another difference: there would have been silence where now Stainmore is loud with the sound of A66 traffic.

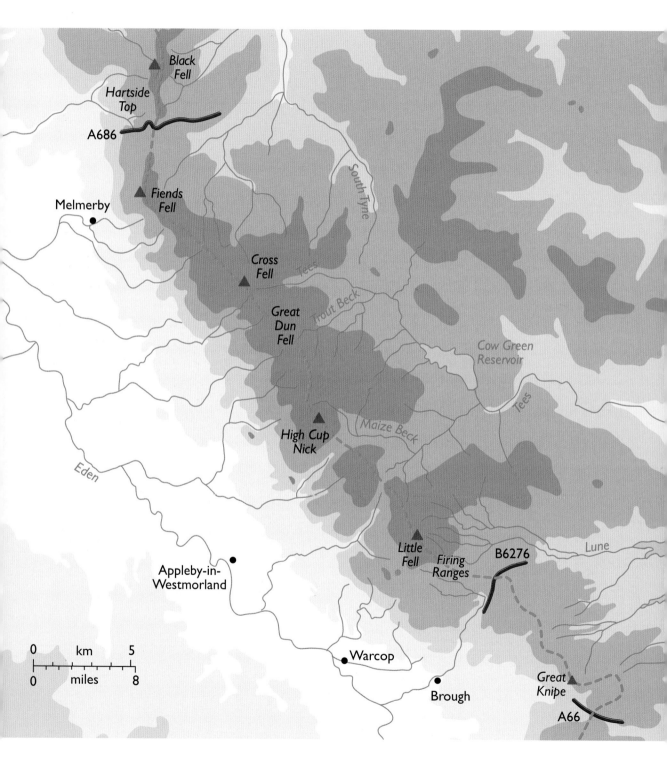

20. LITTLE FELL

B6276 – Burton Fell/Little Fell – Scordale Head – High Cup Nick

North of the minor road which crosses the high moors from Brough to Middleton-in-Teesdale are 24,000 acres of the Pennines dedicated to the arts of warfare. The Warcop training area has been occupied by the military since 1942 when the Ministry of Defence took over the moorland to provide adequate space for army tank crews to prepare for D-Day. The exigencies of war demanded speed: people living on the land being requisitioned were given a month to find somewhere else to go.

And once they'd gone – in the words of one 1946 newspaper report – the firing started: 'It went on day after day, month after month, as thousands of tons of ammunition buried itself in the Pennine moorland, spent but not wasted. Not wasted because it was all fired with one aim – to perfect the fighting skills of the tank crews – an aim which had ultimate justification on the battle fields of Europe.'

Since the war many more tons of munitions of various kinds have been used at Warcop, for after 1945 the army decided to stay on and to keep this area for training purposes. For much of the post-war period, Warcop continued to be used for tank and heavy artillery practice and the high Pennine fells stretching back from Warcop towards Burton Fell and Mickle Fell provided the necessary safety space needed for any overshoots or ricochets. In 1994, however, the focus switched away from tanks and today most of the activity at Warcop is light arms training geared to the needs of new recruits to the army, focused on the lower ground closer to Warcop village.

Nevertheless, the warning signs stay up around a very large slice of Pennine moorland, reaching up almost to the Pennine Way and the valley of Maize Beck. This land has been exempted from the right to roam arrangements of the Countryside and Rights of Way Act and public access is limited to the small number of rights of way which cross the military land, and then only on a very limited number of days a year. You can walk these paths on Sunday afternoons when the firing has stopped, on twelve weekends a year which are given over to public access, and on a further fifteen or so 'short notice' days when for various reasons firing is not taking place.

There are special permit arrangements for those people who want to reach the summit of Mickle Fell, at 2,585 feet (788 m) the highest ground in the danger area. Mickle Fell is a destination both for walkers aiming to tackle all the mountains over 2,500 feet and for nostalgic Yorkshiremen and women paying their respects to what used to be the county's highest point before local government reform in 1974 snatched it away and gave it to Durham.

But the Mickle Fell permit system was little help to me. The watershed here is more perverse, shunning Mickle Fell for the slightly lower ground of Burton Fell and Little Fell to

A long and winding track that leads to a farm on Stainmore.

the south-west, and this area, I was told, was normally out of bounds. I persevered, and a few letters and phone calls later got a positive response: in the interests of literary endeavour I was, it seemed, to be given special authority to be allowed across. I might need to be escorted, and I would certainly need to attend a safety briefing first. I envisaged a morning spent in a bare army training room, with a training officer at the front (peaked cap in place) lecturing me on how to distinguish between bits of metal detritus which could blow up in your face and those which were rusting away safely into the heather. There was a slight sense of anticlimax when the safety briefing turned out to be simply a case of visiting the estate office, reading a short loose leaf folder of instructions and then (the important bit, no doubt) signing my name at the disclaimer at the bottom. By this stage, too, talk of the escort had disappeared and I gathered I was to be trusted by myself. (I did persuade a friend to come with me, however – just in case, you know . . .)

I am happy to report that we made it on to Burton Fell and Little Fell without misadventure, though there was perhaps a certain tentativeness in the way we picked our way through the peat groughs on the way there. The risk, according to the army, is that there may still be stuff left behind here in the peat from the frantic months prior to D-Day. Peat can become eroded, they caution, and things you'd rather not find can be brought back to the surface. Of course, it's hard to assess just how great this risk is and a cynic would say that it suits the army to emphasise the danger, if only to discourage any freelance initiatives up here by walkers.

Little Fell has a trig point, so I was able to acknowledge another stage completed on my journey along the watershed journey. By this stage the maths may have gone wrong, though I thought that this was probably the twenty-seventh trig stone I'd passed. It was a sad sight, barely recognisable, with the concrete pillar almost completely destroyed and with the Ordnance Survey metal frame left perched precariously at the top. Someone must have been using it for target practice. But otherwise Burton Fell and Little Fell were beautiful places, and

When the red flag is flying, walkers should stay away from the army range on Warcop Fell.

beyond them the limestone outcrops on the gradual descent from Little Fell to Scordale Head were a delight to enjoy as well.

The majority of soldiers who come to Warcop never come anywhere near these moors but spend all their time on the firing ranges proper. A few days later I was taken around the heart of the training area by one of the estate staff, in order for me to get a real sense of how the army uses its land. We looked at some of the twenty-six separate ranges and training areas, saw the moving targets installed for shooting practices and examined from a distance the incongruous three-storey house built on a hillock where you learn what it's like to be confronted by a sniper. (The building carried the name Fibua House which I thought might be a tribute by the army to an old farmhouse placename hereabouts; only later did I discover it stood for Fighting in Built-Up Areas.)

We also watched a team of new army recruits in action. Warcop receives new infantry recruits at the very end of their six-month training programme at the main army base of Catterick, and gives them their first taste of training with live ammunition. A helpful officer found a place for me to stand to look down as four trainee soldiers made their way across open ground, pouring fire into two-dimensional figures of the enemy who popped up periodically from behind patches of grass. The exercise ended with a hand-grenade leaving its mark in the long-suffering countryside. Afterwards all the soldiers came down from their adrenaline rush by queuing up at the nearby burger van, given permission to come on to the range to ply what looked like a very profitable business.

The army's continued use of Warcop was controversial in the immediate aftermath of the war when most local people wanted to see the land restored to agriculture, and there was controversy again in the years between 1998 and 2002 when the army decided that it needed to extend the use it made of the area. Until then, every Monday had been left free of firing to allow the local farmers who still held their traditional commoners' rights and who grazed

A molecatcher puts his catch on display, so the farmer knows the job's been done.

livestock on the range to look after their sheep. The range closed for five weeks during the year for the same purpose, and there were also restrictions on night-time exercises. But by the late 1990s the army was finding these limitations frustrating. Their proposal was to buy out the commoners' rights, to close two footpaths and to extend the use of the range to Mondays and to night-time use. The case was heard at a public inquiry and the outcome went broadly as the army had hoped, though they didn't get the right they'd hoped for to extinguish the two rights of way.

The army's use of large areas of countryside is of course more generally controversial. The MoD is one of the largest single landowners in Britain with over half a million acres; together with the land leased (a further 660,000 acres) it has about 2 per cent of the total land area of the country under its control. Not everyone is convinced that the military really need this much land or, indeed, that they manage it very effectively, but there has been no comprehensive attempt by government to look at the issue since 1973 when the report of the Defence Lands Committee (the Nugent report) was published.

Military land use is particularly sensitive in national parks, as is the case in Dartmoor and Northumberland. Warcop does not fall within a national park, but nevertheless it is within the North Pennines Area of Outstanding Natural Beauty and much of the training area has also been designated an SSSI, a Special Protection Area and a Special Area of Conservation. Though the army says that its training needs are paramount, it has tried to polish up its conservationist credentials in recent years. As a 1995 MoD report put it, 'Because much Army land lies untouched by development, the plants flourish, the invertebrates prosper and the birds and mammals find ideal homes.' The line, put at its crudest, is that nature is benefiting from the public being kept out.

For Warcop in particular, this is very much the current message. The Army Training Estate website claims that the army here is undertaking 'careful conservation of a unique heritage'. It goes on, in slightly truncated English: 'Warcop's use as a military training area has preserved a substantial landscape, home to a wealth of rare species of flora and fauna, and also with numerous archaeological remains, and great geological interest, with some of the UK's finest untouched limestone dating 10,000 years from the Ice Age – weathering and preserved condition being thanks to the restricted access for the last sixty years.' Finally, the website offers a check-list of the wildlife currently making their home on the range, including black grouse, red squirrels and bats.

Even if you are hostile to the army's continued occupation of beautiful countryside, you may yet still welcome the fact that the military are prepared to acknowledge and respect their conservation and environmental obligations. Alternatively, you can accept without hesitation the army's case that this land is needed for training purposes and yet feel a slight tendency towards cynicism creeping on. Extensive use of land by the army for training purposes almost inevitably involves an element of rearrangement of the landscape; in some cases (partly when tanks and heavy artillery are concerned) this rearrangement can be quite substantial. It comes down to the question of what our countryside is for: is army use any less legitimate than agriculture, or forestry, or recreational usage?

I left Little Fell behind with one sour thought, however. If the army is right to warn walkers like me of the risks left behind from world war and post-war ordnance training, the reality is that these wild moors are as much contaminated as derelict ex-industrial waste ground. Contaminated land is land which humans have abused and failed to look after properly. And, unfortunately, contaminated land tends to stay that way for a very long time.

21. HIGH CUP NICK TO GREAT DUN FELL

High Cup Nick – Great Rundale Tarn – Knock Old Man – Great Dun Fell

So why does the Pennine landscape look like it does? As each mile followed the last, I found my questions starting to mount: why are there rocky outcrops here – but not over there? Why has the vegetation changed dramatically in the last few hundred yards? Why has that hill over there got a peaky top? For that matter, why are there hills here at all?

To properly appreciate what the land is saying you need to understand the language it is using and, as I looked at the stunning rock formations near High Cup Nick, I knew that I needed an interpreter. I picked up the telephone and rang for help. The person at the other end of my call was Brian Young, for many years the British Geological Survey's district geologist for the north of England – basically, the person responsible for everything under our feet between Tweed and Tees. More recently since his retirement Brian has been energetically communicating the message of geology to the general public, not least through the regular series of geology walks which he leads in the North Pennines area.

I explained my problem, and warned him not to get too technical. Encouragingly, he immediately came back with suggestions for questions I might want to put to him. 'Ask why Cross Fell, which has been a mountain for a long time, is still almost 3,000 feet high. Or why Appleby, a short way away, is only at 400 feet,' he said. Brian had immediately grasped the point. It was these apparently simplistic questions which I wanted to have answered.

We arranged to spend a morning looking at the land near Great Dun Fell. We met at the bottom and made our way slowly up the hillside, giving Brian the opportunity to explain what we were seeing. When it comes to the geology, he told me, the North Pennines hereabouts is like the Lake District with a roof on – he wanted to show me that roof.

One of the initial difficulties for the layperson is that the time frame within which geology operates is so enormously different from that of ordinary human time. The earth as a planet is about 4.6 billion years old. All sorts of things happened over the first four billion years which geologists are gradually starting to understand, but they really get dug in to their subject matter a little over half a billion years back from the present, thanks to the first hard-shelled fossils beginning to appear as evidence. This first geological period is called the Cambrian (leaving everything that came before to be conveniently labelled Precambrian), and the present-day science of geology dates the start of this era at around 540–570 million years ago.

We don't need to go back quite that far for the time being, however. To get to grips with the story of the Pennines, it's perhaps best to start in the geological middle-distance, the years which elapsed between roughly 350 and 290 million years ago. This era is categorised as the Carboniferous period, and Carboniferous rocks make up the vast bulk of the Pennines range.

For Pennine Wayfarers, High Cup Nick is one of the highlights of the walk.

At that point there was no Britain, or anything remotely like the map of the world we know today. What is now this part of northern England was down near the equator, gradually making its way northwards. (As an aside: the world's land masses are still moving around just as fast, it's just that we're not around long enough to notice.) For some of this period, the land – or some of it – was under shallow tropical water. At other times, the land – or some of it – was covered by mud brought down by great rivers, and by sand deposits. Sometimes, forests of trees grew up on the swampy ground. The forests decayed, and the seas rose again, coming in to cover the land.

From this cycle of events came, eventually, different rock forms. Limestone was formed from the limey skeletal debris of the remains of the sea creatures which lived in the tropical waters and which accumulated on the sea-bed. The mud washed down by rivers became shale. Sand, associated with river deltas, hardened and became sandstone. Finally, in some of the places where there had been forests, leaf litter from the trees accumulated as a sort of peat-like organic debris which eventually ended up as seams of coal.

You can look at the edge of the Pennines escarpment, as I did with Brian Young as we climbed up Great Dun Fell, and note how the hillside is made up of layers of different types of Carboniferous rock. Brian pointed them out to me: there a limestone layer, for example

('At certain times of the year, it's even more unmistakable – the grass is brighter green,' he explained), there sandstone, there shale. The strata vary in depth in different parts of the Pennines because, naturally enough, there were some parts of the land which stayed under the tropical seas for longer periods of time (more limestone), or were sandy deltaic areas (more sandstone) or were under mud (more shale). Over the millions of years of the Carboniferous age the cycle became repeated several times, for reasons which geologists still debate. Did sea-levels change as the southern hemisphere ice caps melted and reformed? Did rivers change the routes they took through their deltas to the sea?

I like to think of the northern Pennines as being made, therefore, in rather the same way as you might put together a good lasagne: just as you would pile up gradually the layers of meat and of cheese sauce and of pasta sheets, and then repeat the layers again and again to the top of the dish, so the Pennines is put together with strata of different rocks, with the whole pattern repeating. If you're talking to geologists, however, it may be better not to talk about lasagne but to use the proper term for this, cyclothem.

Under Brian's guidance, the landscape of the escarpment immediately below Great Dun Fell and Cross Fell was beginning to make some sort of sense. But as I'd already discovered at first hand, the countryside varies considerably along the Pennine watershed. I asked a slightly worried question: though we conventionally talk of the Pennines as a single range of hills, was this, geologically speaking, the correct thing to do?

Brian was reassuring. There was, he said, a coherent entity to the whole range, from the Peak District to the Tyne valley, which came from the fact that the rocks all basically date from the Carboniferous period. Earlier geologists tended to categorise these rocks in one of three ways, in order of age, as Mountain Limestone (or Carboniferous Limestone), Millstone Grit and Coal Measures. Non-geologists can just about get away with this usage today, though I got the impression that to do so was to run the risk of being simplistic. Different strata of Carboniferous rock in different parts of the Pennines have been classified in detail and given their own names. You can talk about Millstone Grit, the hard-wearing coarse sandstone which gained its name because it was found to be ideal for grinding corn, for instance, but you can also get more detailed: you can distinguish between say, Kinderscout Grit, Lower Kinderscout Grit, Todmorden Grit, or Parsonage Sandstone, again to give just four examples. Similarly, limestone strata get classified. The significant limestone layer in the Yorkshire Dales which can reach thicknesses of twenty metres or more carries the name of Great Scar Limestone, for instance.

More importantly, later upheavals of the earth which pushed up these Carboniferous rocks to create the range of hills we call the Pennines did so along pre-existing fault lines, rather than evenly. There are several major fault lines which run across the Pennine chain, dividing it into distinctive sections or blocks. As we've seen already, geologists distinguish between the mass of the northern Pennines lying between the Tyne valley gap and Stainmore, and the Yorkshire Dales area directly to the south. When I'd passed over the A66 I had, geologically speaking, been in transition from the Askrigg Block to the Alston Block. And when I would eventually come down off the North Pennine hills to Hadrian's Wall, so Brian told me, I would be arriving at the geological fault line which cuts its way almost due west–east across England and which is known after a small settlement near Hexham as the Stublick Fault.

We had been making our way up Great Dun Fell for some time by this stage, and we turned to enjoy the view. We'd been lucky in our choice of a clear day so that, away across the

Eden valley in front of us, the whole range of the Lakeland fells could be seen, their tops clear of cloud. It was a great view, one of those days when the eye is drawn far away across the country, relishing the sheer delight of distance.

But Brian wanted to drew my attention rather closer to home. 'If you look along the main Pennine escarpment, it's mainly a plateau, an enormous great flat hill,' he said. From right to left, from Dun Fell and Cross Fell north to Knapside Fell and beyond, the Pennines extended before us as an unbroken whole. 'But along the front of the escarpment are lots of pointy hills, just like you find in the Lake District. You'd have to be very unobservant not to notice them,' he went on.

I looked as observantly as I could as Brian identified Knock Pike, the 400-metre roundhead just beside us and, further away, the slightly higher hill that is Dufton Pike. 'The reason that they look like the mountains you find in the Lake District is because that's what they are. The North Pennines is really just layers of Carboniferous rock on top of older Lake District rocks,' he said. Here was the roof he had mentioned earlier.

It was time to turn the geological clock back, another hundred million or so years before Carboniferous times. Geologists call what came after the Cambrian the Ordovician period (roughly 495–440 million years ago), and this is followed in turn by the Silurian (roughly 440–415 million years ago). The rocks which form the Lake District mountains date back to Ordovician and Silurian times, when what eventually became northern England hadn't yet reached the equator on its travels and was still way down in the southern hemisphere, gradually moving away from the ancient continent of Gondwana and for much of the time at the bottom of a deep ocean. In actual fact the Lake District mountains divide geologically into three separate types (the early Ordovician Skiddaw group, the somewhat later Borrowdale volcanic group and lastly the so-called Windermere super group), which helps explain why the Lakeland fells don't all have the same characters and characteristics.

But this isn't the place to get sidetracked into Lake District geology. It's sufficient to say that Ordovician and Silurian rocks almost certainly make up the basement underneath the Carboniferous rocks of the Pennines, and that we can detect this basement in just a few places where these much older rocks put in a very brief appearance on the surface. The conical hills like Knock Pike and Dufton Pike below Cross Fell and Great Dun Fell are one such place. If you look at the geological maps of this area, you'll see them represented in tiny slivers of different colours, representing what is known technically as the Cross Fell Inlier. Knock Pike's rocks, for example, are directly related to the Borrowdale volcanic rocks dating back to Ordovician times. It's the result of pyroclastic activity – or in other words, the result of a volcanic eruption of molten debris. 'It would have been a nightmare place to be, like being sprayed by a giant aerosol full of liquid rocks,' as Brian Young graphically put it.

The early Ordovician and Silurian rocks also peek out further south, close to the line of the modern-day A65, where the North Craven Fault provides the southern boundary of the Askrigg Block of the Pennines. Though I hadn't realised it, I had briefly been on Silurian rock just south of Fountains Fell, on my first day in the Dales. Inliers of these early rocks are brought to the surface along the North Craven Fault near Malham, Stainforth, Horton, Austwick and Ingleton.

How do we know all this? The accumulated knowledge which now makes up the science of geology rests on the shoulders of early pioneers, both natural scientists with an intellectual curiosity to understand the physical characteristics of the world and – just as important – the

High Cup Nick, a classic U-shaped valley, stretching away towards the Eden Valley.

miners, quarrymen and mine engineers whose working lives had given them a profound understanding of the ground beneath their feet. From the mining areas of the northern Pennines came figures such as, for example, Westgarth Forster and Thomas Sopwith, both mining engineers who went on to make their mark as geologists.

One pioneer geologist from an even humbler background, William Smith, came from the other end of the country. He was born in 1769, the eldest son of a village blacksmith in Oxfordshire, and had only a very basic school education. He found work as a surveyor for the growing network of canals in England, and through his work began to take a keen interest in the rock formations he was surveying. He noticed that the different rocks were arranged in regular, and predictable, strata. He also realised that each stratum could often be identified by the particular fossils it contained. He then had the idea of illustrating his findings by creating the first geological map, using different colours for different rock formations – exactly the system used on geological maps today. He travelled the length and breadth of England and Wales recording what he found and, astonishingly, by 1815 was in a position to produce the first-ever geological map of the country. Sadly, if predictably, his work was treated disdainfully by more eminent figures in society, and he became bankrupt and spent time in a debtors' prison. Only late in life was his contribution to the emerging science of geology recognised. These days, if the Geological Society decides to award you the William Smith Medal you know you're at the very top of your academic discipline.

But there's another figure from early British geology more directly connected with the Pennines who also deserves a mention. It was Adam Sedgwick, born in the Dales village of Dent in 1785, who as President of the Geological Society of London was the first to acknowledge Smith's contribution, calling him the Father of English geology. Sedgwick himself is remembered in his home community with an impressive granite standing stone, inscribed simply 'Adam Sedgwick 1785–1873', and I confess that I'd been to Dent many times on visits and walking trips before I first properly took the trouble to find out more about the man behind the monument.

Sedgwick grew up as the second son of Dent's parson and was educated at nearby Sedbergh school before obtaining a place at Trinity College, Cambridge. His interest in geology effectively only started after 1818 when he took up the post of Woodwardian Professor of Geology (those were the days when professorships were obviously awarded more on potential than achievement) but in the years after that he visited all parts of the country, engaging in geological field work. He was in the Pennines in 1822, coming across into Westmorland from Middleton in the Upper Tees valley, and then going on to meet up with William Smith briefly in Kirkby Lonsdale. He was on his way at that time to the Lake District where, among other things, he established a lasting friendship with William Wordsworth. Sedgwick also undertook some detailed studies on the Carboniferous rocks in the Yorkshire Dales a few years later, in 1830, an area which he must have considered his home patch. It's appropriate that his home village was Dent, since there's a lot of significant geology going on immediately around that part of the Dales. Just as the southern edge of the Askrigg Block is defined by the North Craven Fault, so the western edge is identified by another major fault line which runs in a broadly north-south direction very close to Dent village and which is given by geologists the name of the Dent Fault.

Sedgwick is most often remembered for his work on earlier rocks than the Carboniferous ones of the Pennines, however, particularly for his research in Wales. It was Sedgwick who chose the name Cambrian for this geological period, for instance. Later on, he was engaged in an almighty academic row with a former colleague Roderick Murchison over the exact distinction between the Cambrian and Silurian periods, a dispute which later geologists conveniently side-stepped by creating an intervening Ordovician period. Incidentally, the Welsh connection remained, since both the Ordovician and Silurian names come from those of ancient Welsh tribes.

Talking of Ordovician and Silurian rocks brings us back to Knock Pike and Dufton Pike, and the mini re-appearance of the Lake District at the foot of the North Pennines escarpment. Brian Young and I had been gradually making our way towards the Civil Aviation Authority radar station at the top of Great Dun Fell, stopping periodically to look back down at the widening view below us. We'd also been working our way forward in geological time, since we'd moved on from the Carboniferous period to the next two major geological ages, the Permian (which takes over from the Carboniferous about 290 million years ago) and the Triassic (which in turn comes in around 250 million years ago). Conveniently enough, these periods are represented in the view from Great Dun Fell, if you are looking down at the Eden valley. By the Permian time, what was to become northern England had migrated even further northwards and was now well above the equator. The reason why there are attractive red-coloured stone buildings in some of the villages of the Eden valley is because the sand which went to form this sandstone (known as Penrith sandstone) was originally formed in desert areas. The Eden valley also has sandstone from the slightly later Triassic period.

Looking towards the heart of the Eden valley reminded me, however, of Brian Young's initial conversation with me on the telephone. I went back to the questions he'd suggested then that I pose him: what was it that determined that Great Dun Fell was the top of a hill and why was Appleby, by contrast, down in a valley? The answer, he explained, is because of what lies deep under the Pennines. The earth's crust is always restless ('We think of it as static, but that's only because our existence is so infinitesimally short that it looks static to us,' he said), and the movement of tectonic plates long in the past had the effect of raising up the Carboniferous rocks to create what we now think of as the Pennines. The reason why the Pennines stayed higher than neighbouring areas, however, is because they were underpinned by a base level of granite, dating back to around 410 million years ago. Despite what common sense might seem to suggest, granite is lighter – or at least less dense – than other rock forms, so that it behaves a little like a cork does in water. It's almost as though the Pennines, atop this granite base, are able to float above neighbouring areas of England.

Brian Young had one more lesson to impart. By this stage, we'd reached the top of the fell, and he'd led me to the jumbled landscape just to the south of the radar station. Like so many other parts of the Pennines, the high ground of Great Dun Fell had once been a scene of industrial activity. The Silverband mine on the slopes of the fell had for many years been an important centre for lead mining, and there was an unexpected reincarnation of this activity in the later years of the twentieth century when Silverband had been reopened, this time in the quest for baryte, a barium sulphate which is used in the construction industry and the oil drilling industry. (Incidentally, baryte had also been mined after the second world war on Long Fell in the heart of the Warcop army range; on the days when firing was taking place, the miners had to arrive at work early and stay underground for the whole day until the late afternoon when firing was over. Mining is always a risky activity, but the Warcop miners had to cope with this additional hazard.)

The 'golf ball' on Great Dun Fell, actually a radar station for air traffic control.

The Pennine mining industry developed as it did because of what happened at the very end of the Carboniferous period. This was the time when mineral-rich hot water, which had been warmed by the heat from the basement granite rock, found its way through cracks and fissures in the main Carboniferous rocks. As the water cooled, the minerals crystallised inside the fractures, leaving behind the mineral veins. In places, the solution also reacted with the limestone to create 'flat' deposits of minerals. It was these veins and flats which, about 290 million years later on, humans laboriously worked to discover and then excavate in order to extract the commercially valuable ores: lead, iron ores, baryte (and another barium mineral, witherite), fluorspar, zinc ore (sphalerite), and even a small amount of silver.

Minerals are Brian Young's particular field of study. He told me that he was close to completing field work which is seeing him visit and research in detail all the old lead mining areas of the North Pennines, exploring the geological evidence left behind when the mines closed, and though he was too modest to mention it I later discovered that it was on a visit to Brownley Hill mine near Nenthead in the early 1990s that he came across a zinc-based mineral never previously identified by geologists. The mineral, which has since been found in an old mine in Ceredigion in Wales as well as in Austria, Germany, Greece, Japan, Norway and Namibia, needed naming and the International Mineralogy Association had the answer: brianyoungite is now the officially recognised term worldwide.

What's heartening is that the North Pennines is taking active steps to celebrate its geological heritage. As mentioned earlier, approaching 775 square miles of Durham, Cumbria and Northumberland have been designated as the North Pennines Area of Outstanding Beauty, and though the AONB team don't have the same powers or resources as they would in a national park they have been creative and energetic in making the most of their status. In 2003, thanks to their efforts, the North Pennines was formally declared the first 'geopark' in Great Britain, part of a network of around thirty or so European Geoparks which have in turn received Unesco backing for what is intended to be a Global Geopark network.

The North Pennines AONB is a Geopark partly in recognition of its geological significance, but that's only one side of the story. Geoparks also have to commit to having a strategy in place to conserve their geological heritage and to interpret it to the general public. The educational side of the work, in other words, is central to getting your Geopark status confirmed and renewed.

It was Elizabeth Pickett, a geologist who has recently moved to the North Pennines AONB team after working for the British Geological Survey, who filled me in later on some of the activities they'd been undertaking. For example, they'd created three Rock Detective Clubs aimed at children between six and twelve, each with a programme of regular events for the members. 'We thought we might get fifteen kids at each club, but in fact we've now got over 200 members of the clubs,' Elizabeth told me. For adults, the North Pennines AONB regularly organise what they describe as 'geotours' and 'rockwalks' (some of them led by Brian Young), ranging from a half-mile stroll to High Force waterfall to a twelve-mile hike through old lead mining areas, and the AONB has also been organising a series of annual summer geo-festivals called Northern Rocks.

It's appropriate particularly because of the historical importance which geology has played in the story of the North Pennine countryside. Today, most of the 12,000 people living in the AONB area are concentrated in settlements in the dales in small towns like Alston and Nenthead. A hundred and fifty years ago, the same area has 27,000 people, many dependent on mining for their livelihoods. Geology has shaped the landscape, but also it has also shaped the recent social and economic history of this part of northern England.

22. GREAT DUN FELL AND CROSS FELL

Great Dun Fell – Little Dun Fell – Cross Fell

In May 1938, a few weeks after the Hope conference which led to the creation of the Pennine Way Association, Tom Stephenson received a letter in the post. The correspondent introduced himself and went on to say how excited he was about the Pennine Way proposal: 'The idea is to my mind superb,' he said. The letter continued: 'I know the Pennines very well: my particular walking ground used, c.1918–23, to be the Forest of Bowland in the days when nothing less than thirty miles was needed to reach one's objectives and return. Since those days I have backslid in the matter of distances, but have advanced in knowledge.'

The writer went on to get to the main point of his letter, which was to enquire whether the proposed route included the North Pennines ridge walk across Great Dun Fell and Cross Fell. If so, 'I have a small hut on Dun Fell. If it is any good in relation to this 'ridge', I might be able to dispose of it at a nominal figure for the benefit of walkers (and possibly skiers too).'

The person writing to Stephenson was Gordon Manley, who in 1938 was in his mid-thirties and in the process of building what was to be an eminent career as a climatologist. From the late 1920s he had been an academic at Durham University. Later, after the war, he was to move to Cambridge University, become Professor of Geography at one of London university's colleges, and finally the first Professor of Environmental Studies at Lancaster University. He died in 1980 and is remembered particularly for painstaking forensic work which enabled him to combine a series of historical weather records into a continuous database of monthly average temperatures dating back to 1659.

At the time he was writing to Tom Stephenson he was particularly interested in studying the weather of the North Pennines. He'd come to an agreement with the family who owned a shooting lodge at Moor House in Upper Teesdale, just to the east of Great Dun Fell, which enabled him to keep detailed meteorological records there from 1932. Moor House, at 1837 feet (560 m), is high up in the Pennines, but in 1937 Manley decided that he wanted to record weather conditions even higher up, at almost the very summit of the Pennine chain. Thus it was that he came to have his 'small hut' constructed 170 yards south-south-east of the top of Great Dun Fell at, he estimated, 2,710 feet (826 m) above sea level.

Photos of the building show it resembling a large garden shed, complete with an anemometer on the roof and – slightly incongruously – a sliding sash window in one of the gable ends. Its location meant that it copped some serious weather: one photo for example shows it entirely encased with ice. There were other hazards too: a later letter from Manley to Stephenson included the plea, 'Would you mind not telling the Dufton people too widely that my hut is on Gt Dun Fell . . . because the village lads have rather too much spare energy and have done various damage to fell huts in the last year (by fire). I was quite seriously warned to put mine well away

Cross Fell, at 893 metres, is the highest point on both the Pennine Way and the watershed.

from footpaths etc. and not to spread the word too widely where it was!'

To visit his hut and record the weather data collected there involved Manley driving from Durham over the Pennines to the foot of Great Dun Fell, and then making the climb up the escarpment to the summit, a journey which he reportedly made more than a hundred times. On some occasions he bedded down in the building for night or two. He once wrote that 'occasional small misadventures in the darkness, mist, wind and snow of a December night were offset by the many pleasures'.

Great Dun Fell can be a very windy place. The Met Office reported a gust of 133 mph here on 17th January 1993, and an average hourly wind speed of 105 mph on another January day, this time in 1974. However, Manley was particularly interested in one particular climatic phenomenon associated with this part of the Pennine ridge, the Helm wind.

The Helm is the nearest England gets to having its own notorious wind, a Cumbrian equivalent perhaps to France's mistral. Because it only affects a small area of the North-West – basically the North Pennine ridge and the Eden valley settlements immediately to the west – it's not particularly well known but those who encounter it do not easily forget the experience. Here, for example, is how one correspondent in The Times put it in an article published in September 1935:

> It is an uncanny sensation to be out in the Helm. With terrific force, paralysing cold, and a frightening noise like the roaring of a tempestuous sea it swoops down the steep face of the Fell and rages over the cultivated slopes beneath. One can hardly stand against it: breathing becomes difficult. Every few yards you must turn your back to it, or bend low on your knees with face to ground to get a breath, and are fain to seek the friendly shelter of a house as soon as ever may be. The vortex seems to have created a vacuum.

David Uttley, a local writer from whose book *The Anatomy of the Helm Wind* I have extracted that account, also records in his book a series of interviews with local people about their own

One of the many curricks dotted around Cross Fell.

experiences. One story is of a heavy agricultural roller being blown out of a farmyard and down a hill, another of a stationary tractor beginning to move, another of a border collie blown head over heels down a track. Then there's the case of the local resident who stepped out into his garden during the Helm wind but who 'had to retire because it became too dangerous due to the Brussels sprouts being blown off their stalks and ricocheting around the garden like green machine gun bullets'.

What is particularly distinctive about the Helm wind is that while people on the Pennine fellside and in the houses directly below can be encountering weather conditions like this, a few miles further to the west all may be calm and quiet. The Helm wind is a highly localised phenomenon.

The Helm wind can be identified when it is blowing by the presence of an apparently stationary cloud above the top of the Pennine ridge: this is the 'helm' itself (the word coming from the same Old English root as helmet, and with the same meaning of the covering of the head). As well as the helm cloud there is in addition a 'helm bar' of cloud parallel to it but slightly out from the hillside. Another eye-witness account, this time from the late eighteenth century, described how 'the Bar appears in continual agitation as boiling or struggling with contrary blasts; while the Helm all this time keeps a motionless station'.

It was Gordon Manley, in an academic study of the Helm wind published in 1945, who first came close to explaining the phenomenon, which is partly attributable to the gentle gradient on the eastern side of the ridge and the much more pronounced slope on the Eden valley side. The Helm only blows when there is a stable high pressure zone over the North Sea and a wind of at least force 5 blowing from there in a broadly south-westerly direction. At the summit of the ridge, the cold air represented by the visible Helm cloud is held under a layer of warmer air which effectively traps it. The wind continues to push the cold air down the western flank of the escarpment, where it increasingly picks up speed. Then, at the bottom of the fells the cold air is turned back up again where the moisture it carries condenses and the distinctive 'bar' cloud forms in mid-air, constantly rotating like, as it were, a mid-air whirlpool.

The Helm can blow for an hour or two but it can also last for days or even weeks. As well as the physical hazards of coping with a high wind, the incessant noise of the wind howling can be intensely depressing. As David Uttley puts it, 'Life suddenly becomes harder when the Helm Wind blows'.

Gordon Manley's research work at Moor House and on Great Dun Fell was to have a long and important scientific legacy. On Great Dun Fell itself, Manley's tradition of taking weather readings was continued by the Civil Aviation Authority when it put up a radar station there in 1948. The tradition of using the base as a centre for academic study continued when in the mid-1980s this radar station was replaced by the present large white 'golf ball', used to control aircraft movements through much of the UK's airspace and now under the control of staff of the National Air Traffic Service. Today the Centre for Atmospheric Science at Manchester University uses Great Dun Fell for work focused on monitoring the behaviour of clouds.

Great and Little Dun Fell, together with Moor House itself where Manley had begun his work, were included within the boundary of one of the first official nature reserves in England. Among its other provisions the National Parks and Access to the Countryside Act 1949 introduced for the first time the concept of national nature reserves, to be overseen by Nature Conservancy (later the Nature Conservancy Council), and this area of the Pennines, it was decided, was to be a pioneer. Moor House national nature reserve was designated in 1952 three years after the Act was passed and is now linked administratively with a second nearby reserve, Upper Teesdale, which received its nature reserve status in 1963. Moor House and Upper Teesdale reserves are significant among other things for the range of rare alpine plants to be found here, leftovers from ice age times, of which perhaps the most important is the marsh saxifrage. This attractive plant is to be found growing in the damp flushes running down the hillsides.

National nature reserves are designed to protect important and rare habitats, but the 1949 Act also identified another aim, that of providing opportunities for scientific research. At the Moor House reserve, this second objective has historically been the more important function (until it was closed at the end of the 1970s, the building at Moor House itself was a thriving research centre, on occasions with as many as thirty people working from it). Scientists have come and gone, and so too have the issues they have come to study, which have tended to reflect the particular concerns of the time. In the 1950s and 1960s, the pressure was to explore ways to make the high moorlands more productive agriculturally. Later the emphasis switched to monitoring acid rain and atmospheric pollution.

These days, the focus is very much on climate change. Where once Gordon Manley took weather readings, today at Moor House you're likely to find John Adamson or one of his team from the Centre for Ecology and Hydrology based at Lancaster on one of their regular field visits. The old Moor House building was condemned as unsafe and demolished in 1999 so instead today's researchers have made their lab in a small outhouse. It is from here that John and his colleagues are continuing the tradition of weather recording at the site, using both hourly automatic instruments and weekly-read ones. There's also equipment to monitor atmospheric and precipitation chemistry – or in other words, what the chemical composition is of clouds and rain. Hydrological sampling similar to that I saw way back on Bleaklow is being carried out, too, for example on the river water coming down Trout Beck from its source on Great Dun Fell. Peat – or more precisely the water in it – is regularly analysed for its chemical content.

And that's just the start. The Moor House site is one of twelve sites being closely watched as part of the UK Environmental Change Network programme, an initiative launched in 1992 which is aiming to collect and analyse long-term data which could identify trends in environmental and climate change. The data identified as potentially useful include a wide range of variables so that at Moor House animals, birds and insects are monitored, too, in order to detect any increase or decrease in their population. There's a bird count twice each breeding season, and a record kept of the dates when frogs spawn and tadpoles develop. Ground beetles and spiders are caught in pitfall traps and counted. Bats and butterflies are counted. Spittle bugs (the insects to be found inside the distinctive frothy bubbles often seen on grass stems) are counted in June and August. Fish, invertebrates and plankton in the streams are monitored. The population of rabbits, grouse and sheep is also subject to careful recording. 'Rabbit monitoring is probably the least favourite task,' John Adamson told me. Since it's not really possible to count the rabbits themselves in a very scientific way, what you do is to assess the evidence that they are there – or, put another way, you see how many rabbit droppings have built up on a designated stretch of the moorland over a two week period. The problem, of course, is that this land has to be guaranteed free of all existing droppings first. 'The job of clearing the droppings isn't very popular,' John admits.

The statistics which the Environmental Change Network is collecting at Moor House and at its other sites across Britain are already turning into an invaluable database which is helping to identify changes to our natural environment. But thanks to Gordon Manley's pioneering work, we already have a seventy-year run of weather data for Moor House to work on.

As John Adamson explains to me back in his office on the edge of Lancaster University campus, the evidence from this should give us pause for thought. For example, if you compare Moor House temperature trends since 1931, you find that average annual temperatures are now well over half a degree warmer than they were in Manley's day. The graph isn't a directly linear one: there was a slight increase between the 1930s and the 1950s, and a slight fall in the 1960s and 1970s. However, since the 1980s, there's been no mistaking a pretty steep rise in the temperature graph. The highest temperature ever recorded at Moor House was in August 2003, when the thermometer was reading 27.6°C (the temperature at Great Dun Fell summit was only a little less, at 24°C).

You get a similar story if you look at other weather data. For example, between 1931 and 1979, there were on average 133 days at Moor House when there was frost. Look at the period from 1991 to 2000 and this falls to 101 days. Or you can examine the records for the number of 'snow days' (days when there is snow lying at midday) each winter: here again the trend line is clearly downwards, with the current average down to something around 40 days a year.

The conclusion seems fairly unmistakable. To quote the ministerial preface to an influential report by the UK Climate Impacts Programme, 'Evidence is growing that the UK climate is warming and we expect this trend to continue. . . . Adaptation will be an essential part of the response to the threat of climate change.'

What does adaptation mean in relation to the northern Pennine moorlands? It means, among other things, that the prospects for those rare alpine plants like the marsh saxifrage which have hung on since immediate post-ice age times are not looking particularly rosy – and that in turn raises a host of conservation dilemmas about intervention or non-intervention which environmentalists have to wrestle with. John Adamson tells me that a 1°C rise in temperature is equivalent to a 15- or 20-kilometre shift northwards in terms of the equivalent climate zone, or an uphill move of about 100–150 metres. In other words, plants and creatures which have historically been comfortable half way down Great Dun Fell might be better off migrating higher up the hill. Those on the summit already, in what is known as a montane environment, clearly may have difficult times ahead.

Of course, climate change has been a feature in the past. As we have already seen, temperatures are thought to have been warmer by one or two degrees for several millennia in prehistoric times, a period known technically as the postglacial hypsithermal interval. Then, in the three millennia before the Romans, the weather changed and it got colder and wetter. The Romans generally had a slightly better deal from the British climate, but conditions deteriorated again for three or four hundred years during the so-called dark ages. And so it continued: a dry period around 1290–1410, for example, and cooler and wetter conditions during the 'little ice age' of around 1500 to 1850. Within these periods, there have also been shorter term fluctuations in the weather.

Tough as it may seem for the marsh saxifrage, you might want to maintain that the present trend towards higher temperatures is simply another turn of the climatic wheel of fortune. The prospect (as Gordon Manley suggested) that skiers might need to find accommodation on Great Dun Fell looks increasingly remote, but perhaps walkers will be able to enjoy more opportunities for sun-bathing as they plod the Pennine Way.

In fact, as the whole world is becoming all too aware, the evidence this time is that much of the change in climate is the result not of natural but of man-made factors, particularly our proclivity to fill the atmosphere increasingly with greenhouse gases. In 2002 the UK Climate Impacts Programme published four computer-modelled scenarios for climate change in Britain and, using this report, we can plot the likely way ahead for weather for the North Pennines. The worst case ('high emissions') scenario suggests that there could be a possible increase of 3.5°C in average temperatures by the 2080s, combined with a decline in summer rainfall of 40 per cent and an increase in rain in winter of 25 per cent.

Of course, worst case scenarios do not always come to pass. Nevertheless, there is increasing concern that even a small increase in average temperatures on the Pennine moors could have a highly damaging effect on our ability to control global warming. The reason? The peat.

The peat bogs of the Pennines are a superb storage place for carbon which would otherwise escape into the atmosphere and for several thousand years they have fulfilled this extremely useful function. The anxiety now, to put it bluntly, is that peat bogs will stop working. Worse, if the peat dries out and disappears, it will release its accumulated store of carbon back into the atmosphere. As more greenhouses gases are released from peat bogs, the more likely it will be that temperatures will rise still further – truly, a vicious circle.

It's perhaps the most important issue which any book on the Pennine moors has to cover, and it deserves a chapter of its own. But not just yet. First it is time to return to the watershed itself.

Manley was right, in that the Pennine Way when it was finally opened did come over Great Dun Fell – though sadly his hut had long gone by the time the route was officially opened in

The top of Cross Fell isn't so much a summit as a broad plateau. A walker investigates trig point number twenty-nine on the watershed.

1965. It's the first time since Pen-y-ghent that the Pennine Way has chosen to follow the line of the watershed, and it joined us just south of Great Dun Fell coming up from Dufton (the village whose young people's leisure pursuits caused Manley some concern). The reunion will not last long, however, for after little more than three miles the Pennine Way will be making its own way again, heading for the lower land of the South Tyne valley.

But first there is a highlight to share. Just to the north of Great Dun Fell is Little Dun Fell, and just to the north of here we arrive at the highest point of all on both the Pennine watershed and the Pennine Way, Cross Fell. At 893 metres (2930 feet), this is a mountain which deserves respect. It's higher than many well-known Lake District hills: higher than Blencathra, for example, than Coniston Old Man, High Street, Fairfield, Great Dodd or Steeple and a metre higher than Pillar. Only the highest Lakeland mountains can better it.

I arrived on Cross Fell in good weather, fortunately avoiding the Helm cloud and the other clouds which hug the summit all too frequently. It meant that I could enjoy the view to the full. The Lake District mountains were a superb sight, stretching round towards the south to meet up with the Shap Fells and the Howgill Fells. Behind me, directly south, were the distinctive shapes of Wild Boar Fell and the Mallerstang hills still in sight, while closer to hand was another watershed landmark I had already crossed, Little Fell. To the east, too, the view was beginning to open up, down to farmland and the valleys below. On these eastern moors is a watershed, not *the* Pennine watershed but an important one nevertheless: here, within a very short distance of each other, rise both the Tyne and Tees.

23. THE CUMBRIA RIDGE

Cross Fell – Green Fell – Knapside Hill – Hartside Top

It was the afternoon of the day I had been a guest of the army at Warcop. In the morning, I'd been watching young lads training to become soldiers. An hour later I was talking to Tom Pickard about poetry. Nobody can claim that the Pennine watershed doesn't offer variety.

Previously, as a walker you couldn't carry on from Cross Fell along the top of the escarpment unless you were in disobedient mood. Now with the coming of open access rights the hillside is there for all to enjoy. The team at the North Pennines AONB have produced a leaflet *Discover Open Country* to mark the new legislation. I noticed that they'd named the hilltop walk north from Cross Fell the Cumbria Ridge.

When you first leave Cross Fell and the Pennine Way there's a path of sorts to follow. But somewhere near the slight rise known as Green Fell (a slight rise compared with Cross Fell: it's still higher than Kinder Scout by several hundred feet) the trod peters out. After that, you make your way as best you can, past innumerable numbers of the curious stone curricks erected like sentinels in the landscape. The ancient bridle track known as Maiden Way, a through route between Eden and Tyne dating back to the Romans (or, who knows, perhaps earlier) crosses the watershed line. The watershed itself keeps a steady northerly direction. You look across the moors in anticipation of being able to see the traffic on the Penrith–Alston road but the road comes into sight later than you expect. There are several more miles of moor to cross first. Finally, the trig point shown on the map arrives (the modern map calls this Fiend's Fell, but I'm not convinced: Fiend's Fell was reportedly the name originally for Cross Fell itself). From the trig point – number thirty – it's a steady descent down, at last, to the main road, and a very welcome break for refreshments.

Hartside Top, at the very summit of the A686 from the Eden valley to Alston, is not necessarily the most obvious place to erect a café, but there's been one here in one shape or another since 1902. It was invaluable originally as a place to give your horse a rest; then it became invaluable when your car had struggled up the hill and your engine was boiling. Now, rebuilt after a fire in 1974, it's a popular port of call for motorbikers, for mountain bikers tackling the cycle version of the Coast-to-Coast, and indeed for almost anyone who travels this way. Kathryn Renwick, who has been running the café since 2001, has a varied clientele. Pensioners on coach trips call in. Grouse shooters have breakfast here. Gypsy horse wagons pull up *en route* to the annual horse fair at Appleby. Even, on occasions, a RAF mountain rescue helicopter has dropped by, literally, landing in a field at the back so that the crew could pick up an order of bacon butties they'd phoned through earlier.

So Hartside Top seemed the ideal place for me to meet up with Tom Pickard. Tom has been living up on the watershed, not so far away from the café, since the summer of 2002. He told

On a sunny weekend at the café on Hartside Top, motorbikes outnumber cars.

me, or I thought he told me, that he must be the poet with the highest address in England, and I replied that there could surely be no competition. Then I realised he'd said that he was perhaps the *person* with the highest address, a rather different matter, but even so I thought he was quite possibly correct.

We settled down for a lengthy conversation beside one of the big picture windows in the café, looking out over the Hartside moorland. I was interested in asking Tom how the landscape affected his work, and he replied by talking mainly about the ever-changing weather which came over the hills. He talked of the winds which blew – not just the Helm wind, he said, the Helm was just one many. He talked of the night when the wind reached over 100 mph and part of the roof of his house came off: 'I couldn't believe it, I was very excited by it.' He described how his bedroom could feel like a tent when the weather outside was raging. He described, too, the experience of lying down in among the heather and moorland grasses, photographing the same view again and again as the clouds swept by and the rain came and went.

Later, he gave me a photocopied note he'd written for a local writers' workshop, which provided a more formal response to the question I'd been trying to ask: 'I'm not sure, as an 'artist', how I relate to the landscape of the North Pennines and frankly don't want to – other than in what is produced. But as a man I live at almost 2,000 feet above sea level and walk out most days, whatever the weather, on to the hills and it always, without fail, restores my spirit. Most all of my poetry of the last four or five years has arisen in the landscape and much of it written outside in the landscape, or at least begun there,' he'd written.

It's been a long time since Boulsworth Hill and the Brontë moors, when I last looked at the way the Pennine landscape has influenced writers. Earlier on, when first planning the book, I'd expected that I would be mentioning some of Ted Hughes' powerful poems set in his own home landscape of the South Pennines; but in the end, the chapter was written and the next begun before Hughes's work found its rightful place. So when it comes to poetry and the Pennines, up to now all you've been offered is a snatch of dialect verse by Samuel Laycock and the Blackstone Edge song by chartist Ernest Jones.

Time to redress the situation. Time, perhaps, first to mention W.H. Auden who knew and loved the northern Pennines. He was born in York in 1907, though his family moved almost immediately to the Midlands and he spent most of his childhood at prep school in Surrey and public school in Norfolk. However, he once commented that 'Between the ages of six and twelve I spent a great many of my waking hours in the fabrication of a private secondary sacred world, the basic elements of which were (a) a limestone landscape mainly derived from the Pennine moors in the north of England, and (b) an industry – lead mining.'

His long conversational poem *New Year Letter*, written from New York in wartime and bearing the dateline 1st January 1940, suggests a similar obsession with the northern Pennines and their landscapes:

> Whenever I begin to think
> About the human creature we
> Must nurse to sense and decency,
> An English area comes to mind,
> I see the nature of my kind
> As a locality I love,
> Those limestone moors that stretch from Brough
> To Hexham and the Roman wall,
> There is my symbol of us all.

A few lines on, he continues in same vein:

> Always my boy of wish returns
> To those peat-stained deserted burns
> That feed the Wear and Tyne and Tees . . .

Auden's fascination with the remains of the lead mining industry provides the artistic focus of several early poems, including one written when he was about twenty and which – since it bears the title 'The Watershed' – surely has to claim its space here. The poem includes a mention of Cashwell, an old mine a short distance north-east of Cross Fell close to the old road over the hill, so the 'crux' of line one, it has been suggested, may be Cross Fell itself. The poem, like many Auden wrote at the time, is heavy with an atmosphere of unspecified danger and discontent. Those interested can find it in standard Auden collections, so I will quote just the first few lines:

> Who stands, the crux left of the watershed,
> On the wet road between the chafing grass
> Below him sees dismantled washing-floors,
> Snatches of tramline running to a wood,
> An industry already comatose,
> Yet sparsely living . . .

Auden's fascination with the North Pennines was that of someone living and writing from a distance. Basil Bunting by contrast was originally from Newcastle, and was living once again in the North-East when he came to write his best-known poem Briggflatts, the language of which has something of the rhythms and accents of Northumbrian speech. Though the poem ranges over fifty years of time and is set in part in Italy, Briggflatts has a strong whiff of the Pennines about it and the legend of Erik Bloodaxe's death in Stainmore is a recurring motif. The poem takes its title, Briggflatts, from an early Quaker meeting house in the Howgill Fells near Sedbergh, and it is in the landscape there beside the river Rawthey that the poem commences.

Though Bunting was Auden's senior in age by seven years, the former's intensely pared-down style of poetry seems to make his the more modern voice. It is Bunting that Tom Pickard gives as one of the artistic influences on his own work, but in fact Pickard himself – in his teens at the time – had a role in encouraging the writing of Briggflatts. Briggflatts was given a first reading by Bunting, by then in his mid-sixties, just before Christmas in 1965 in Newcastle, in an old building attached to the medieval walls of the city known as Morden Tower. This was (and indeed, still is) a venue for poetry, a sort of jazz club for words rather than music, which had first opened in 1964. Its presence in the city of Newcastle as a focus for the spoken word helped encourage Bunting to rediscover his poetic voice.

Morden Tower was, in part, Tom Pickard's idea, and it played a significant role in the poetry revival in Britain in the 1960s. Through his involvement he became friends with many contemporary American poets, including Allen Ginsberg, Robert Creeley and Ed Dorn, all three of whom gave readings at Morden Tower. Pickard's own poetry has been influenced in part by the American modernist movement in poetry, particularly the mid-twentieth-century movement known as the Black Mountain poets.

Tom Pickard's journey from working class teenager in Newcastle to his current home in the North Pennines has been, in tabloid journalise, colourful. He has lived for periods of time, among other places, in London, in Warsaw and in the States. He has written a number of radio documentaries and written and directed a number of film documentaries. He collaborated with Alan Hull of Lindisfarne in the 1974 BBC play *Squire*, and later played a part in the development of Paul McCartney's symphonic poem *Standing Stone*. Sometime during those years there was a creative writing fellowship and time spent studying social history at Ruskin College, Oxford. Sometime, too, there were divorces and a couple of bankruptcies.

But you want me to get back to the Pennines. Tom Pickard's recent collection of poetry, *The Dark Months of May*, in part charts a relationship break-up, the one which brought him to his present life on the high moors. This is how one American reviewer has described these particular poems: 'The poet anchors his calls, cries and ruminations in the landscape, the fierce, windblown area called Fiend's Fell in the North Pennine hills on the English/Scottish border. In deft, delicate lines he charts the bleakness of inner and outer weather.'

But it is a ballad from Tom Pickard's latest collaborative project with which I propose to close this chapter. The wonderful new Sage concert hall in Gateshead was the venue in 2005 for the first performance of a powerful folk opera for which Tom contributed the libretto and composer and saxophonist John Harle the music. The Northern Sinfonia, the Sage's resident orchestra, were there to perform it, and they were joined on stage by one of the North-East's best known folk musicians, the Northumbrian piper Kathryn Tickell, another one of Tom Pickard's circle of friends and collaborators. Kathryn Tickell's involvement was appropriate, for the opera itself *The Ballad of Jamie Allan* tells the tale of a man who was both one of the most celebrated performers on the smallpipes in his day and a complete scoundrel.

Jamie Allan's life was one long tale of thievery, horse-stealing, desertion (he allegedly joined the army several times and scarpered as soon as he had the proffered cash), and imprisonment, interspersed with numerous sexual encounters, but interspersed too with a period when his mastery of the pipes led to him becoming the piper for the Duke and Duchess of Northumberland in Alnwick castle. After his death in 1810, Allan's life story was the subject of numerous chapbook histories and he took on something of the mantle of a popular criminal hero like Dick Turpin or (later) Jesse James.

For the opera libretto, Tom Pickard explained to me, he'd tried to get back to the authentic story of Jamie Allan, and had spent time at the National Archives in Kew researching among other things Allan's army records. The libretto itself is not necessarily typical of the compressed style which Tom Pickard often brings to his poetry, but takes its feel from the traditional ballads of the English and Scottish borders. You have to hear Pickard's ballads set to John Harle's music to appreciate them fully, but here are the lyrics of one. It is entitled 'Hawthorn'.

> there is a hawthorn on a hill
> there is a hawthorn growing
> it set its roots against the wind
> the worrying wind that's blowing
> its berries are red its blossom so white
> I thought that it was snowing
>
> there is a hawthorn by a wall
> that looks down to the valley
> its berries are red its thorns are sharp
> it's where we said we'd marry
> its berries are red its blossom is white
> and the hail makes sharp weather
> without her now I'll make my bed
> in the bleeding heather
>
> come with me oh come with me
> come with me my darling
> the berries are red the thorns are sharp
> and the corbies are craawing
> don't send me out don't cut me down
> don't exile me my darling
> the thorns turn red kill the blossom dead
> and the tethered wind is snarling
>
> there is a hawthorn by a wall
> that looks down to the valley
> its berries are red its thorns are sharp
> it's where we said we'd marry
> its berries are red its blossom is white
> and the hail makes sharp weather
> without her now I'll make my bed
> in the bleeding heather.

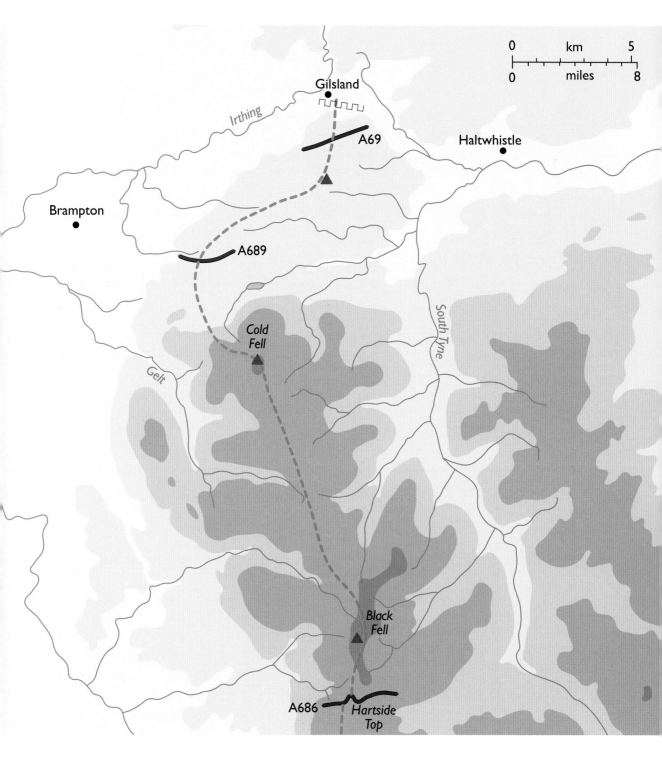

24. GELTSDALE

Hartside Top – Black Fell – Gillingbrigg Gate – Great Blacklaw Hill – Cold Fell

Steve Downing had seen a female hen harrier the previous Thursday and again on the Sunday before I met him. He was hopeful I would be lucky too, and took me out late one afternoon to one of his regular observation places. We sat quietly for an hour or two, but I wasn't in luck: no hen harriers that evening.

On the other hand, there was nobody out committing crime either which at least was a plus, for Steve's work means that he spends much of his time patrolling some of the remoter and wilder areas of the Pennines – and further afield, too – making sure the law isn't being broken. Steve's background is as a police officer, working first in South and more recently in West Yorkshire, and now, although he is technically a civilian, his job still involves policing work. The particular law he is concerned with is the Wildlife and Countryside Act 1981, or more precisely the part of it which protects wild birds, and it is the hen harrier which is the main focus of his attention.

Steve is part of a very small team of police and civilians who make up the National Wildlife Crime Unit. The unit is concerned about a number of problems: the illegal importing of live animals and birds such as parrots, for example, the importing of ivory, the illegal destruction of bat roosts, and the taking of wild birds of prey for collectors or falconers. However, high on the list of priorities, because of the persecution it has experienced, is the hen harrier. In 2004 the police launched a national campaign Operation Artemis, focused specifically on this bird. Steve, to all intents and purposes, *is* Operation Artemis.

You might imagine that hen harriers would be a relatively common sight along the Pennines. The bird is widely distributed in Scotland, and in recent years has been doing well in Wales, Northern Ireland and the Isle of Man. There are about 750 breeding pairs in the UK as a whole. But in England, it's a different story. Although one study suggested that the habitat could take well over 200 pairs of birds, the last few years have seen only between seven and fifteen successful breeding pairs in England. In other words, hen harriers remain one of England's rarest birds of prey.

They suffered historically, particularly at the hands of gamekeepers. Hen harriers eat a range of food, and are happy to snack on a plump field vole or a meadow pipit, for example. However they are also partial to red grouse chicks, and it is this proclivity which brought about their complete removal as a breeding bird from England. If you were trying to maximise grouse on a grouse moor, you were not pleased to have your moors shared with hen harriers. You also had means at your disposal to make sure the birds disappeared.

That was the past. Under the 1981 law it is now illegal to shoot or poison a hen harrier, to remove eggs or to disturb a nest. Nevertheless, Steve Downing told me, persecution continues. He told me of a case in the North-East where a hen harrier had disappeared in suspicious circumstances; a few days earlier, a man had been seen in the nearby countryside wearing camouflage gear and a full face mask. He also mentioned another recent case from Derbyshire, where two males had disappeared just at the time when their mates were nesting. Were the males killed? The suspicion has to be that they were.

Steve Downing himself prefers not to draw unnecessary attention to his movements, though the large metal aerial which he often carries in his hand is not precisely inconspicuous. As well as being ringed, many of the fledgling hen harriers in England have also been equipped with miniature radio transmitters and high-visibility coloured wing-tags. It means that, at least until the battery goes and the transmitter stops working, there's a chance to track their movements, hopefully get them in sight and then identify them. Steve had his aerial and receiver with him as he walked with me across the moors, but all that was coming back was static. Nevertheless, radio tracking has proved successful. I'd already read the story of how three young hen harriers born in the North Pennines in 2005, a male and two females, had been followed during their first winter: the male had died in December in Northumberland, but one of the females had been tracked to the east coast, at Teesmouth, where it stayed for the autumn before crossing back across the Pennines to Settle and then moving to the Forest of Bowland. The second had, probably, got as far as Somerset before returning north, also to Bowland.

Radio tracking is better than nothing but what really enables you to know where a bird is at any one time is satellite tracking, and in 2007 a pilot programme was introduced for the first time in England to enable ten hen harriers to be equipped with the necessary kit. This is one way in which it's hoped that technology can be used to build up a much more detailed picture of hen harrier behaviour. DNA sampling is another major new idea. Recent years have seen the beginnings of the creation of a major DNA database of hen harriers in Britain, which should very soon reveal much more information about the migratory and mating habits of the birds. The work, begun in 2006, is being coordinated from the forensic science department of the University of Central Lancashire.

I asked Steve the obvious question: how do you set about getting a hen harrier's DNA? The answer, he told me matter-of-factly, was by getting a mouth swab. You use a special extra large cotton bud, which you carefully poke inside the bird's mouth. It was, I got the impression, not difficult. DNA sampling has been carried out for several years on other birds of prey including peregrine falcon, and it has already helped reduce crime levels.

The young birds who had been electronically spied on during their winter journeys had grown up in the RSPB's Geltsdale reserve in the North Pennines, a large area of the moors at the very northern end of the Cumbria Ridge which I entered on my penultimate day on the Pennine hills. I'd left the Hartside Top café, making use of new stiles put in as a consequence of the access legislation to walk along the moorland fence to the trig point at Black Fell, and then continuing to the boundary marker named on the map as Tom Smith's Stone. My later attempts to find out more about Tom Smith failed dismally, but nevertheless his stone marks a historic boundary. It is carved on its four sides with letters, A on the south face which I took to stand for Alston Moor parish, K on the northern (probably for the combined parish of Knaresdale with Kirkhaugh), and W and C or G on the east and west flanks respectively, both these letters leaving me puzzled. But the important boundary here is the one between Cumberland/Cumbria and Northumberland. Although I would be

Dave O'Hara spotting black grouse at the RSPB reserve of Geltsdale.

crossing back into Cumbria after a few more miles, it felt good at last to be in my destination county of Northumberland. I stayed close to the county boundary past Gillingbrigg Gate, over Merelaw Hill and Three Pikes to the curious pile of stones marked as Hornby's House. I know as much about Hornby as I do about Tom Smith, I'm afraid, but if I were him I would look for a new home.

The Cumbria Ridge ends inside the RSPB's reserve at Cold Fell where, in effect, the Pennines stop too. It means that, weather permitting, Cold Fell has great views to offer, down to the Tyne valley below, across to the hills of Galloway and ahead across Kielder Forest towards the Cheviots. I was fortunate, the weather was good and the views were there, rolled out below for me to enjoy.

Cold Fell is another place which officially wasn't accessible before the 2000 law change, though Dave O'Hara, who heads the RSPB team at the Geltsdale reserve, says that previously there had been tacit acceptance of walkers. Although this land is a Site of Special Scientific Interest, a Special Protection Area and a Special Area of Conservation (chapter 7 will refresh your memory if necessary), Dave welcomes walkers on the RSPB's reserve. 'We want people to enjoy the uplands. Geltsdale is a wonderful place for birds, and I have no problem with open access. There may sometimes be conflict with conservation needs, but I tend to think it's exaggerated,' he says.

The hen harrier is one of the main reasons for the RSPB's presence at Geltsdale, which goes back to 1975 but which was expanded considerably in 2000 when Geltsdale became one of the organisation's most significant upland reserves in England. Some of the moorland has been purchased by the RSPB but some of the reserve – and there is a nice irony here – the RSPB controls by dint of having acquired the shooting tenancy rights. The moors are actively

A dry-stone wall snaking up a flank of Cold Fell.

managed by the RSPB's Geltsdale team, though not in quite the same as a gamekeeper would set about the task. Dave O'Hara describes, for example, the way that they are experimenting with heather cutting as an alternative to burning.

As well as the hen harrier, nine other birds of prey can be found on the reserve, including the buzzard, peregrine falcon and short-eared owl. Geltsdale is also important for golden plover, curlew, lapwing and other waders, and there's one other special bird to be found here, the black grouse. Black grouse are much larger and much rarer than their red cousins. Their numbers have dropped dramatically in England in the past century but they are beginning to make a comeback in the North Pennines and northern Dales. The magnificent display by male bird, the blackcock, is known as the lek and is one of the most impressive native British ornithological treats.

I had arrived too late in the year to see the main leks, and too late as well to see the two hen harrier chicks which, rather disappointingly, had been the total hen harrier achievement for Geltsdale for that year – the outcome of just one breeding pair. But later, when I met up with Dave O'Hara in the nearby RSPB office, I was able at least to watch the chicks on the CCTV footage recorded during the year. The RSPB and other conservation bodies take no chances during the nesting season. At Geltsdale, hen harrier nests are permanently monitored by teams of staff and volunteers, as well as by sets of CCTV cameras. Filming continues throughout the night, using an infrared camera.

It might seem a little excessive, but the Geltsdale team have reason to take precautions. In 2005, the bodies of two buzzards and a peregrine falcon were found near the reserve. It seemed they died as a result of poisoning, a dead rabbit laced with the poison having been used as the bait. In 2001, six eggs disappeared from a harrier's nest. In 2000, a female harrier was shot. In 1999, another female bird had been poisoned. The year before, the corpse of a shot harrier had been found in the reserve. The year before that, a male hen harrier had been shot. And the list goes on. As the RSPB has said, someone in the area has had a callous disregard for wildlife.

Hen harriers are agile and acrobatic birds, able to swoop very low over the ground to take their prey. The males also put on particularly spectacular aeronautical displays in March and April as a way of attracting females, a mating display which has given the bird the nickname 'skydancer'. For many years their main breeding area in England has been the Forest of Bowland, where the bird has been chosen for the logo for Bowland's Area of Outstanding Natural Beauty, but in recent years they have successfully bred in Pennine areas as well, in the eastern Yorkshire Dales and the Peak District as well as in the Geltsdale reserve.

But nevertheless they don't seem to be making the comeback in the Pennines which had been hoped for when, in 2001, English Nature prioritised the bird and set up the Hen Harrier Recovery Project.

It should be said that this project, even with the extremely limited results it has achieved to date, has been highly controversial with some people. The respectable shooting organisations and shooting estates know they have to abide by the law, but the law doesn't demand that they have to *like* hen harriers, and by and large they most definitely do not. When a hen harrier is seen flying over a grouse moor, the thoughts of most gamekeepers will be on dead grouse chicks, not on skydancing displays.

The Game Conservancy Trust went as far in 2004 as to say that English Nature (as it then was) needed to rethink its whole hen harrier recovery programme. The Trust claimed that originally it had believed that an increase in harriers would be likely to have only a minor effect on grouse stocks – 'an inconvenience rather than a threat'. But the Trust now thought that the effect of harrier predation on grouse had been significantly underestimated, and it pointed to the experience of a pilot experiment in Langholm, Dumfriesshire in the 1990s where, it claimed, an increase in hen harrier numbers had led to the complete collapse of grouse shooting. 'If unchecked, predation by hen harriers on grouse stocks could be severe enough to bring an end to driven grouse shooting in England,' it argued. 'We think it is essential to pursue harrier conservation in a way that does not jeopardise moorland management.'

For the Trust, the idea that the English uplands and moors could accommodate more than 200 breeding pairs was also unrealistic, and the Trust proposed an 'imposed ceiling' of no more than 72 pairs. It also wanted to see the bird's population restricted in the shooting areas of the north of England and instead introduced into new areas away from grouse moors such as Dartmoor. (To achieve this would require applying for formal derogation from the relevant part of the EU's Birds Directive).

It has to be added that the Game Conservancy Trust wasn't too happy about the work of Steve Downing and his colleagues, even though it and other shooting organisations had originally been signed up as supporters to the police campaign: 'We think that solely pursuing an aggressive law-enforcement approach to hen harrier conservation on grouse moors is counter-productive. . . . High-profile, zero-tolerance style campaigns like Operation Artemis are counter-productive in the long run even from a hen harrier conservation perspective.'

I put this point to Steve as we sat chatting, listening to the static coming in on his radio receiver and looking through binoculars at an empty sky. He made a sort of harrumphing noise: 'To talk of derogation to the Birds Directive when we have about ten breeding pairs in England is bizarre. It's quite hard to find a logical argument. Hen harriers do have an impact on grouse numbers, but it's not significant – they also eat voles and small birds,' he told me. The problem, he claimed, was more that some heather moors had been overgrazed and poorly managed. And he also thought that some of the anti-harrier sentiment came from a visceral emotional response: 'People perceive them as evil birds,' he said.

I nodded in agreement. Attributing evil intentions to a wild bird was no doubt simply another form of human beings' desire to anthropomorphise creatures, to endow them with human attributes. On the other hand, I did have to add, wasn't it true that they could be aggressive birds, particularly when nesting or with young? I recounted my first sighting of a hen harrier one spring some years back in the Forest of Bowland, when a female harrier introduced herself to me by attacking me repeatedly, dive-bombing my head. 'Hmm, the best technique is to get a stick, put a bobble hat on it, and go on to your hands and knees; then it will simply whack the hat,' Steve counselled me.

Steve's work on behalf of the hen harrier is a mix of days spent out on the moors and time dedicated to giving talks to groups of bird watchers or presentations at conferences. He says that he is not unsympathetic to the position which gamekeepers find themselves in, but he is also determined that the persecution which the hen harrier has suffered has to stop. 'This is a species in difficulty,' he says. 'Since Operation Artemis came in, we've had no nests destroyed, and that's a major success.' But he admits that the battle against wildlife crime is on-going, and is never going to be completely won.

25. THE PEAT BENEATH OUR FEET

Cold Fell

Somewhere south of Cold Fell I became intimately acquainted with a bog. One moment I was striding along, talking to the friend I was with, and enjoying the countryside. The next I was up to my waist in gloopy water.

I extracted myself, damp and a little dirty with little pieces of sphagnum moss clinging to my clothes. No harm done. We carried on. And, once I'd had the time to dry off a little and I'd thought about it, in a way I was pleased that the bog was there. Compared with the dry peat deserts I had traversed on my first few days on the Pennine watershed, this was an altogether different, and much better, example of a peatland habitat. I'd encountered a blanket bog in pretty rude health.

If you've read this far, you'll know that there are a number of reasons why it's considered important that our Pennine peat moorlands are in good condition. One is because a healthy blanket bog leads to greater biodiversity of plant and animal life. A second reason is because a large percentage of the population of northern England gets its drinking water from off the peat moors, and peat erosion leads to both discolouration and an increase in the presence of particles in the water.

But there's another reason, arguably even more important, which I briefly mentioned a few chapters back. Peat bogs act as a superb store for carbon which could otherwise escape into the atmosphere as carbon dioxide or methane, fuelling the greenhouse effect. If we lose our peat bogs, we risk increasing still further the problems we face of global warming.

School children learn the basic principle of photosynthesis, whereby plants convert carbon dioxide and water into oxygen and glucose. When plants die and decay, under normal circumstances, the carbon held by the plant is released back into the atmosphere. In certain circumstances, however, especially where the ground is very waterlogged, lack of oxygen prevents micro-organisms from getting to work and the process of decomposition doesn't take place. Dead plants are instead slowly turned into peat, with the carbon safely retained in the soil. Peat, in other words, is what's known as a carbon sink.

This is the reason, of course, why peat has over the centuries been dug, dried and used as a fuel. As with coal, the carbon it contains is combustible and can be used to provide heat and light. This is also why, when peat-covered moorland catches fire, environmentalists are concerned: carbon dioxide is escaping into the atmosphere in much the same way it does from coal-fired power stations.

Peat formation is a slow process – perhaps a centimetre of peat each ten years – but Britain's peat has been building up for several millennia which means that the amount of carbon trapped within peat bogs has become quite significant. An academic at Durham

An isolated farmstead, backed by the bulk of Cold Fell.

University, Dr Fred Worrall, has come up with a striking way of looking at this, so striking that you can now find his phrase quoted again and again in publications. I'm happy to repeat it one more time: there is more carbon held in British bogs, Dr Worrall says, than in the forests of Britain and France added together. In his own words, 'peat is much more vital in terms of carbon storage than forests'.

The Pennine moors make up a small part of what are called the northern peatlands, which stretch around the world from Siberia through Scandinavia to northern Canada and Alaska. It's been estimated that the land masses of the planet hold three times the amount of carbon currently in the atmosphere, with much of this carbon held within the soil itself; and of this, the northern lands hold at least 20–30 per cent of the total. This is one reason why recent reports from Siberia and elsewhere of the rapid melting of the permafrost and the apparent destruction of peatland habitats has been causing concern to scientists worldwide.

What about our own bogs? For peat to be accumulated in the Pennines, the right sort of climate conditions have to be in place. When I'd talked to John Adamson of the Centre for Ecology and Hydrology about his work at Moor House, he'd told me that there were four key criteria for successful peat formation. The first is that there has to be plenty of rain: about a thousand millimetres a year as a minimum. (At present, Moor House with about 2,000 mm easily meets this; the Peak District moors do too, with average annual rainfall of 1,200–1,500 mm). Secondly, there has to be a minimum of 160 wet days. Thirdly, the average temperatures in the warmest summer months shouldn't be too hot: a mean of less than 15°C is required. And finally, there needs to be relatively minor seasonal fluctuations in the climate. Meet all these conditions and you will have the right sort of waterlogged conditions to prevent vegetation from decomposing.

When everything is working well, I'd gathered, a healthy peat bog can fix about 50 grams of carbon per square metre each year – about 50 metric tonnes per square kilometre. (This by itself is not an enormous quantity: it equates very roughly with the amount of extra carbon released into the atmosphere from air travel if twenty-five people make a holiday trip to the Caribbean and back. Fortunately, as anyone walking the watershed will testify, there are many thousands of square kilometres of Pennine peat moorland to take into account.) However, what's not clear is the extent to which peat is still being accumulated; are our peat bogs still acting as carbon sinks?

All of the country's soil was carefully assessed and measured for its carbon content as part of the National Soil Inventory which took place in the late 1970s, and it was recently sampled again in a study by the National Soil Resources Institute to check whether carbon levels had increased or decreased since then. The findings, reported in 2005, were that the soils of England and Wales, taken together, were losing carbon each year at an average rate of 0.6 per cent, a rate of loss which equates to around four million tonnes of carbon a year. If true (and it should be added that the study has since come in for some criticism from other academics) this would be unexpectedly grim news: the apparent loss of carbon from the soil would be cancelling out any successes which Britain has been having in reducing greenhouse gas emissions.

The question that's relevant to us is what's happening specifically with peat. Because of its significance as a carbon sink, researchers have been paying particular attention in recent years to upland peat and the land around the Moor House reserve has been a major focus for their work. There's a sense, perhaps, of academics today building on the past generations of researchers going right back to the time of Gordon Manley. Durham University, for example, has had sophisticated measuring devices up on the Moor House reserve trying to trap and measure the gases which are leaving the peat to enter into the atmosphere. This is the most direct way in which carbon dioxide (and other greenhouse gases such as methane) escape, but it is not the only route. Carbon can also be taken away through the streams and rivers which drain the land, either dissolved in the water (dissolved organic carbon, DOC) or in particulate form (particulate organic carbon, POC). To measure levels of DOC and POC you need some of the hydrologists' toolkit of equipment which I saw in place out on the moors near Bleaklow, though I was intrigued to discover that it's not only high-tech kit which gets used: a good way to measure levels of particulates, I learned, is to put a small mat of Astroturf down in a stream and wait to see what gets caught on it.

Trout Beck, a stream south-east of Great Dun Fell which flows into the Tees has been especially targeted by researchers, including the man-with-the-quote Dr Fred Worrall himself. In a 2003 study he and a number of colleagues carefully measured the levels of DOC and POC escaping down the stream, looked also at levels of methane and inorganic carbon coming from the peat, and concluded that here, at least, the peat moor was functioning adequately as a carbon sink. Their research suggested that each year on average about thirteen tonnes of carbon per square kilometre were becoming stored within the Pennine peat – rather less than the target of fifty tonnes, perhaps, but still on the right side of the balance sheet.

What worries soil scientists and hydrologists however is that, increasingly, peatlands will start giving out more carbon than they take in: that they will become carbon sources, not carbon sinks. There are a number of reasons for this, but climate change is the key factor. The two particular dangers are hot dry summers with drought-like conditions and very wet winters. Dry summers bake the peat, cause it to crack open and allow oxygen in through these fissures to oxidise the carbon below. Wet winters make the rivers and streams 'flashy', eroding peat banks and carrying the peat away down the hillside. Unfortunately, as you may recall, computer modelling of Britain's future climate carried out by the UK Climate Impacts Programme suggest that both these eventualities will become increasingly likely. The worst case for the North Pennines saw a significant increase in average temperatures by the 2080s, a decline in summer rainfall and an increase in rain in winter (to refresh your memory, see page 172).

The really frightening scenario is not just that global warming will stop new peat from forming, it is that the carbon already stored in existing peat will increasingly start to be unlocked allowing it to enter the atmosphere. What could happen, in other words, is a climatic equivalent of the sort of screeching feedback you can get when a microphone is placed too near a speaker. The world gets hotter. Result: peat bogs start giving up their carbon stores. Carbon dioxide (and, worse, methane) enters the atmosphere. Result: the world gets hotter still. The cycle speeds up, and gets faster and faster. This is why journalists have started using terms like the 'carbon time bomb'. What should give pause for thought is that the fuse on this bomb is short.

I recalled one conversation I'd had as I'd progressed my way along the watershed. I'd been talking to an ecologist working for Natural England who had responsibility for one of the Pennines moors' Sites of Special Scientific Interest. Our conversation had moved from the work he was doing to encourage biodiversity on his moorlands on to the subject of climate change. 'The people who are doing the research work tell us we have only about a decade's breathing space,' he told me. 'Climate change is irreversible, and our peat bogs could become a source, rather than a sink, of carbon in a decade's time.'

It's true that, as a society, we are becoming increasingly conscious of the risk of carbon emissions. But the importance of the Pennine bogs, and those of Scotland, Wales and Ireland too, is not yet widely understood. 'You can plant a tree to salve your conscience. But what you should really be doing is looking after the peat bogs,' he said. 'If we act now, we can at least ensure that the impact is less severe.'

So how do we do this? It comes back to a theme which this book has focused on several times already, good moorland management and moorland restoration work. It means many things. It means trying to prevent peat from becoming eroded. When erosion has occurred, it means trying to bring back vegetation. It means in some places trying to lessen the impact brought about by visitors to the countryside. It means avoiding overgrazing, and being sensitive to the effects which can come from heather and grass burning.

It particularly means trying to avoid the peat drying out. Maintaining a high water table in blanket bog land is critical and sphagnum moss, because it acts like a sponge, is one of the key species which help to achieve this. Where peat has already become dry, as in the Peak District and the South Pennine moors, the strategy has to be to take steps to rewet the moor. Ironically,

Between Cold Fell and Hadrian's Wall, the moors give way to a more benign, farming landscape.

government grants were widely available in the 1980s to dig drainage channels in moorland, to reduce the water level and to make the land more productive agriculturally (and incidentally more productive for grouse shooting). Now, only a generation on, it's become clear just what a disaster this policy has been. Moorland grips (drainage ditches) began as narrow channels but have become eroded so that in some places they are as wide as roads. Today government funding is available not for creating grips but for blocking them, so that the moors have a chance to become waterlogged once again. And some ecologists are suggesting that companies should join in the funding of this work too, supporting grip blocking programmes and bog management systems as a way of offsetting their CO_2 emissions. Plant a tree if you like. Protect a bog as well.

There are grounds for some optimism. Manchester University's Martin Evans has, like Fred Worrall, undertaken research on the land drained by Trout Beck, and his findings support the suggestion that this area could be working better as a store of carbon than it was a generation ago. Of course, this may yet be reversed again as we suffer from climate change. But Martin points out that the northern Pennine moors seem to be healthier now than they were in the second half of the twentieth century. Eroded areas have disappeared and vegetation has come back. If this can happen in the North Pennines, perhaps it can happen further south as well.

As I'd found out at first hand, there are areas of the Pennine moors which today are very healthily boggy and wet. That's the way they need to be. We need to learn to love our peat bogs.

26. HADRIAN'S WALL

Cold Fell – Coalfell (A689) – Blenkinsopp Common – Gapshield – Gilsland

And after all that, I arrived at Hadrian's Wall.

I'm not sure there's much to say about the last day. I was with a friend Richard Blakeley who had also accompanied me on my day in Stainmore, and by dint of careful checking of timetables we'd worked out that we could start and finish at Brampton, getting a bus out around nine o'clock on the Alston road and returning later in the afternoon from Gilsland. We got off the morning bus in the small settlement of Coalfell (the name is significant: there were several coal mines providing work for several hundred miners directly below Cold Fell) and made our way along a bridleway across a low moor called Greenside Rigg and Folly Rigg. We were barked at by a dog. We met a retired farmer, who stopped for a chat: she was, she said, helping a neighbour bring in the yows. We looked slightly half-heartedly and without success for a set of cup-marked rocks shown on the map. We also reached the very last trig point of all, a modest 289 metres above sea level. It was, I'm almost certain, the thirty-third I had passed.

Having decided to start this journey at Mam Tor, it seemed appropriate to finish it at Hadrian's Wall, another historic landmark. Ideally, the Romans would have built a major fort exactly on the line of the watershed, providing book authors two thousand or so years later with a fitting climax to their books. Sadly, they didn't. Richard and I went to look at the remains of the turret and milecastle just to the east of the watershed, but there wasn't much to see. Then we turned west and went as far as Birdoswald Fort to the west of Gilsland, which is a very much more impressive site, but which involves *crossing running water* and is therefore well beyond the remit of any account of the watershed. On the way back, we stopped and talked to three men whose work it was to repoint Hadrian's Wall, a slow and apparently never ending task which they undertook for a contractor who in turn undertook it for English Heritage. Ray Craig, who'd been doing the same work to the wall on and off since the Ministry of Public Building and Works was in charge back in 1970, talked of the special lime-based mortar used for the pointing work and how it was imported from a particular centre in France and how it was chosen for Hadrian's Wall because it was porous and breathable. This was interesting. But Ray revealed that he had already told his story for Hunter Davies' book on the Roman wall, and anyway we were still some distance from the watershed. So I closed my notebook, shook hands and Richard and I returned to Gilsland.

The watershed squeezes its way through just to the east of the town, between the Tyne tributaries and the west-flowing Irthing, the gap in the hills here being recognised by the name given to the settlement of The Gap. Of course, the watershed doesn't stop here. Beyond, it

Birdoswald Fort, near Gilsland: the site once housed a thousand Roman troops.

carries on towards Scotland, making a big sweep round to the east to accommodate all the Irthing's tributaries, passing through Kielder Forest, climbing once more to Cheviot outliers such as Sighty Crag and Glendhu, crossing the Border near the village of Newcastleton and then heading off into the Borders, not so very far from that other, Scottish, Pen-y-ghent/Pennygant mountain. And on, further.

But I had reached the geological divide which Brian Young had told me about, the Stublick Fault, and that meant the Pennines had come to an end. It was time to stop. Richard and I decided that the best way to finish the journey was with a drink in one of Gilsland's pubs.

And anyway we had more than an hour to wait for the bus.

SOURCES AND ACKNOWLEDGMENTS

This is a book which will, I hope, be read for pleasure, and it wouldn't have been appropriate to have weighed down the text with the sorts of footnotes or source attributions appropriate to an academic work.

But I'm also aware that books on the countryside can sometimes suffer from a surfeit of throw-away authorial assertions which turn out to be based on hearsay rather than evidence, a trap which I have tried my best to avoid. Any factual information I give in the text is intended to be able to withstand scrutiny, and for any mistakes which, despite my efforts, have crept in, I give my apologies now.

This section of the book, therefore, is designed to help those readers who want to know the sources I have used or to have suggestions for further reading. This is where I will be unpicking the stitching of the book, to show the threads which I used in putting it together in the first place.

As will be clear by now, the book is structured around a journey north along the Pennine watershed, focused on people and places along the way. But although this is what drives the narrative forward it would not, I think, have helped the book if I had chosen to stick too rigidly to the details of my own particular journey. A little literary structuring has had to be carried out, in the name of readability. I intend, therefore, at this point also to take my exercise in deconstruction a stage further and, for those readers who may be interested, to give the actual details of how I got from Mam Tor to Hadrian's Wall.

For I did indeed make the journey along the watershed. The whole trip was originally broken down into eighteen day-long legs, though in the end I concertina-d four days in the North Pennines into two. So in total, I had sixteen days out on the hills. The legs were undertaken between August and October 2006, sometimes by myself but more often in the company of friends, and sometimes walking but more often fell-running. Mostly I did each of the sixteen legs sequentially, starting in the south and making my way gradually northwards; two or three legs were done out of order, however. My day on the Warcop firing range, for example, had to coincide with a public access weekend there.

I estimate that I walked or ran about 250–260 miles in the course of researching this book. About two miles of the whole watershed were left unwalked, however. This was a stretch between the northern edge of the Warcop range and High Cup Nick, which simply got squeezed out. When I was at High Cup Nick, which I'd reached from Appleby, I wanted to head north not south; and my day on Warcop took me as far as Scordale Head before it was time to turn back, to catch the last of the daylight, leaving the short northern section as I thought for another day.

Some readers may be shocked by this admission. In reality, I could easily have returned to complete this missing gap on one of the many later visits I made to the North Pennines. I decided not to. I've decided to leave the journey uncompleted in this way – perhaps it's better like that.

Kinder Scout

The nineteenth-century quotation about Kinder is taken from:

Jennings, Louis J., (1880). *Rambles Among the Hills* (John Murray).

For any account of the Kinder trespass, the starting point is Benny Rothman's own beautifully illustrated account produced for the fiftieth anniversary, which has long deserved to be reprinted:

Rothman, Benny, (1982). *The 1932 Kinder Trespass* (Willow Publishing).

Kinder is covered enthusiastically in Howard Hill's guide to the access struggles:

Hill, Howard, (1980). *Freedom to Roam* (Moorland Publishing).

For a more jaundiced account from another part of the rambling movement, see Tom Stephenson's posthumously published memoirs:

Stephenson, Tom, (1989). *Forbidden Land: The Struggle for Access to Mountain and Moorland* (Manchester University Press).

For a comprehensive guide to the history of the British outdoor movement and its quest for access, see:

Taylor, Harvey, (1997). *A Claim on the Countryside* (Keele University Press).

Benny Rothman's personal archive is preserved in the Working Class Movement Library in Salford. Among his papers are his notes of his intended speech to the Derby Assizes and a typed report of the actual speech he made at the earlier committal proceedings. The extensive set of correspondence in the run-up to the fiftieth anniversary of Kinder in 1982 is particularly interesting.

The words to the song 'For, by Kinder . . .' etc. are in a letter to Rothman from another trespasser George Sumner dated 19th April 1982. (It has been suggested elsewhere that Ewan MacColl might have been the song's author.) Also from the Working Class Movement Library archive comes Rothman's recollection of cycling in the Lakes, his comments on his parents (from a letter sent to Jerry Pearlman), and a newspaper cutting of Sol Gadian's letter about the trespass.

A short biography of Benny Rothman 'Not Just a Rambler!' written by Bernard Barry is available on-line at www.wcml.org.uk/people/benny_r_intro.htm.

Although I choose not to focus on an earlier period in the story of Kinder Scout and the rambling movement, one useful source (from the Sheffield side) is:

Sissons, David (ed.), (2002). *The Best of the Sheffield Clarion Ramblers' Handbooks, 'Ward's Piece'* (Halsgrove, Tiverton).

My thanks to Melanie Tebbutt of Manchester Metropolitan University for sharing with me her work on the Sheffield Clarion rambler G.H.B. Ward in her paper:

Tebbutt, Melanie, (2006). 'Rambling and Manly Identity in Derbyshire's Dark Peak, 1880s–1920s', *Historical Journal*, 49, 4.

I chose one of the hottest days of the year to begin the journey described in this book, and I only just about had enough water with me. My train out from Manchester, as I report, was to Edale. After crossing Kinder and reaching Snake Pass I returned via the Doctor's Gate track to Glossop, pausing briefly to try to cool off in the waters of Shelf Brook. From Glossop I caught a train back to Manchester. This leg I undertook by myself, though the hills themselves were full of others enjoying themselves.

Bleaklow

For much of this, and the following, chapter I have to thank the staff of Moors for the Future for their support, advice and time. I particularly acknowledge the help proffered by Chris Dean, Jonathan Walker, Aletta Bonn and Matt Buckler. Most of the resources produced by Moors for the Future are currently on their website www.moorsforthefuture.org.uk. Among documents I found useful are the 'Moors for the Future Partnership Interim Report 2003–2005' (n.d.), and the set of Moors for the Future Research Notes, particularly 'Breeding Bird Survey of the Peak District Moorlands' (May 2005), 'Peak District Moorland Gully Blocking in Deep Peat' (September 2005),

'Peak District Moorland Stream Survey' (September 2005) and 'Heavy Metal Pollution in Eroding Peak District Moors' (September 2005).

I also acknowledge the help offered by Penny Anderson of Penny Anderson Associates. For my introduction to the Peak District's hydrology and geomorphology, my thanks go to Dr Martin Evans of Manchester University, and to Andy Keen of Penny Anderson Associates, who took me out for a morning's site visit on the slopes of Black Hill.

The establishment of the Moors for the Future project followed earlier moorland restoration work, documented in a series of reports including:

Anderson, P., Tallis, J.H. and Yalden, D.W., (1997). *Restoring moorlands. Peak District moorland management project phase III report* (English Nature).

The *Overexposed* plane crash has been widely written about; the best account is in:

Collier, Ron. and Wilkinson, Roni, (1979, republished 1990). *Dark Peak Aircraft Wrecks 1.* (Barnsley Chronicle Newspaper Group, 1979, Wharncliffe Publishing, 1990, Leo Cooper, later editions).

In addition to my time spent with Peter McGrory, I crossed Bleaklow on a day which began with a train ride to Glossop (and a slow pull up Doctor's Gate) and ended with a bus trip to Huddersfield on bus 310 from Holme village. My thanks to Richard Leonard who came with me and helped keep me on the right route through the Bleaklow groughs. The bus driver was understanding of our peat-encrusted sweaty state.

Black Hill

This chapter forms something of a diptych with the preceding one, and most of the acknowledgments and sources given for Bleaklow apply here too.

Wainwright's experience of Black Hill is in:

Wainwright, A., (1968). *Pennine Way Companion.* (Westmorland Gazette, 1968, Frances Lincoln, 2003).

For the story of Holme Moss TV transmitter, I used the press cuttings at Huddersfield reference library and an undated booklet (1960s?) from BBC North Region entitled 'Holme Moss brings Programmes on BBC Television and VHS Sound to Your Home'. This, and a 1951 booklet, are available on http://tx.mb21.co.uk/gallery/holmemoss/. For the Woodhead railway history I used www.wikipedia.org; another site is www.thewoodheadsite.org.uk. For the E8 long-distance footpath, see the European Ramblers' Association website, www.era-ewv-ferp.org.

My day spent running the watershed from Holme Moss to Blackstone Edge and then onwards to the Calder valley turned out to be the longest leg of the book, and has ended up worth four chapters. Once again my thanks go to Richard Leonard for sharing it with me. Thanks too to Jane Scullion who took a roundabout route to work to drop us off at Holme Moss; she has contributed much else besides to the book.

Standedge

For background on the effect of the American Civil War on the cotton industry I used the following:

Law, Brian, (1995). *Fieldens of Todmorden* (George Kelsall).

My edition of Samuel Laycock's *Collected Writings* was published in 1908. I include a little more about Laycock's verse in my book *The Pennine Divide: Walking the Moors between Greater Manchester and Yorkshire* (Frances Lincoln, 2005). Perhaps the most convenient place to find the full text of Laycock's poem 'Welcome Bonny Brid!' is in the extended edition of Glyn Hughes's book *Millstone Grit: A Pennine Journey* (Chatto and Windus The Hogarth Press, 1985).

Two complementary books with much useful detail on Standedge are:

Stonehouse, W.P.B., Chadderton, David (ed.), (2001). *The Prehistory of Saddleworth and Adjacent Areas* (Saddleworth Archaeological Trust).

Booth, Ken, (2001). *Roman Saddleworth* (Saddleworth Archaeological Trust).

For the story of Standedge Tunnel I used:

Gibson, Keith (2002). *Pennine Dreams: The Story of the Huddersfield Narrow Canal* (Tempus Publishing).

Also informative are two websites:

www.penninewaterways.co.uk/huddersfield/index.htm

www.huddersfieldcanal.com

My thanks to Fred Carter and his colleagues, and also to Rowena Pemford (British Waterways).

White Hill

I am not aware of any detailed history of the Pennine Way, so much of this chapter is based on primary source material in the Ramblers' Association archives, held at the London Metropolitan Archives. The letters between Stephenson and Royce are in folder LMA/4287/02/398. Other correspondence, including that from the walking clergyman Rev C.E.V. Hodge is in folder 02/399, as is the comment from Stephenson (to Gordon Manley) about a contemplated Pendle/Bowland routing. Information about the 1938 Hope conference is in various folders, especially folder 02/395/1 and (for the agreed statement) 02/397. The campaign against the PW routing on Kinder was led by a well-known rambler from Sheffield Phil Barnes (see folder 02/401).

The early guidebook quoted is:

Wright, Christopher, (1967). *A Guide to the Pennine Way* (Constable).

Two other interesting early books I consulted are:

Oldham, Kenneth, (1960, 1964). *The Pennine Way* (Dalesman Publishing)

Wood, John, (1947). *Mountain Trail* (Blackfriars Press).

Otherwise this chapter uses Tom Stephenson's memoirs and Wainwright's *Pennine Way Companion*, mentioned earlier.

Blackstone Edge

The report of the Blackstone Edge Chartist rally is in the Northern Star dated 8th August 1846. Jones' poem was printed in the newspaper two weeks later, and is reproduced in:

Kovalev, U.V., (1956). *Anthology of Chartist Literature* (Moscow).

An introduction to Ernest Jones and his writings, including the text of part of his speech at Blackstone Edge, is:

Saville, John, (1952). *Ernest Jones: Chartist* (Lawrence and Wishart).

For a general introduction to Chartism, I consulted among others:

Thompson, Dorothy, (1984). *The Chartists* (Maurice Temple Smith).

Briggs, Asa, (1998). *Chartism* (Sutton Publishing).

I also need to acknowledge the help given by Harriet Dell, Dr Mike Sanders (University of Manchester) and – for the experience of participating in the singing of 'The Blackstone Edge Gathering' – the members of the Yorkshire Chartist Choir and of Corista.

On the South Pennine Moors

The article in the *Yorkshire Life* edition of September 1968 was by Hilda Gledhill and was entitled 'Valley of the Shadow'. It has been reproduced on a personal website run by a former resident of the area, at www.dawtrina.com/personal/barkisland/valley.html. My thanks to Diana Monaghan of Hebden Bridge local history society for bringing this to my attention.

Information about the South Pennine Moors SSSI, including condition reports, are on Natural England's website, www.naturalengland.org.uk (under 'Conservation'). For the SPA and SAC records, see the Joint Nature Conservancy Council, www.jncc.gov.uk. The JNCC has a useful directory of all protected site designations (www.jncc.gov.uk/page-1527).

For the Rochdale canal, I used primarily a booklet entitled simply 'The Rochdale Canal', undated (around 1990?) and unattributed to any author, published by the Waterway Handbooks Company. The story of Hollingworth Lake has been told in:

Colligan, A.W., (1998, second edition). *The Weighver's Seaport* (George Kelsall).

My thanks to Sean Prendergast and his workmates for making space for me in their van and for answering my questions.

I decided to do the leg of my journey between the White House and Cliviger by myself one Sunday, finishing in the Cliviger gorge in time for a drink at The Ram Inn. (This was another hot day.) Buses serve both the start and finishing point, and I should really have made use of them. Instead I drove to the White House and was picked up by a friend in Cliviger.

Todmorden Moor

I'm grateful for Peter Drew for the time spent showing me round the Astronomy Centre. Their website is www.astronomycentre.org.uk. For light pollution, more information from the Campaign for Dark Skies (www.britastro.org/dark-skies/index.html) and from the Campaign to Protect Rural England (www.cpre.org.uk).

The Headwaters of the Calder(s)

For the etymology of the Calder, I have relied on *The Oxford Dictionary of British Place Names* (A.D. Mills, 2003 edition). An interesting introductory essay, 'Leadmining in East Lancashire', by Jack Nadin, was printed in the *Burnley Caving Club Review* (2004), available at www.burnleycavingclub.org.uk. I chose not to go deeper into the history of Thieveley lead mines, but the two key sources would be:

France, R.S. (ed.), (1951). *Thieveley Lead Mines 1629–1635* (Lancashire and Cheshire Record Society series 102, 83).

Roe, Martin, (2000). 'The Archaeology of Thieveley Lead Mine', in *British Mining,* no. 67 – Memoirs (Northern Mine Research Society).

A short account of Hill Top Colliery, by Alex Potts (2004), is available on the Miners' Advice activist website, www.minersadvice.co.uk/hill_top.htm

The Todmorden Moor Restoration Trust has a comprehensive website, http://todmordenmoor.org.uk, with some shocking photographs of the fly-tipping problems members have confronted. Information about Coal Clough was taken from the Renewable Energy Systems website, www.res-ltd.com

Boulsworth Hill

For details of early plans for the Pennine Way, see my notes above. Tom Stephenson describes the background to the Boulsworth 1956 enquiry in his memoirs, *Forbidden Land*, already mentioned. For details of early access agreements in the Peak District, I have used Howard Hill's book *Freedom to Roam*, also mentioned above. The government quote on the 1949 Act is borrowed from Hill.

My information for the Yorkshire Dales national park involves recalibrating the data contained in a Yorkshire Dales National Park Authority press release, which stated that the implementation of the Countryside and Rights of Way Act saw an increase from 4 per cent to 62 per cent in land where access is permitted (YDNPA press released, The Dales opens up to walkers, 28th May 2005). Prior to CRoW, access agreements in the Dales had been negotiated with the Duke of Devonshire for Barden Fell and Barden Moor

The account of viewing Blackpool from Boulsworth by F.A. Leyland is quoted extensively by a later Halifax writer, Whiteley Turner:

Turner, Whiteley, (1913, third edition). *A Spring-Time Saunter Round and About Brontë Land* (Halifax).

Despite the best efforts of the helpful staff of Halifax reference library, I have been unable to find Leyland's original article in the *Halifax Courier*. My thanks, however, to Katie Warrinder at the library for tracking down an obituary of Leyland (Halifax Reference Library: Sutcliffe newspaper cuttings folder, vol. 3).

For the eighteenth-century vogue for the picturesque, I used:

Andrews, Malcolm, (1989). *The Search for the Picturesque* (Scolar Press).

Also relevant and stimulating is Robert Macfarlane's study of changing human attitudes to high places:

Macfarlane, Robert, (2003). *Mountains of the Mind* (Granta Books).

Edmund Burke's *A Philosophical Enquiry . . .* is available in several modern editions. My quotation from Thomas Gray is from:

Gray, Thomas, (1775). *The Poems of Mr Gray, To which are prefixed memoirs of his life and writings, by W. Mason* (London). A facsimile edition of this book is available at www.thomasgray.org.

Ian Simmons' fascinating study which will be mentioned again is:

Simmons, I.G., (2003). *The Moorlands of England and Wales, an Environmental History 8000 BC – AD 2000* (Edinburgh University Press).

The clag was definitely down when, with James Riley, I made my way from Cliviger over Boulsworth to Cowling. Looking back, I find that this was the leg of my journey where I made fewest notes – not surprising, we could hardly make out each other, let alone the landscape around us. Cars again provided our transport.

Beyond Watersheddles

My thanks to David Airey for his help and advice. My thanks also to Richard Betton, who farms in Upper Teesdale, who also took time to share with me his thoughts on the future of upland farming, and to Richard George and Rachael Gillbanks of the NFU.

Recent studies on hill farming used include:

Institute for European Environmental Policy (IEEP), Land Use Consultants and GHK Consulting (2004). *An Assessment of the impacts of hill farming in England on the economic, environmental and social sustainability of the uplands and more widely*.

Cumulus (2005). *Assessment of CAP reform and other key policies on upland farms and land use implications in SDAs and DAs in England – Final Report*.

Burton, R. *et al.*, (n.d., 2006?). *Social Capital in Hill Farming, Report for the Upland Centre*.

EFTEC (Economics for the Environment Consultancy), (2006). *Economic Valuation of Environmental Impacts in the Severely Disadvantaged Areas – Final Report*.

For an overview of current government thinking of support for hill farmers see:

Defra, (2006). *Rural Development Programme for England 2007–2013: Uplands Reward Structure*. Consultation Document.

All the above can be accessed through the Defra website, www.defra.gov.uk, which also has full information on the Single Payment Scheme, HLS/ELS, Hill Farm Allowance, etc

For the NFU viewpoint, see:

NFU/CPRE, 2006. *Living landscapes: hidden costs of managing the countryside*.

A short introduction to traditional sheep and cattle farming on the uplands is included in:

English Nature (2001). *The Uplands Management Handbook*.

The Swaledale Sheep Breeders' Association have a website at www.swaledale-sheep.com. The UK National Sheep Association are at www.nationalsheep.org.uk . The information on farmers' average age in the Dark Peak is to be found in the IEEP study, vol 3.

Emmott Moor

My information on wild fires in the Peak District is taken from:

Centre for Urban and Regional Ecology, University of Manchester, (2006). *Climate Change and the Visitor Economy, technical report 3, Moorland Wild Fires in the Peak District National Park.*

This has been supplemented by a slide presentation to the Moors for the Future research conference by Julia McMorrow *et al.*, 'Moorland wildfire, visitors and climate change'.

For the history of both medieval hunting and later grouse shooting, I recommend Simmons (2003), *op. cit.* Lord Lovat was the Chairman of the Committee of Inquiry on Grouse Disease whose final report 'The Grouse in Health and in Disease' in 1911 ran to a weighty two volumes.

For controlled burning, my sources include:

Glaves, David J., and Haycock, Nicholas E., (eds) *et al.*, Science Panel Assessment of the Effects of Burning on Biodiversity, Soils and Hydrology (2005). *Burning Review Science Panel Report: Report to Defra.*

Defra, (2005). *Review of the Heather and Grass Etc (Burning) Regulations 1986 and the Heather and Grass Burning Code 1994 in England.* Consultation document.

MAFF, (1992). *The Heather and Grass Burning Code.*

The CLA response to the consultation document was found on the CLA website, www.cla.org.uk. The quote from Defra on burning pros and cons is from the Defra website, www.defra.gov.uk.

Nick Wigmore and I chose poor weather to make our way from the A6068 to Barnoldswick. Embarrassingly, I misread the map near Earby, and ended up much too far south heading towards Sheep Hill. Using Colne as the starting point, we used the hourly bus towards Keighley for the outward journey and returned on one of the frequent buses from Barnoldswick. Barnoldswick, incidentally, carries the stress on the second, nor first, syllable – or you can use the alternative local name for the town of Barlick.

Earby

My thanks to Peter Hart. For the story of lead mining, I used particularly:

Raistrick, A., and Jennings, B., (1965). *A History of Lead Mining in the Pennines* (Longmans, Green and Co.).

Raistrick, A., (1975). *The Lead Mining Industry of Wensleydale and Swaledale* (2 vols) (Moorland Publishing Co.).

Gill, M., (2001). *Swaledale, its Mines and Smelt Mills* (Landmark Publishing).

The song 'Fourpence a Day' was collected by Ewan MacColl and Joan Littlewood. I have used the version published in:

Lloyd, A.L. (compiler), (1952). *Come All Ye Bold Miners: Ballads and Songs of the Coalfields* (Lawrence and Wishart).

It is also printed in Ewan MacColl and Peggy Seeger's 1960 selection of folksongs for children *The Singing Island*, where they add this remark: 'Local legend has it that the mine-owners reacted to the song by temporarily closing the pits and importing leadminers from Germany'.

To the Dales

For the Leeds and Liverpool canal, I used Mike Clarke's enthusiastic history:

Clarke, M., (1990). *The Leeds and Liverpool Canal* (Carnegie Press, Preston).

The quotes from the Yorkshire Dales national park are taken from its website, www.yorkshiredales.org.uk. For an introduction to karst landscape I recommend the national park's booklet:

Waltham, Tony, (1987). *Karst and Caves* (Yorkshire Dales National Park).

The text and background documents about the European Landscape Convention are most easily obtained from the Council of Europe website: www.coe.int/t/e/Cultural_Co-operation/Environment/Landscape/

Information about the Character Areas and the text of *Landscape: Beyond the View* can be found, if you persevere, via www.naturalengland.org.uk. Another good site is www.landscapecharacter.org.uk, the site of the Landscape Character Network. The final quote in the chapter is from Professor Carys Swanwick writing in *LCN News* (Autumn 2006).

The Newcastle study is:

Willis, K.G., and Garrod, G.D., (1993). 'Valuing Landscape: a Contingent Valuation Approach', in *Journal of Environmental Management*, 37, pp. 1–22.

Details of Ian Simmons' book are given above.

I was joined by Trevor Smith for the leg from Barnoldswick to Hellifield, which we organised by starting in Skipton and using buses. The next leg of the journey involved a day's run across Fountains Fell almost to Pen-y-ghent, using the train out to Hellifield station and coming back from Horton-in-Ribblesdale. Roger Haworth was with me for this. Trevor and I chose a pleasant day; Roger and I were less lucky, and the cloud was down almost all the way. On Fountains Fell we were somewhat taken back when an apparently large beast emerged out of the mist towards us. As we got closer it was revealed to be a small terrier, keeping two men who were engaged in dry-stone walling company. The wallers looked equally taken aback to see us, ghostly figures emerging from out of the weather.

Pen-y-ghent

Wainwright's quote is from *Pennine Way Companion*, mentioned earlier. For the origins of Pen-y-ghent's name I referred to a paper given by Dr Mary Higham at a Scottish Place Name Society conference in 1998 (details at http://www.st-andrews.ac.uk/institutes/sassi/spns/perthconf.htm).

The 2005 England Leisure Visits survey is available on the Natural England website. Information on employment in the Lake District is in the IEEP report on hill farming (see above). The Yorkshire Dales 'difficult balance' quote is from the national park's education sheet Tourism; other information is taken from the YDNPA State of the Park report 2005.

For footpath repair history and techniques I used:

Davies, P. and Loxham, J. with Huggon, G., (1996). *Repairing Upland Path Erosion* (Lake District National Park).

Also informative is 'Information Note 10, Managing Public Access and Footpaths', in English Nature, *The Uplands Management Handbook*, mentioned above. A technical Pennine Way report 'Aggregate and Mineral Paths and Tracks' is currently available at http://nationaltrail.co.uk/PennineWay/uploads/Pennine%20Way%20aggregatepaths.pdf.

It was a pleasure to be accompanied by my daughter Joanna over Pen-y-ghent and Plover Hill. We left the car in the national park car park in Horton.

Cam High Road and Beyond

My quote about Cam Houses ghosts is from:

Pontefract, E., and Hartley, M., (1938). *Wharfedale* (Dent).

I am grateful to Cosima Towneley for taking time to talk to me of her mother's life and work and providing me with a copy of her mother's account of the 1986 ride 'Here be dragons'. For information on the Towneley history I used the booklet prepared by Burnley borough council 'Tracing the Towneleys', available at www.burnley.gov.uk/towneley. Information on the Pennine Bridleway is available at www.nationaltrail.co.uk.

Thanks to Matt Dinsdale of Dinsdale Moorland Services for sharing with me a contractor's view of the construction of the Pennine Bridleway.

Rachel Skinner and I took the train to Ribblehead, picking up the line of the watershed beyond Cam Fell. There were fine views of Ingleborough for much of the first two-thirds of our route, which saw us arrive at Garsdale station about five minutes after a train had left. The Moorcock Inn provided the welcome for the two hours or so we had to wait for the next train.

North of Great Knoutberry

My thanks to Nick Parker, and to Amanda Anderson of the Moorland Association. Information about red grouse (in sickness and in health) can be found among other places on the website of the Game Conservancy Trust, www.gct.org.uk. I was shown the Abbeystead estate game book, recording the size of the August 1915 shoot, by the estate manager Rod Banks for my earlier book *Forest of Bowland* (Frances Lincoln, 2005). (This information is also in Simmons, 2003.) The survey mentioned in the last paragraph is:

PACEC, (2006). *Shooting Sports: Findings of an Economic and Environmental Study*.

Garsdale Station

Plenty has been written on the Settle–Carlisle line, but I've used an early account:

Houghton, F.W., (1948). *The Story of the Settle–Carlisle Line* (Norman Arch Publications).

The illustrated booklet *The Settle Carlisle Railway*, published by the Settle–Carlisle Railway Development Company (2006), sold by volunteers on the train, is also informative.

I say more about Lady Anne Clifford in my book *Wensleydale and Swaledale* (Frances Lincoln, 2006). Among sources about her are:

Holmes, Martin, (1975). *Proud Northern Lady* (Phillimore).

Bouch, C.M.L., (1954). *The Lady Anne*, (published by the author).

Bill Mitchell is among those to recount the story of the Lady's Pillar:

Mitchell, W.R., (1991). *High Dale Country* (Souvenir Press).

My reference to Wainwright this time is to his *A Coast to Coast Walk* (1987).

My thanks, of course, to Nick Chetwood. My companion along the Mallerstang section of the watershed was Ben Crowther, and appropriately enough we were able to use the railway: a train out from Keighley to Garsdale with a train back from Kirkby Stephen. You'll have gathered from my account of the fine views that we were lucky – it was good weather, a fine August day.

Stainmore

Much of this chapter uses the comprehensive report of the 1989–91 archaeological project at Stainmore:

Vyner, B.,(2001). *Stainmore, The Archaeology of a North Pennine Pass* (Tees Archaeology and English Heritage).

Climate information is from Simmons (2003), *op. cit*.

For Kaber Rigg, I used:

Greaves, Richard, (1986). *Deliver Us from Evil* (Oxford University Press).

Hopper, Andrew, (2002). 'The Farnley Wood Plot and the Memory of the Civil Wars', in *Yorkshire Historical Journal*, 45, pp. 281–303.

Richard Blakeley was with me for the leg from the minor road near Nine Standards Rigg to the B6276, both of us just managing to cross the A66 without becoming roadkill under the tyres of the lorries passing by. I noted down immediately afterwards the fine views which opened up across the Vale of Eden beyond Great Knipe – best views yet?, say my notes.

This was not a leg where public transport was much help, although we saved the need for a second car by arranging for a taxi from Kirkby Stephen to pick us up at the day's end.

Little Fell

My thanks to Major Tam Campbell and John Woods for facilitating my visit to Warcop. The post-war newspaper article ('Westmorland's Contribution to D-Day') dated 14th December 1946 was given me by John Woods, and is attributed to *The Herald* (presumably *The Cumberland and Westmorland Herald*). The ATE website quoted is www.army.mod.uk/ate/public/warcop.htm.

I have used Rachel Woodward's interesting academic essay dissecting the MOD's use of landscape and conservation issues in relation to the army lands for background information as well:

Woodward, R., (1999). 'Gunning for Rural England: the Politics of the Promotion of Military Land Use in the Northumberland National Park', in *Journal of Rural Studies*, 15/1, pp. 17–33.

I also consulted:

Goodwin, S., (1997). 'East of Eden', in *Rambling Today* (Spring 1997).

Particular thanks to Nigel Smith who came with on to the Warcop lands, and who tiptoed with me through the heather waiting for the loud bangs that never came.

High Cup Nick to Great Dun Fell

The North Pennines AONB Geodiversity Audit and Action Plan 2004–9 provides a comprehensive introduction to the geological heritage of the area (available to download from www.northpennines.org.uk). I also used the excellent AONB publication Discovering Geology and Landscape in the North Pennines, designed particularly for cyclists.

The North Pennines is covered in *British Regional Geology Guide 7: Northern England* (published by the British Geological Survey). *Guide 8: The Pennines and Adjacent Areas* covers the southern half of the Pennine watershed.

For the story of Adam Sedgwick, Colin Speakman's book is recommended:

Speakman, Colin, (1982). *Adam Sedgwick, Geologist and Dalesman* (Broad Oak Press, Geological Society of London, Trinity College Cambridge).

Particular thanks are due to Brian Young. My thanks too to Chris Woodley-Stewart and Elizabeth Pickett of the AONB team.

Richard Leonard and I took the train to Appleby, using the footpath from Harbour Flatt up High Cup Gill to reach the watershed and from there crossing Great Dun Fell, Cross Fell and Fiends Fell to the café at Hartside Top. A taxi took us back to the Settle–Carlisle line at Langwathby station. A great day on a magnificent ridge.

Great Dun Fell and Cross Fell

My thanks for John Adamson of the Centre for Ecology and Hydrology for his help. I have used one of his recent slide presentations 'Climate Change in the North Pennines'. I have also used his article on Gordon Manley 'A Moor House Pioneer', in *ECN News* issue 6 (Spring 1995), from which the 'small misadventures' quote is taken and his article on Moor House in *ECN News* issue 5 (Autumn 1994). Both these are available at www.ecn.ac.uk. Also interesting is the article by John Adamson 'Environmental Research at Moor House in the Cumbrian Pennines', in *Conserving Lakeland* (Summer 1999). The correspondence between Manley and Stephenson is in the Ramblers' Association archives (see above), file LMA/4287/02/399.

For the Helm wind see:

Uttley, David, (2000). *The Anatomy of the Helm Wind* (Bookcase, Carlisle).

For past climate changes I have used again Simmons (2003). The UK Climate Impacts Programme quotation, and the four scenarios, can be found in:

UKCIP, (2002). *Climate Change Scenarios for the United Kingdom; the UKCIP02 Briefing Report* (available at www.ukcip.org.uk).

I must also thank Chris McCarty of the Moor House/Upper Teeesdale NNR for his time and interest.

The Cumbria Ridge

For Auden I have used the text in his *Collected Poems*, edited by Edward Mendelson (Faber, 1976). Auden's comment about the North Pennines is from his *A Certain World* (Viking, 1970; Faber, 1971). Basil Bunting's poem 'Briggflatts' was published by Fulcrum Press, 1966. 'Hawthorn' is published in Tom Pickard's *The Ballad of Jamie Allan* (Flood Editions, Chicago, 2007). I've used the author's latest text; a slightly different version is in his collection *The Dark Months of May* (Flood Editions, Chicago, 2004).

The reviewer quoted is Maureen N. McLane of Harvard University; the review was published in *The Chicago Tribune* (24th April 2005).

The Ballad of Jamie Allan was performed at the Sage in 2005 by Omar Ebrahim and Sarah Jane Morris; John Harle conducted the Northern Sinfonia.

I came across one of the nineteenth-century chapbook histories, *The History of James Allan*, which was reprinted by Alan Brignull, Hedgehog Press, in 1981 in time for the 250th anniversary of Allan's birth. As action-packed as a comic!

Particular thanks to Tom Pickard, not least for allowing me to reproduce the text of Hawthorn. Thanks too to Kathryn Renwick and the very welcoming staff of the Hartside Top café.

Geltsdale

Data on hen harrier numbers in Britain are taken from the RSPB website, www.rspb.org.uk. The 2005–6 radio tagging story is told on the news release dated 22th March 2006 'Round Britain tour for Pennine Harriers' (www.daelnet.co.uk). Past persecution near Geltsdale is recounted in the RSPB press release dated 26th May 2005, 'Birds Poisoned in North Pennines'. Information of recent breeding numbers is included in the English Nature press release 'Five years on and still slow progress for hen harriers', dated 11th September 2006. Operation Artemis has its own website, www.savethehenharrier.com. The Black Grouse Recovery Project in the North Pennines is reached via www.blackgrouse.info.

The Game Conservancy Trust document mentioned, 'Hen Harrier Recovery in England: Submission to English Nature from the Game Conservancy Trust', is dated 6th August 2004. See www.gct.org.uk.

Thanks to Steve Downing and Dave O'Hara. I was with Richard Leonard again for this penultimate leg of my journey. We drove to Hartside Top, ran over to Cold Fell and beyond, caught one of the very occasional buses to Alston from near Tindale on the A689 and then had a taxi ride back up to the café in the clouds. The day started unpromisingly but the weather cleared later, certainly in time for Cold Fell. The Haltwhistle Wednesday walking group were out on Cold Fell, too.

The Peat Beneath our Feet

For this chapter, I am particularly indebted to Martin Evans (Manchester University), John Adamson (Centre for Ecology and Hydrology) and Chris McCarty (Moor House NNR).

Among the academic literature I looked at were:

Evans, M., and Warburton, J., (2007). *The Geomorphology of Upland Peat: Erosion, Form and Landscape Change* (Blackwell).

Garnett, M.H., Ineson, P., Stevenson, A.C., (2000). 'Effects of Burning and Grazing on Carbon Sequestration in a Pennine Blanket Bog, UK', in *The Holocene* 10/6 (2000) pp. 729–36.

Worrall, Fred, *et al.*, (2003). 'Carbon Budget for a British Upland Peat Catchment', in *The Science of the Total Environment* 312, pp. 133–46.

Evans, M., Warburton J, Yang J., (2005). 'Eroding Blanket Peat Catchments: Global and Local Implications of Upland Organic Sediment Budgets' (ScienceDirect, www.sciencedirect.com)

Evans, M., and Warburton, J., (2005). 'Sediment Budget for an Eroding Peat-moorland Catchment in Northern England', in *Earth Surface Processes and Landforms*, 30, pp. 557–77.

Bellamy, Pat H. *et al.*, (2005). 'Carbon Losses from all soils across England and Wales 1978–2003' *Nature*, 437/8, pp. 245–8, (September 2006).

Fred Worrall's quote can be found in various places, including the press release dated 3rd March 2006, 'Peat uplands in the spotlight for environmental protection', www.dur.ac.uk/news/research/?itemno=4125. For a calculation on carbon emissions on flights to the Caribbean I consulted various websites, including www.climatecare.org.

The phrase 'carbon time bomb' was used for an article by Fred Pearce, *New Scientist*, 7th July 2004. Also from *New Scientist* comes the article 'Soil May Spoil UK's Climate Efforts', by John Pickrell, 7th September 2005. For a more general wake-up call on climate change and global warming I recommend:

Pearce, Fred, (2006). *The Last Generation: How Nature will take her Revenge for Climate Change* (Transworld).

INDEX